GUIDE

Velázquez

MUSEO DEL PRADO

Written by:

Javier Portús
Curator, Museo del Prado

Foreword

A hundred years ago, on the occasion of the third centenary of Velázquez's birth, the Museo del Prado decided to dedicate the large basilican room off the central gallery (Room 12) on the second floor to the permanent exhibition of the painter's work. Until that time that large, stately area had contained a selection of the museum's masterpieces but with its new purpose came the symbolic confirmation of something which critics, writers and painters had long been saying: that the artist whose memory is most closely associated with the history of the Prado is Velázquez. This was not only because the setting for the painter's "discovery" in the 19th century had been the Prado's rooms but also because the Museum's fame is directly related to its prestige as the place which houses the work of an artist raised during that period to the summit of the artistic Olympus.

Velázquez continues to be the main point of reference for the Museographical Plan currently dictating the institution's functions, and Room 12, dedicated to him throughout this century and now with an additional three rooms to enable the visitor to view his work in a more satisfactory manner, continues to be reserved for the painter. It is in line with this that the other collections – now being arranged according to criteria combining chronological order with the concept of "national school" – have been located. On the top floor Velázquez's painting is perfectly within its context. Very close is the Flemish Baroque school with the work of Rubens – who not only gave the Sevillian such cause for admiration but also taught him so much – shining with a light of its own. The large Central Gallery is reserved for Velázquez's three great Spanish contemporaries: Zurbarán, Ribera and Murillo. The inner rooms adjacent to those which contain paintings by Velázquez are to be devoted to the work of his contemporary or immediately subsequent Spanish fellows and arranged according to theme. This additional step with respect to the arrangement of a century ago thus situates the painter's work within its creative context.

But the reorganization of the collections of the last few years must be accompanied by a major effort to further the knowledge and diffusion of Velázquez's work so that the visitor will find the greatest possible number of keys to understanding the paintings he or she can see and admire. This involves various features: lecture programmes intended to bring the Museum closer to the public, activities for specific groups of visitors coordinated by an Educational Section, wall charts and labels explaining each room and each work, and finally the publication of visitor's "Room Guides" to serve as a complement to all information from other sources. At this time of the fourth centenary of the painter's birth I am very pleased to be able to introduce this book; it is not only intended as a guide for the visitor while at the Prado but also to serve as a reminder that in the Prado Museum in Madrid it will always be possible to enjoy Velázquez's painting.

Fernando Checa
Director

Introduction: An Intelligent Approach

The idea we now have of Velázquez is the result of constant reflection on his work by generations of critics and artists. Although, over the years, assessment of Velázquez has been contradictory, today no-one would hesitate in describing him as one of the great figures in the history of painting. Our knowledge of Velázquez as man and artist is based on more than one hundred and twenty confirmed works, the memory of several more, and a small number of written records. And even though we are now able to discuss the most relevant facts of his biography, to study the different artistic and intellectual influences which affected him throughout his career, and to describe the historical, political, cultural and creative context in which he lived, there are still many questions, some of which can only be partially answered through hypothesis and conjecture. The lack of personal writings and records means that we have few clues to Velázquez's character or to specific aspects of his psychological and intellectual make-up. And when historians have attempted to compensate for this lack of documentary evidence with reflections on his work, the result has always been one of conflicting interpretations. Some have written of his life in almost hagiographic terms, making him out to be a painter receptive not only to visual stimuli but also to the human and social reality of his times. It has also been suggested that he was deeply religious, compassionate with his more unfortunate fellow men, and even the possessor of an anachronistic social conscience. But the very facts on which such interpretations are based have been used by others to describe Velázquez as an artist only concerned that no-one should overshadow him, and as haughty, proud, disdainful and much more interested in his career at Court than in the misfortunes of his fellow men.

There is nothing really surprising about this disparity of opinions, for the same might be said of artists like Goya or Rembrandt on whom a great deal of biographical information, much of it of a highly personal nature, actually exists. Furthermore, judgements of the character or personality of these painters by posterity are sometimes no more than a reflection of the psychological profile of the historians who made them or the times they lived in.

Thus, instead of attempting vainly to identify the strings which moved the painter's will or the people who influenced him, I believe it is more useful in these introductory pages to discuss his biography in general terms. The reader can then form his own opinion of the painter through the few facts that are available and from the conclusions to which reflection on Velázquez's paintings will lead him.

Velázquez's life can be described quite briefly. Not just because that lack of biographical records prevents us from doing so at length, but also because his life was marked with so few milestones, apart from the daily miracle of his artistic production. Basically his story can be told in terms of the three different stages in which he ascended the artistic and social scale. As a background we have the Spain of the 17th century, the Golden Age of its culture and socially, economically and politically a very complex period. The country was still a major European power – despite the fact that with the passing of the years it lost some of its influence – having to maintain a costly presence on the continent which, with the fluctuations of a basically agrarian economy dependent on the wealth of the Americas, prompted severe economic and demographic crises. In the more important cities a very varied, heterogeneous society grew up whose (basically conservative) ideology was tightly controlled through forms of expression catering for the masses such as the theatre or *fiestas.* The roots of the ruling classes lay basically in catholic militancy, a belief in absolute monarchy as the ideal form of government, and blind faith in the virtues of a system based on social strata and organized according to a highly codified system of privileges that assigned to each and every one his "natural" place in the world.

The first stage or setting in Velázquez's life was Seville, where he was born in June 1599. He began his studies in 1610 at the workshop of Francisco Pacheco, who was more than a

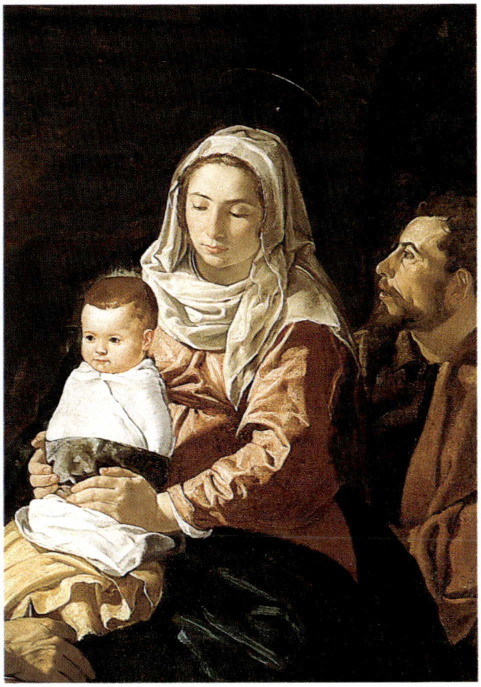

The Adoration of the Magi *(detail).*

simple painter for he was also a highly cultured man, a writer of poetry and a member of the city's intellectual elite. Without doubt Pacheco passed on his tastes to his pupil, who in 1618 became his son-in-law when he married Pacheco's daughter Juana. The previous year Velázquez had begun working on his own and had been admitted as a master into the Seville painters' guild. During those years he painted about two dozen pictures with an almost tenebrist use of light, a definite preference for naturalistic detail and a small range of earthy tones, as may be seen in such well-known works as *Christ in the House of Martha and Mary, Old Woman Frying Eggs, The Water Seller of Seville, Peasants at Table* and *The Adoration of the Magi.* During that period religion was the most important theme in his work – as it was for all the other painters in Seville and indeed in the whole of Spain. He also became extremely proficient at painting portraits, a field he continued to work in for the rest of his life, and this may be seen both in his individual portraits and in the naturalist precision with which he constructed the faces of many of the personages in his religious and genre paintings. This period also saw the appearance of a facet of his work that was to be constant throughout the whole of his career: a predilection for scenes involving double meanings or supposed narrative paradoxes (such as the window or mirror in *Christ in the House of Martha and Mary*) drawing the spectator into an ingenious game of interpretation. Another constant characteristic of his work was his originality. It is a fact that the painters of those years took their inspiration from the art of the 16th century then prevalent in the

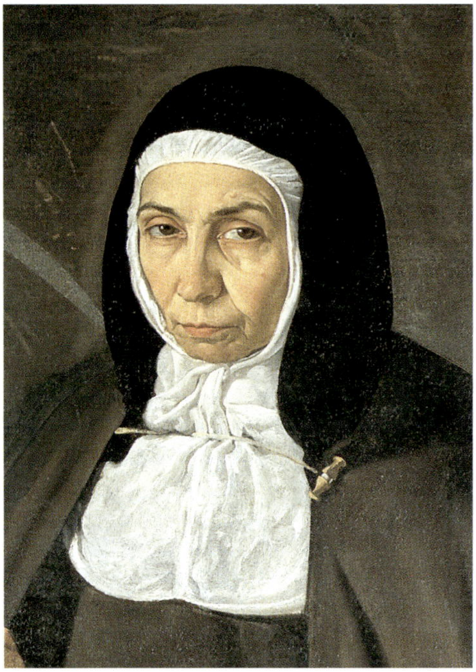

city and from the work of the still-living masters. Indeed there would be no explanation for many of the characteristics of Velázquez's art if we did not take this or the most general tendencies in the European painting and culture of his age (such as an interest in naturalism and chiaroscuro) into account. However, it is also true that, in spite of such influences, Velázquez's Seville pictures bear no similarity to any painted in the city or in the rest of Spain at the time.

Mother Jerónima de la Fuente *(detail)*.

Pacheco may have been only an average painter but he was a shrewd teacher, a man of experience who immediately realized that his son-in-law's extraordinary talent deserved to be allowed to develop in more ambitious and favourable surroundings than in Seville, on the banks of the Guadalquivir – even though it was one of the greatest cities in the Iberian Peninsula. He therefore encouraged Velázquez to travel to Madrid, which the latter did for the first time in the spring of 1622 in the hope of gaining entry into Court circles. Philip IV had ascended the throne the previous year and had chosen as his right-hand man the Count-Duke of Olivares, whose Andalusian background must have raised Pacheco's hopes for his son-in-law. Velázquez painted Luis de Góngora's portrait at Court and visited El Escorial, but, failing to find definite employment, he was finally forced to return to Seville.

He went back to Madrid the following summer, and after painting a portrait of his contact in Madrid, the courtier Juan de Fonseca, was allowed to paint Philip IV, who in October appointed him his painter. From then on the Spanish Court was to be the main setting for Velázquez's career as an artist and the King his principal patron. The new circumstances brought new developments. From the artistic point of view, access to the royal collections was very important to his stylistic evolution, and working in the King's service compelled him to specialize in portraits, which meant that he devoted little time to religious painting and somewhat more to mythological scenes. While working as a painter, he also embarked on a career in the administration which served to consolidate his position at Court and to fulfil social aspirations which in Velázquez were always highly pronounced. The most important points in his career in this respect were his appointment as Usher of the Chamber in 1627, House and Court Bailiff in 1633, Gentleman of the Wardrobe the following year, Superintendent of Royal Works and Gentleman of the Chamber in 1643, and Chamberlain of the Royal Palace in 1652. From the 1640s he was a key figure in the extensive refurbishment of the Alcázar and other Royal Seats, including the Monastery of El Escorial. Although the execution of such duties brought him honours, he was left with little time to

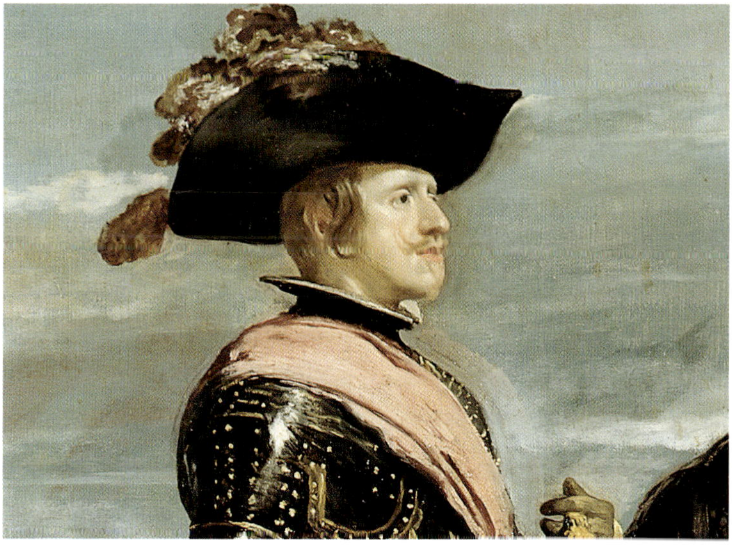

Philip IV on Horseback *(detail).*

paint, which explains the relatively small number of works in the last two decades of his life.

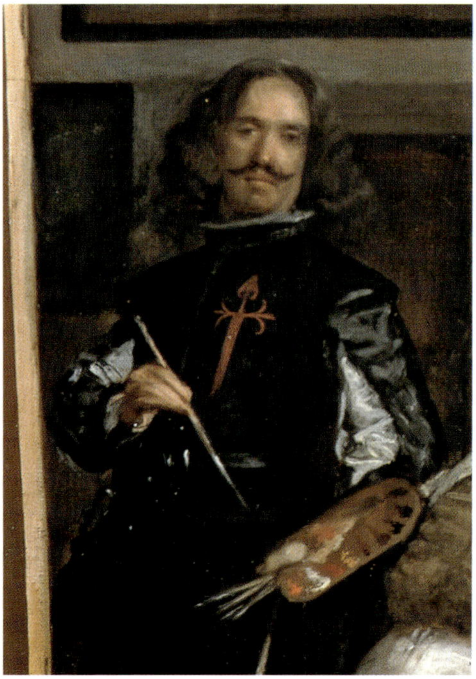

Las Meninas *(detail).*

The culmination to Velázquez's social ambitions came in 1658, when he received the habit of St James. The inventory of his possessions made on his death two years later proves very useful to our knowledge of his intellectual pursuits, for it mentions his library, which contained 154 volumes on a wide range of subjects, including architecture, astronomy, astrology, physiognomy and poetry. It reveals that Velázquez was a cultivated painter interested in many fields of learning.

Although after 1623 he worked mainly as a Court painter in Spain, two periods extremely important in his life and decisive to his career took place in Italy, for he travelled there in 1629 and 1648. On the first journey, made for purposes of study, he saw 16th-century Italian painting, ancient sculpture and the work of his counterparts in Rome; it was an experience which had an immediate effect on his art, to the extent that where style is concerned there can be said to be a "before" and an "after" to that journey. He embarked on his second Italian journey twenty years later, when in his artistic prime, on that occasion to purchase paintings and sculptures for the Alcázar and to prove his worth on what was the main stage for the European painting of the times.

Whether in Italy, Seville or at Court, Velázquez was extraordinarily receptive to visual stimuli and reflection on the world around him underlies all his work. In his Seville paintings the city itself was the point of reference while, once established at

Court, it was the great paintings belonging to the royal collections. Among these he saw works by the Venetians, particularly Titian, whose influence on him was to be the strongest of all. And as the royal palaces gradually became enriched with modern works of art by Rubens, Ribera and the Italian painters, Velázquez processed their influence mentally. We have already mentioned the great importance of his journeys to Italy as a source of methods and ideas. From the stylistic point of view, Velázquez subscribed to the Western tradition which gave priority to the value of colour and insisted on reflection on vision as the main object of the painting. Titian and Rubens, his two great masters, also subscribed to this view. However, Velázquez was always an original artist, not only due to his absolutely personal style but also to his unique approach to pictorial motifs.

Traditionally the painters of the Modern Age have been classified as "realists" and "idealists" or "classicists" and for a long time Velázquez was assigned a prominent position among the former. However, in contrast with the traditional view of the Sevillian as an artist who sought uncompromisingly to capture visual experiences, over the last few decades it has become ever more clear to historians that different terms must be used when referring to his work. He was not an incorruptible realist but a painter with an intelligent approach to both artistic tradition and the visual experience who consequently painted pictures which in many cases are of great intellectual complexity and display deep reflection not only on reality but also on the laws of representation, on narrative and on the history of art itself. As an alternative to the naturalism v. classicism dilemma, Velázquez proposed a third approach partly related to the trends of the Spanish culture of his times. This was *conceptismo*. There are numerous examples of how far he involved in this process not only the spectator's aesthetic experience or culture but also his wit and intelligence and his knowledge of the history of art. While *Las Meninas* ("The Maids of Honour") is an extremely complex painting with various levels of interpretation involving concepts of all kinds – politics, art history, biography, etc. – underlying *The Fable of Arachne (Las Hilanderas)* is reflection on artistic ability, mythology, Rubens and Titian, and on Velázquez's own place within the artistic tradition. Furthermore, *Aesop* and *Menippus* cannot be properly understood if we do not take into account where they were intended to be hung (in the Torre de la Parada) and their similarity to Rubens's *Heraclitus* and *Democritus*. *The Topers* is possibly a retort to the courtly art circles as well as a reflection on the pictorial genres and the confrontation between realism and classicism. The equestrian portraits can only be properly interpreted as a possible reflection on an iconographic tradition represented by Titian and Rubens. *The Surrender of Breda* involves a profound discourse on war and peace and the providential role of a Spanish monarchy believed capable of embodying such deeply-rooted concepts of Christian tradition as the good governor, etc. But the most extraordinary thing is not that one painter should have wished to express such concepts but that such a wonderful convergence of intellectual originality with an unequalled gift for artistic narration actually took place.

The History of Velázquez at The Museo del Prado

In a monograph on Velázquez the art historian Denys Sutton wrote some years ago that no room in any museum in the world offers so pure and refreshing a note as that dedicated to Velázquez in the Museo del Prado in Madrid. He added that one immediately feels a change in the atmosphere. This impression is due not only to the unique aesthetic aspects of Velázquez's work but also to the characteristics of that special place which continues to display his paintings and even to its historical personality. Although the Prado possesses unrivalled collections of the work of some of the most important artists in the history of painting – Titian, Hieronymus Bosch, Rubens, Goya... – the artist most closely connected with its history since its creation as a picture gallery is Velázquez. And this is due to the fact that in the Prado rooms visitors from all over Europe discovered the existence of a powerful, original and hitherto unknown painter who also acted as a guiding light for various generations of artists and critics, providing them with an apparently free and sure method for approaching the visual experience. It was inevitable that such an encounter should take place there, for its approximately fifty paintings by the Sevillian account for over forty percent of his authenticated pictures and almost all his most ambitious compositions. No other institution in the world can boast such an essential, irreplaceable part of the works of one of the most important figures in the history of painting, a part without which a complete understanding of Velázquez the artist would be impossible.

Inauguration of the Velázquez Room in 1899.

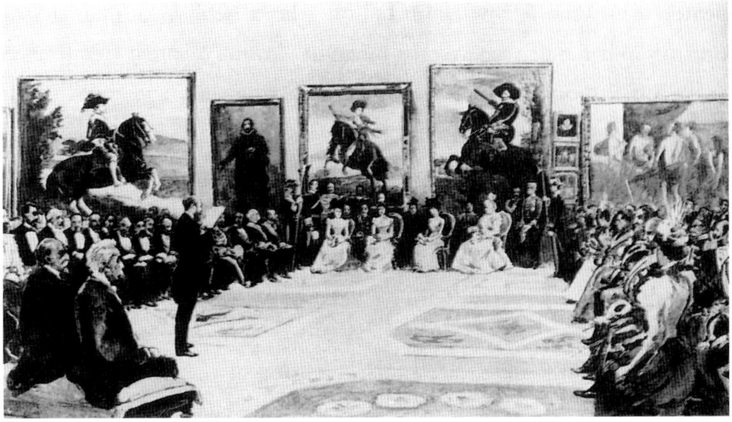

As regards his reputation, Velázquez is a creation of the Museo del Prado – just as the museum is partly a creation of Velázquez's – in the sense that like a magnet his name drew many of the greatest artists of the 19th century to Madrid and made of the building on the Paseo del Prado what the painter Ricketts described as a "Mecca" for modern artists and critics. Attracted by the museum's prestige – due particularly to its paintings by the Spanish school – the travellers and writers who came soon began to realize how rich the collection of paintings by other great European artists was. Indeed, at the end of the 19th century, one lady tourist was heard to exclaim: "I have heard people talk of it since the very moment I knew what art meant".

Thus, studying the history of Velázquez's work in the museum means coming into contact with some of the most important episodes in the history of the institution itself, for the painter and his "house" have led parallel lives. Such a relationship has been referred to by many visitors to the Prado, one being J. Rikard, who in 1922 said that essentially the Museo del Prado was Velázquez.

One of the reasons for this interdependence can be found in the painter's own biography, for he lived most of his life under the protection of the King, Philip IV, for whom he did the majority of his paintings. For a century and a half these works hung in various Spanish royal residences, and although some left the country as a result of the Peninsular War, most of them continued to be the property of the crown. Thus, when Ferdinand VII decided to convert the Prado building into a museum of painting and sculpture and to use the old royal collections to this end, a large number of Velázquez paintings were included among the exhibits. Unlike the rest of Europe, Spain had always been aware of this painter's crucial importance to its art. Great writers and historians of the late-18th and early-19th centuries – such as Ponz, Jovellanos and Ceán Bermúdez – had stressed this fact, for they realized that the rest of Europe had forgotten our history of art and in fact one of the main reasons for creating the Museo del Prado was to bring our "national glories" the recognition they deserved. And among these the Sevillian took pride of place. The result was that for the opening of the museum in November 1819, the rooms adapted for exhibition were devoted to the Spanish school only and the catalogue for that year listed 18 paintings by Velázquez, three of which – landscapes with hunting scenes and royal seats and the head of an old man – are now believed to have been painted either by his school or his son-in-law, Juan Bautista Martínez del Mazo. In the next catalogue (1821) 44 paintings were listed, at least 12 of which are now ascribed to other artists. However, by then almost all Velázquez's great works could be viewed at the museum and his mastery of all the genres he applied himself to appreciated.

Throughout those years the museum continued to incorporate works from royal palaces and residences into its collections, Velázquez's paintings being no exception. Thus, in 1827 several – including *Pablo de Valladolid* (1198), *Don Juan de Austria* (1200) and *Mars* (1208) – which had been at the Academy of San Fernando since 1816, were added to the collection. Consequently, by the time Pedro de Madrazo signed his first catalogue in 1843, the Velázquez collection consisted of 61 paintings – the largest number attributed to him in any Prado catalogue and twelve more than those listed in the latest edition (1996). This does not, of course, mean that the Prado's treasures have diminished since 1843 but simply that further study of Velázquez's production has led to the elimination of several paintings. Here it might be interesting to discuss briefly those works no longer considered attributable to the painter so that the reader will be able to identify what is characteristic of "Velázquez's art". Some of these pictures were copies of originals either lost or known to have been painted by Velázquez, such as the *Boar Hunt in El Hoyo* (1230) or the portrait of *Don Luis de Góngora y Argote* (1223). Others came from his prolific workshop and

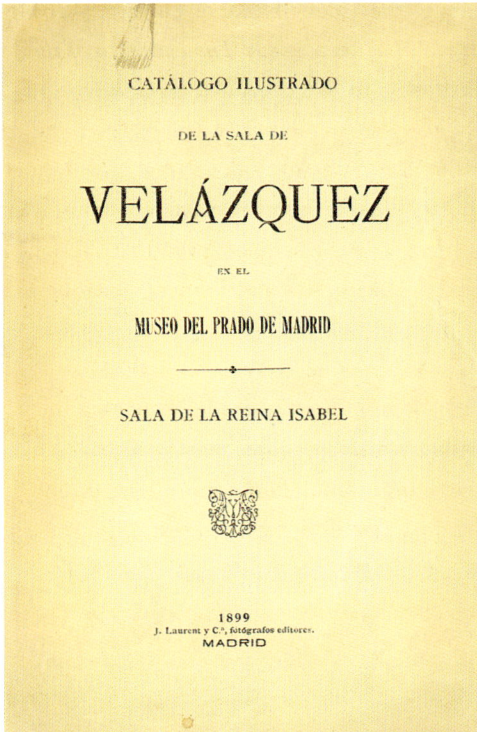

CATÁLOGO ILUSTRADO

DE LA SALA DE

VELÁZQUEZ

EN EL

MUSEO DEL PRADO DE MADRID

SALA DE LA REINA ISABEL

1899

J. Laurent y C.ª, fotógrafos editores.

MADRID

Catalogue of the Velázquez Room.

include *The Fountain of the Tritons in Aranjuez* (1213) and portraits of Philip IV and Maria Anna of Austria, both in an attitude of prayer, and the Dwarf Don Antonio el Inglés. Several can be attributed to Velázquez's son-in-law, Juan Bautista Martínez del Mazo, the artist whose style was closest to the master's. This is the case of *View of Saragossa* (889), whose groups of figures for a long time were said to have been painted by Velázquez. Other examples are: one of the portraits of Baltasar Carlos; another of the Infanta Margarita; and a number of landscapes attributed to Velázquez in the first catalogues, including *The Arch of Titus in Rome* (1212), *Palace Garden* (1216), and *Landscape with Mercury and Herse* (1217). A number of other paintings are now attributed to painters with similar stylistic features who were at Court at the same time as Velázquez. In this respect, two portraits of girls (1227 and 1228) by José Antolínez were believed for a long time to have been painted by the Sevillian. Finally, of the paintings attributed to Velázquez in the 1843 catalogue, some, such as the *Head of an Old Man* (1226) by Pier Paolo Bonzi and a *Portrait of a Lady* (1285) are now known to be the work of foreign artists.

One copy of the 1843 catalogue contains handwritten notes which provide us with extremely useful information on the Velázquez paintings of greatest interest to visitors to the museum at that time. The notes take the form of comments limited in some cases to no more than a short observation or an adjective and were probably written by the owner as a reminder of his visit. The observation *Ojo* ("Attention)" was used for the portrait of

Maria Anna of Austria and the equestrian portraits of the Count-Duke of Olivares (1181), Philip III (1176) and Margaret of Inner Austria (1177) as well as for *The Fountain of the Tritons in Aranjuez* (1213, a painting now believed to be from Velázquez's workshop) and highly ambitious compositions like *The Forge of Vulcan* (1171) and *The Fable of Arachne* (1173). The owner of the catalogue regarded certain other paintings deserving of a more explicit and enthusiastic observation than the simple *Ojo*. He seems to have much admired the equestrian portraits, for in addition to the works mentioned, he believed that special attention should be paid to the pictures of Philip IV and Elizabeth of France, which he described as "superb". The works he praised most highly of all are among the great compositions and include *Las Meninas*, next to which he wrote "very noteworthy", *The Surrender of Breda* (1172) – a "capital painting" – and *The Topers* (1170), which he described as "extremely beautiful". His views were very much in agreement with the aesthetic tastes of an age which attached the utmost importance to the more realistic and naturalistic aspect of Velázquez's work and took a great deal of interest in historical painting.

The 1843 catalogue lists most of the paintings by Velázquez which came to the museum from the royal collections, but not all of them, for it was not until late in 1848 or early in 1849 that the portraits of *Philip IV in Armour* (1219) and *Queen Mariana* (1191) arrived from El Escorial.

Although historians are increasingly taking into account the existence of an extremely industrious workshop at Velázquez's service, the painter's powerful, original style nevertheless makes identification of his paintings an easy task. It is a task, however, which continues to keep historians occupied, and there is no reason to believe that the situation will be different in the future, even though it can be said that by the end of the last century, the Museo del Prado's catalogue was quite a reliable one. Thus, comparison of *The Illustrated Catalogue of the Velázquez Room* (published in 1899 for the third centenary of the painter's birth) with the 1996 catalogue reveals few changes. Of the works attributed then to the Sevillian but now to other artists there are only the portrait of Don Antonio el Inglés (1203) and one of Maria Anna of Austria. Now believed to have come from the workshop, both have been in the possession of the Musée du Louvre for almost fifty years. The opposite has also happened, i.e. some paintings now definitely attributed to Velázquez, such as the *Buffoon Don Cristóbal de Castañeda y Pernia (Barbarroja)* (1199) or the supposed *Self-portrait*, were then attributed to him with certain misgivings.

The Museo del Prado's dependence on the Austria and Bourbon monarchs as collectors was essential, for its best collections are due to them. However, the Prado's holdings have also increased thanks to private donations of major works and a rather inconsistent purchasing policy. Which explains, for example, the collection of works by Goya, which consisted of very few pictures in the early years of the museum's existence but is now made up of around one hundred and fifty paintings, almost five hundred drawings and a large number of prints – ample proof of Spanish society's generosity towards the Prado. The case of Velázquez's works has not been the same, however, due to the fact that few have ever been in private hands. Nevertheless, with the passing of time a small number of paintings of this kind have been incorporated into the museum's collection. The first of these – none other than *Christ Crucified* (1167) – came to the Prado thanks to the generosity of a private owner. It was given to Ferdinand VII by the Duke of San Fernando in 1829 and the King immediately had it reserved for the museum. The portraits of *Don Diego del Corral y Arellano* (1195) and *Doña Antonia de Ipeñarrieta* (1196), which had belonged to the Villahermosa Collection in the Palace of Zarauz until the mid-19th century, were donated in 1905 by the Duchess of Villahermosa. The museum acquired the portrait of *Mother Jerónima de la Fuente* (2873) after the Civil War, purchasing it in 1944 from the nuns of the Convent of Santa Isabel in Toledo and thus making up, to a certain extent, for the shortage of Seville works, for there were few in comparison with works from other stages in Velázquez's career. Two years later the nuns of the Convent of El Sacramento in Madrid donated the small *Christ on the Cross* (2903) to the state in gratitude for the reconstruction of their church and the painting was sent to the museum. The last acquisition was a *Head of a Stag* (3253), donated by the Marquis of Casa Torres and exhibited since 1984. It may have originally come from the old Madrid Alcázar, which again underlines the Museo del Prado's almost total dependence on the royal collections.

Velázquez's importance to the historical and aesthetic identity of the Museo del Prado is very interestingly reflected in the history of the location of his works within the building. The museum's collections have always been arranged according to the criterion of a national school – a golden rule in many Western museums. Consequently, during the first decades, Velázquez's paintings were exhibited in preferential positions together with works by his most important 16th-, 17th- and 18th-century compatriots. This arrangement was generally maintained, although a few small changes, affecting some of the parts but not the whole, were subsequently made. Thus in the 1850s the large basilican room off the Central Gallery on the second floor

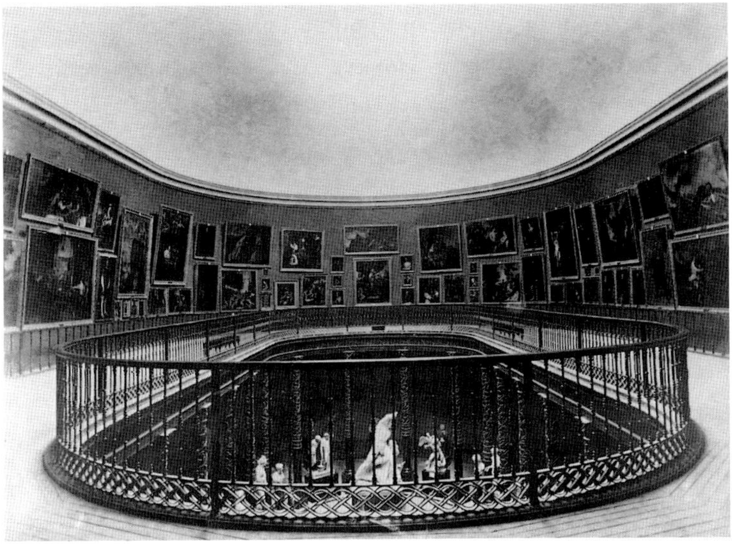

The Queen Isabel Room.

(now Room 12) was devoted to a selection of great works. Called the "Queen Isabel Room", it was opened in memory of Ferdinand VII's Portuguese wife, who is regarded as the driving force behind the creation of the museum. Here emphasis was placed on the predominant concept of art in the 19th century – that of the "masterpiece" – with the result that several paintings by Velázquez were exhibited alongside others by Raphael, Titian, Dürer, Van Dyck, Zurbarán, Ribera and Sebastiano del Piombo. Indeed, according to the incomplete records existing on this area, it seems that the painter best represented was Velázquez with *The Fable of Arachne, The Sculptor Martínez Montañés, The Cardinal Infante Don Fernando as a Hunter, Mercury and Argus, Philip IV as a Hunter, The Topers* and *Pablo de Valladolid.* The idea of the anthological room had various precedents and references to such rooms can be found in the records of many modern museums. One well-known example of this is the "Tribuna of the Uffizi", which brought together the Florentine palace's most select works.

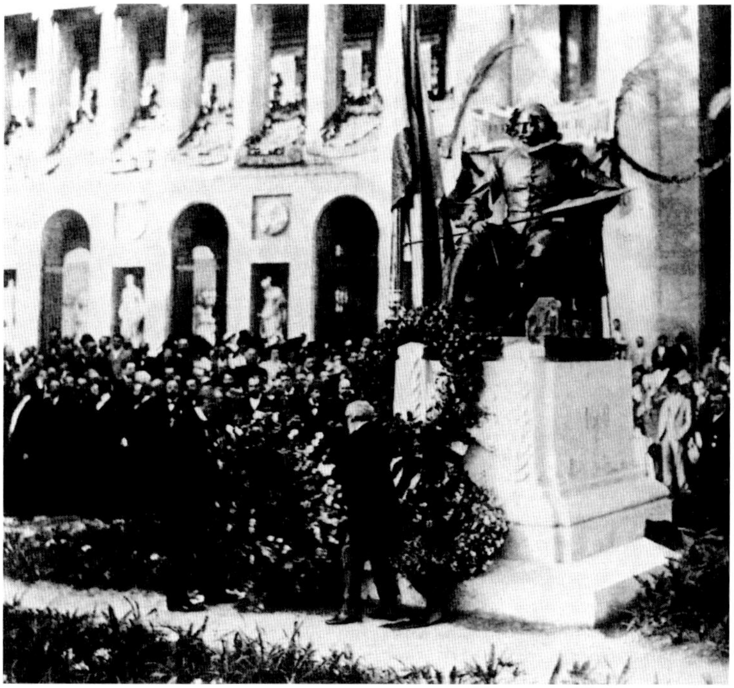

Unveiling of the statue of Velázquez in 1899.

As we shall see, by the end of the 19th century Velázquez had become a major point of reference not only for art historians but also for painters, and his work, furthermore, had been "discovered" in the rest of Europe, all of which increased the Prado's prestige. Fully aware of how intimately linked was the museum's fortune to that of the painter, the museum trustees then decided to take a further step in the exaltation of the Sevillian by dedicating to Velázquez the room where only the most important works of art had hitherto been exhibited. With this decision an important move was made from the idea of the "masterpiece" to that of the "work of the capital painter", and in this way Velázquez's work was assigned the most important area in the museum – at its very heart. To commemorate the third centenary of his birth in 1899, all his paintings were arranged in this room in chronological order, beginning with *The Adoration of the Magi* and ending with *St Anthony Abbot and St Paul the Hermit.* A special illustrated catalogue (the museum's first, mentioned above) was printed and a celebration was held whose guests included politicians and whose activities included readings of poetry. Some days later Aniceto Marinas's bronze statue of the painter was unveiled in front of the museum before a public which included a number of famous foreign artists, among these Carolus-Duran and Jean Paul Laurens. Although the poet Rubén Darío complained in the press that the celebration had been a poor one, one century later we are still reaping its benefits: Marinas's powerful figure of the artist in front of the solemn Doric entrance is an essential part of the Prado's image and, as far as the basilican room is concerned, it has never occurred to anyone that it should contain paintings other than Velázquezs. In other words, the centenary celebration confirmed – not only symbolically but also effectively – Velázquez's status as "King of the Museo del Prado", as he has been called on so many occasions.

Similar examples of the establishment of close links between an institution and its national "artistic glories" can be found at other European museums. The Rijksmuseum in Amsterdam, for example, reflected the nation's pride in being the homeland of Rembrandt through a room that had much of the shrine about it; and at the heart of the building the *Night Watch* was hung.

Before going on to discuss the vicissitudes of the Velázquez collection in the 20th century, we might pause for a moment to consider a question mentioned indirectly in previous pages – the fact that the Prado became a very special place where 19th-century European artists, men of letters and art lovers discovered the painter and ultimately broadened their aesthetic horizons.

In terms of international prestige, Velázquez can be regarded as a creation of the 19th century and more specifically of some of the most advanced artists of that age. To understand their interest it is necessary to know something of the general opinion of Velázquez and his work at that time. According to a historiographic tradition dating from the 18th century, Velázquez was the "painter of reality" par excellence, the artist who most skilfully and sincerely committed the pure visual experience to canvas. Although views have now changed and historians point to the carefully thought-out intellectual process behind that apparent realism – a process with hints of *conceptismo*, double meaning and constant reflection on reality and appearance, representation and its laws – it cannot be denied that the 19th century inherited and promoted that image of Velázquez as an

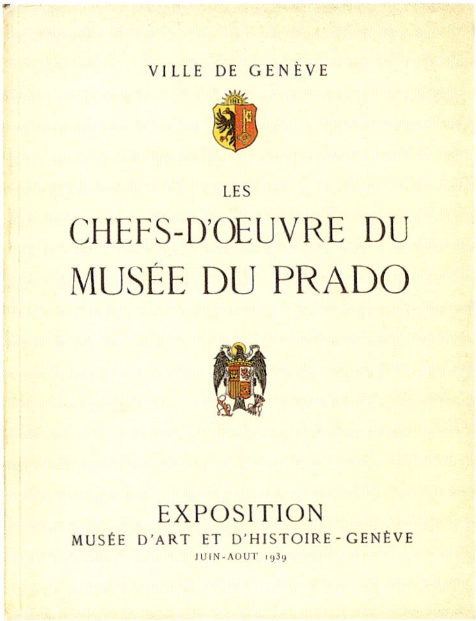

Catalogue of the 1939 Geneva exhibition.

absolute realist. In the 18th century this had won him a certain amount of contempt from writers like Mengs, but in the next century the painter became a champion for new artists who aspired to break away from the traditional classicistic limitations and sought precedents to free them from academic conventions. And in their search some visited Madrid and found Velázquez.

Interest in the painter spread relatively slowly in the first three decades of the museum's existence. From time to time artists came along who immediately realized his great importance, one being the Scotsman David Wilkie, who in the late 1820s wrote that his last seven months in Spain had been the best in all his career. It is said that he spent three hours a day in front of *The Topers* and that Velázquez changed his style, that his paintings became bolder and his colours richer. Other British painters like John Frederick Lewis and John Phillip followed in his footsteps, adopting compositions similar to Velázquez's in their portraits. However, it was due to famous writers rather than artists who visited Spain that Velázquez's name reached other countries. This was the golden age of the "journey through Spain", a land to which Europeans, faced with the onset of an industrial age, avidly came, hoping with romantic nostalgia to recover in southern regions customs, habits and settings by then lost in their own countries. Of those numerous visitors, some were exceptionally cultivated and perceptive and it was they who disseminated knowledge of Spanish culture on the continent. Such was the case of Richard Ford, who in addition to writing a number of splendid passages in his *Handbook for the Traveller through Spain,*

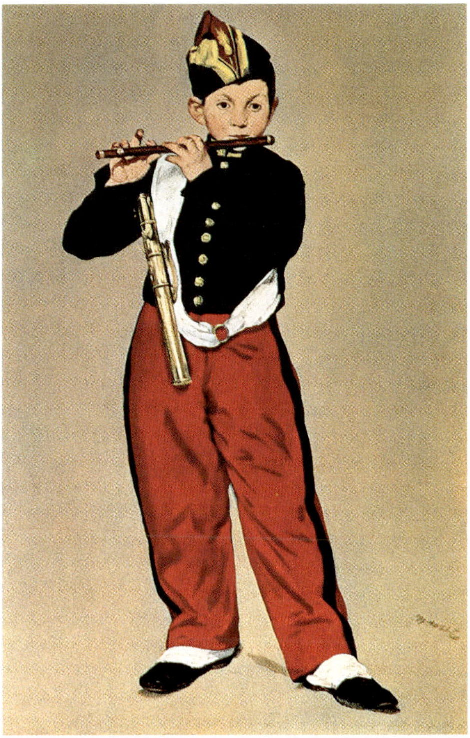

Edouard Manet, The Fifer. *Paris, Musée D'Orsay.*

dedicated a monographic article to Velázquez, and of the French writers Prosper Mérimée and Louis Viardot, authors of studies of the museum.

During those decades, the Museo del Prado and Velázquez became two recurrent themes in the many accounts of journeys through Spain and, together with exhibitions of works by the Spanish school of the Golden Age held abroad, caused great expectation in Europe. This gave rise in the middle of the century to the "pilgrimage" to the Prado to study Velázquez, by then a true point of reference for painters whatever their views on art. A glance at the names proves just how interested the most important artists of the age were in his work.

There is evidence of the painter's influence in France – one of the most important settings for pictorial renovation – between the 1830s and the end of the century. His influence not only reached representatives of the purest academic tradition like Carolus-Duran, but also staunch realists and Impressionists. Deeply aware of Velázquez's influence, Leon Bonnat went so far as to write that he had been raised in the cult of Velázquez. But it was the Impressionists who made the Sevillian their champion, discovering an older brother to rally around in their quest for the pure visual experience. Having studied paintings in Paris believed to be by the Spanish painter, Manet in 1865 decided to travel to Madrid to visit the Prado. His observations are well known and virtually described the experience in terms of a revelation. He did not hesitate to call Velázquez "the painter's painter" and said that looking at his pictures gave him "great hope and complete confidence" in the aesthetic path he had embarked on in Paris as he had found "the realization of his ideal in painting".

Manet is universally acknowledged as the immediate precursor of the painters who most aptly claimed the title of "Impressionists". He passed on to them not only his technical and aesthetic formulas but also his veneration of Velázquez, who became a kind of guiding light to those artists. At some point in their lives the most important Impressionists travelled to Madrid expressly to visit the Museo del Prado and admire the Sevillian's work. Degas had already painted his *Hommage à Velázquez* when he visited the Prado in 1889 and wrote: "Nothing, absolutely nothing can give even a rough idea of what Velázquez is." Renoir, who came at around the same time used similar terms: "When you've seen Velázquez you lose all desire to paint. You understand that it's all been said". The list can be extended to Toulouse-Lautrec, who said: "There is only one painter... and that is Velázquez", or to Claude Monet, who by 1904 an old man longed: "To go to Madrid to see the Velázquezs". Monet made his visit and Aureliano de Beruete wrote of it to Joaquín Sorolla: "He came out marvelling at El Greco, Velázquez and above all Goya.
The rest made no great impression on him".

The above examples are generally well-known because they were written by some of the most important painters of their century, representatives of an aesthetic movement which was to gain popular support. Indeed, although it is now a cliché of historiography to consider Velázquez the harbinger of Impressionism, the Spanish painter's aesthetic interests were in fact somewhat different. Furthermore, as Velázquez won not only the admiration of the Impressionists but also that of many of their contemporaries, such enthusiasm should not therefore be used (as it sometimes has been) to differentiate between Impressionism and other movements but rather to seek the common features defining the pictorial aspirations of almost the whole century.

Thus, it is easy enough to find similar displays of admiration from British, Northern European or American artists. Of these we might cite William M. Chase, who visited Madrid several times and said that no living painter could produce work more pleasing to the eye of the modern critic, or Eakins, who said that *The Fable of Arachne* contained the most beautiful fragment of painting he had ever seen. Or Mary Cassats, or Sargent, or Haley, who painted a portrait of himself as Pablo de Valladolid. From northern regions came Egron Lundgren, Ernst Josephson and also Anders Zorn, who in 1900 made the journey to Madrid because, he said, after seventeen years without seeing Velázquez he

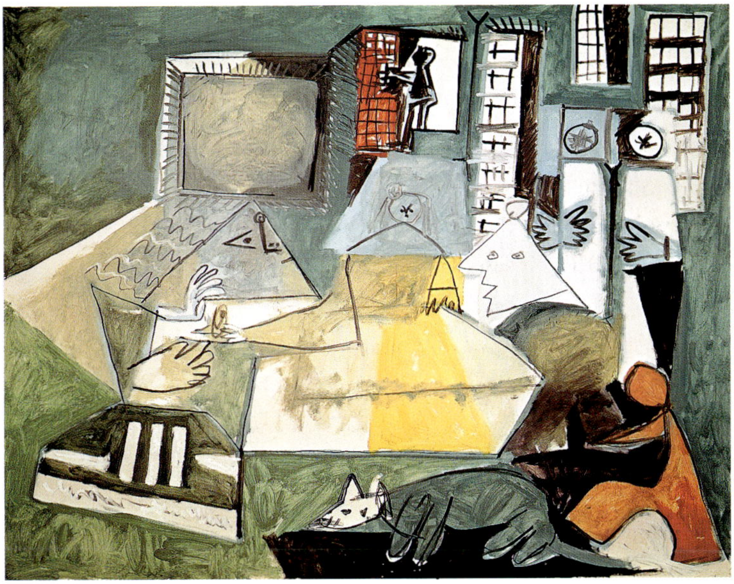

Picasso, a painting from the Las Meninas *series. Barcelona, Museu Picasso.*

missed him. Other visitors were the Dutchman Josef Israels, the English Pre-Raphaelite Millais, and the Germans Von Marées and Lenbach.

By the beginning of the 20th century, the story of the critic or artist standing spellbound in front of Velázquezs in the Museo del Prado had become a cliché. There is no better proof of this than a famous extract from *Trip to Spain* by the German critic Julius Meier-Graefe, who in 1910 rather wickedly evoked what we might call the "anti-image", i.e. his deep disappointment on finding himself in the Madrid museum surrounded by Velázquezs and not feeling that extraordinary sensation: "All that mattered was the great, the one and only Velázquez! I felt as if for years I had lived for no other reason than to experience that moment. But from the very instant I entered the Velázquez room I felt that something painful and absurd was taking place. I had never expected that (...) I tried again with each painting. I would have been satisfied if I had felt drawn to even one!". Although Meier-

Graefe's words were not prompted solely by a critical option, for there was an element of professional rivalry in them (with Justi, for example), their great rhetorical effectiveness is nevertheless based on mockery of the by then deeply-rooted "Museo del Prado-Velázquez-amazement" association.

Although aesthetic criteria and interests have changed greatly since Impressionism, it is true that many 20th-century artists have also expressed their admiration for Velázquez. As the Sevillian had by then joined the pantheon of the great artists, in many cases their comments lacked the poetry (and sometimes what might almost be described as the heroism) of their colleagues before them. Be that as it may and Velázquez's technical achievements apart, his art has also interested artists for other than strictly stylistic reasons and has captivated many whose work, from the formal point of view, has apparently little in common with it. Of the dozens of examples, in this respect we might cite three: Pablo Picasso, who painted a large series of reflections on *Las Meninas*; Francis Bacon, who was obsessed with *Innocence X*; and Nicolas de Staël, who in 1954, one year before his death, wrote in Madrid: "He maintains the miracle of each touch, without hesitating to hesitate (...) and gives the clear impression of being the unbreakable pillar of free, free painting. The king of kings".

Returning to our story of the vicissitudes of Velázquez's paintings in the Museo del Prado, few changes have been made to their location since the decision to exhibit them all together in the large basilican room. More interestingly, adjacent rooms have gradually been assigned to the collection in order to exhibit it in the best possible way, and indeed for a long time *Las Meninas* was displayed on its own in Room 15 A, where there was a mirror (which many will still remember) on the wall opposite to highlight the optical illusion within the painting. The most important changes that have taken place during this century must not, then, be sought in the location but in the position within the general distribution of the collections. The decision to locate Velázquez in a central position like room 12 has subsequently affected the location of paintings by other artists and has made it the backbone of the museum's structure. Thus, it is logical that the large central gallery should have been devoted to the Spanish Baroque school and the southern section of the building to Goya. The careful organization of the exhibition rooms so typical of Sánchez Cantón's sub-directorship and directorship was due in part to the view that the Velázquez Room was the centre of the museum and its backbone. And it continues to be so.

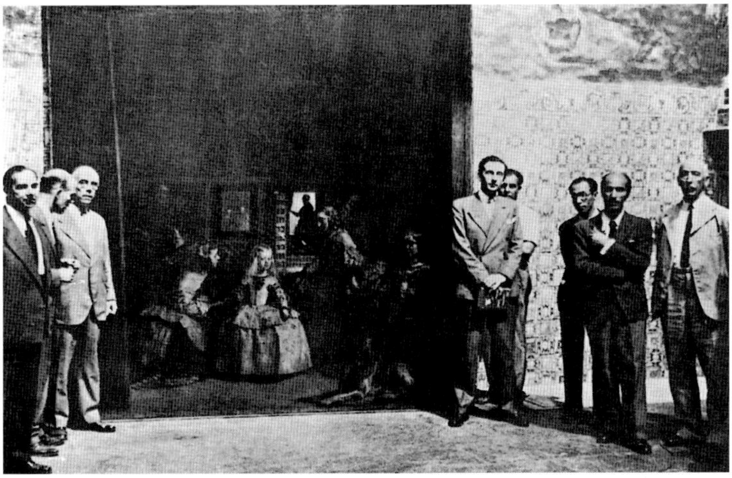

F. Nenyon, T. Pérez Rubio, G. J. Mann and others with Las Meninas *in Las Torres de Serranos, Valencia.*

The Prado's recently approved "Museographical Plan" contemplates the carefully considered distribution of the collections according to a combination of chronological criteria and national schools. Velázquez is to keep the "shrine" referred to by Denys Sutton, while all the 17th-century European painting is to be arranged around it, with the central gallery devoted to his three great contemporaries: Zurbarán, Ribera and Murillo. Collateral rooms will exhibit works by other Spanish artists of his time. Close to Velázquez will be Rubens, so greatly admired by the Sevillian and an artist from whom he learned so much, and the south section will continue to be dedicated to Goya – thus establishing a continuous line of the Spanish school from Ribera to Goya with Velázquez at its centre. Velázquez's influence also explains one of the great projects for the future: the use of what remains of the Buen Retiro Palace as an exhibition area. At present the Army Museum, its heart, the *Salón de Reinos*, was previously dedicated to the Spanish monarchy, the principal points of reference being *The Surrender of Breda* and the Sevillian's five royal equestrian portraits.

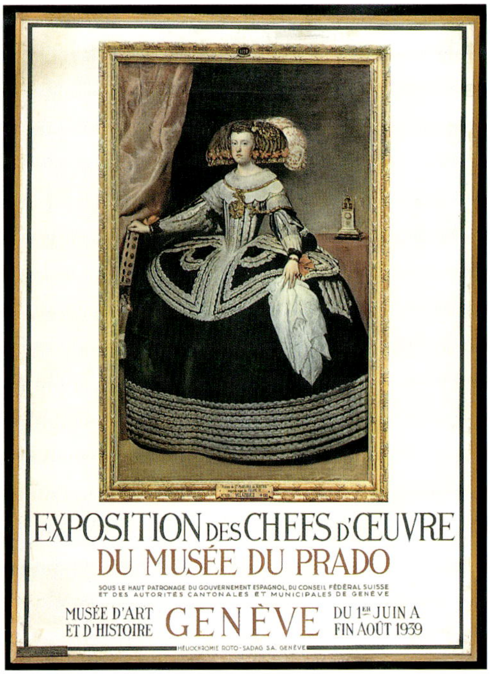

Poster for the 1939 Geneva exhibition.

Like the museum, the Velázquez collection has been very sensitive to Spain's vicissitudes in the course of this century. The Civil War was a difficult time during which it became necessary for the works to be removed from the building on the Paseo del Prado to a place of greater safety. At the end of 1936 the necessary arrangements were made to transfer them to Valencia Museum, where they were stored in the Las Torres de Serranos and the Colegio del Patriarca. Subsequent events made it necessary to transfer them to Catalonia, and from there beyond Spain's frontiers under the supervision of the League of Nations. The presence of such a wealth of painting led to a major exhibition at the Musée d'Art et d'Histoire in Geneva in which a small number of pictures from the Academy of San Fernando, the Royal Palace and the Monastery of El Escorial were exhibited alongside those from the Prado. As this exhibition brought together a large number of masterpieces, it proved to be a major cultural event and was visited by over four hundred thousand people. The most interesting aspect of this exhibition, however, was the Velázquez collection. Although the work of great masters from all the schools was exhibited, a special effort was made to link the name of the Prado with the Spanish painters, so that Goya with 38 works and Velázquez with 36 were the most generously represented.

The Geneva exhibition was a successful mass event thanks mainly to the public's interest in works like *Las Meninas*, and in this respect acted as a precedent for two of the most important events connected with Velázquez and the Museo del Prado that

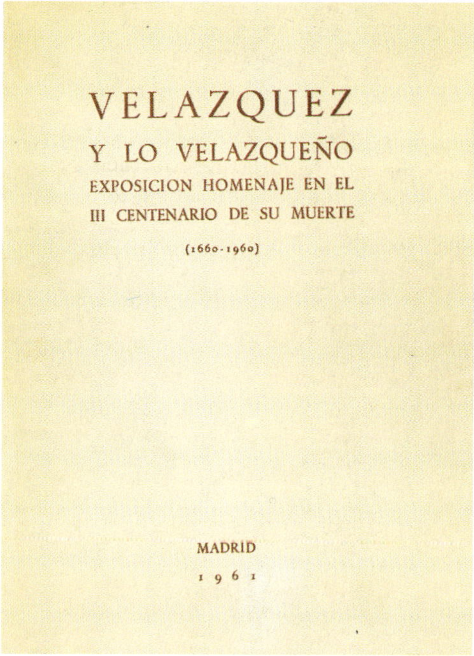

Catalogue of the Velázquez y lo velazqueño *exhibition.*

have been organized in the last few decades. Here I refer to the other multitudinous exhibitions whose success proves just how much interest in the great figures of the history of art has been shown by large sections of society during the second half of this century. In 1961, to commemorate the third centenary of the painter's death, the *Velázquez y lo velazqueño* exhibition in the Casón del Buen Retiro brought together over four hundred items, consisting of works of art and records covering Velázquez's production within the context of his age and society. Of the paintings, more than thirty were originals and included *Venus at Her Mirror, Joseph's Bloody Coat Brought to Jacob* and *The Temptation of St Thomas Aquinas.* In order to facilitate comparison with authenticated Velázquezs, a large number of doubtful paintings at some time associated with the artist were also exhibited. The Prado did not take part officially in the exhibition (it would have been ridiculous to transport such a large number of works over so short a distance) but the event was a fine complement to the museum's collection.

Almost thirty years later, in 1990, the Prado was the venue for a second great anthological exhibition of Velázquez's work. Of the 79 paintings, thirty were loaned to the museum especially for the occasion. One of the cultural events of recent years that is etched most deeply on the memory of Spaniards, it is still remembered for the endless queues which affected the approximately half a million visitors. Further proof of the great interest in the event is that over three hundred thousand copies of the catalogue were sold. Although a number of multitudinous cultural events

Queues for the 1990 Velázquez exhibition.

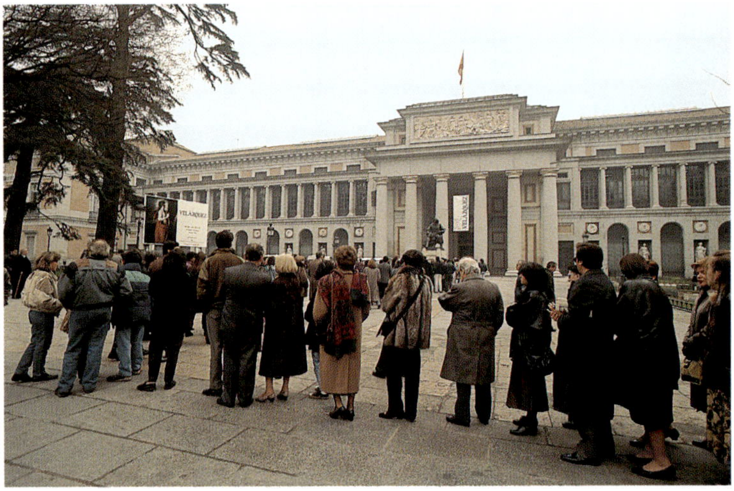

connected with the history of painting have been held in Spain in the last few decades, this one was the supreme illustration of how the work of a long-dead artist is capable of drawing huge crowds. Various factors account for this phenomenon, one of the most important being the association of an institution – in this case the Museo del Prado, for more than a century a focus of Spanish national pride – with an artist regarded as a symbol of national identity.

The Seville Stage and The First Journey to Court

The Adoration of the Magi
Portrait of a Man with a Goatee (Francisco Pacheco?)
Mother Jerónima de la Fuente

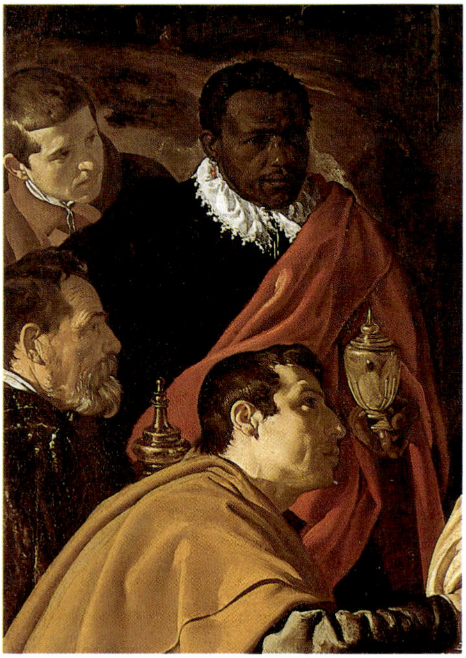

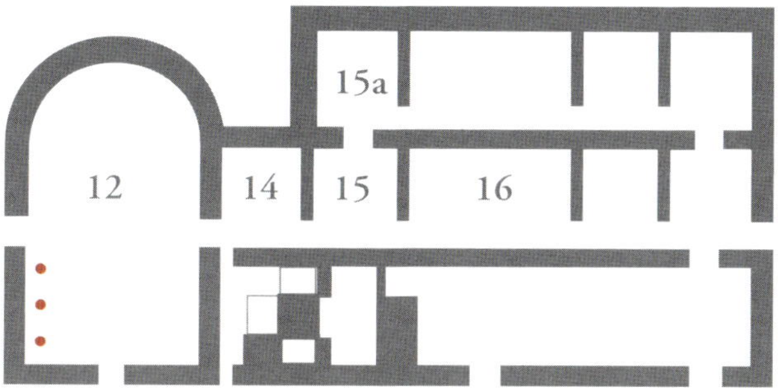

❦ The Seville Stage and The First Journey to Court ❦

Velázquez's professional biography, unlike that of many widely-travelled painters of his age, can be written in terms of three stages. The most important period was spent at Court in Madrid, where he lived for approximately thirty-five of his sixty-one years. Although short, the two visits he made to Italy proved essential to his development as an artist. The first stage in his life, however, took place in his native city of Seville, where he spent his childhood and youth and received his early training as an artist.

With a rich urban tradition hundreds of years old and the monopoly on trade with the Indies, Seville was the most important city in the Iberian Peninsula at the time of Velázquez's birth. Its strength was not only economic, social and demographic, however, but also cultural, and the city on the banks of the Guadalquivir where writers like Fernando de Herrera, Juan de

Arguijo, Cervantes, Lope de Vega, Jáuregui and many more were born or came to live was one of the most important settings for the so-called Spanish Golden Age.

From the artistic point of view Seville was an extremely important centre which for more than a century had welcomed artists from the two most influential focuses of artistic creation in Europe – Flanders and Italy. It is essential to bear not only this in mind when studying Velázquez's career as an artist but also the fact that this cosmopolitan city with its cultivated community was the best culture medium for the intellectual activity Velázquez was to develop throughout his life and accounts for his high regard for art. Furthermore, the opportunity offered him by the city to compare different aesthetic models proved extremely useful to his training.

Historians are increasingly aware of how indebted Velázquez was artistically to his native city and although on some occasions he has been called a "loner" (according to another artist, Ramón Gaya) who developed his own style independently and was indebted as an artist to no man, he was extraordinarily receptive to external stimuli. In fact, personal reflection on such stimuli was one of the driving forces in his career.

But what artistic stimuli did he find in Seville and where did they come from? During the 16th century an influential school had developed in the city, a school characterized chiefly by a combination of forms and expressive resources which had originated with the Renaissance and Mannerism in Italy and had been adapted to the Flemish taste for detail, realism and meticulousness. Men like Sturmio, Pedro de Campaña and Luis de Vargas had created a pictorial tradition which had influenced Velázquez's immediate predecessors, among them his father-in-law, Francisco Pacheco, whose workshop he entered at the end of 1611. Due to his technical skills and, above all, his education, Pacheco was one of the most influential artists in the city. The prototype of the scholarly painter, he was well-placed socially, acquainted with the city's most influential intellectuals, and had written a major treatise on painting. And at Pacheco's workshop the young apprentice would have witnessed his master's high esteem for the art to which he was subsequently to devote himself. From the stylistic point of view, Pacheco cultivated realism in the Flemish tradition, paying great attention to detail. A very different case was that of Juan de Roelas, who had probably travelled to Venice, for his treatment of colour and the arrangement of his compositions reflect a knowledge of the masters of that Italian city.

Such a background explains many aspects of the young Velázquez's style. His detailed manner of painting human beings and inanimate objects owes much to the influence of

Flemish art in Seville. His interest in naturalism and the depiction of everyday objects and events can be associated with Roelas, while his predilection for conceptual games, double interpretations, the inclusion of different scenes and spatial areas in the same painting (as for example in some of his biblical scenes) was due to his own reflection on the artistic stimuli around him. Furthermore, he was almost certainly influenced by paintings reflecting the tenebrist techniques then in fashion in many parts of Europe and which explain the contrast of light and shade so typical of many of his paintings.

The cultural sophistication of some of the city's social circles and a long local history of exposure to a diversity of forms and styles would also explain the favourable reception given to those paintings in which Velázquez distanced himself from Classical and academic ideals of beauty. This he did in order to capture the real and everyday in infinite detail while maintaining that conceptual and compositional interplay of his which put the spectator's intelligence and wits to the test.

All these factors help us to understand the artistic and social background to Velázquez's early painting but in no way do they tell us what it is that makes his work so exceptional. Nor do they explain how he acquired his insuperable technical skill in recreating textures, his extraordinary compositional rigour, his knowledge of how to obtain the greatest degree of expressiveness from a very limited range of colours, or his ability to involve the spectator in extremely subtle games of appearance and reality. With both the existing styles of painting and the new, recently arrived techniques as his starting point, from a very early age he painted works which were not only of extraordinary high quality and personality but also almost completely different from anything else being produced at that time in Seville and in some respects from what he later painted in Madrid or Italy. But now as then, and in spite of stylistic differences, the common denominator of all his pictures is that of having been painted by an artist whose eyes were permanently open to external influences and who had the creative capacity to develop his own, unique artistic personality.

Of Velázquez's production during the six-year period between his admission into the painter's guild (14th March 1617) and establishment at Court, we know of a score or so paintings – approximately one-sixth of his production. Of these the Museo del Prado possesses only three, which makes this period (after that of the second journey to Italy) the most meagrely represented. Furthermore, among the paintings that do not belong to the Prado are masterpieces of exceptionally high quality and interest like *Old Woman Frying Eggs* (Edinburgh), *Christ in the House of Martha and Mary* (London), the "men at table"

(St Petersburg and Budapest) and *The Water Seller of Seville* (London). Only the Prado's *Adoration of the Magi* can compare with these. The reason for this relative paucity lies in the origin of the Prado's collection of Velázquezs, for the vast majority of the paintings came from the old royal collections, i.e. the very reason why the Prado possesses so many pictures from the period when he worked for the King of Spain accounts for the scarcity of paintings of the time when he was a young painter in his home town.

Paintings Exhibited

The adoration of the magi
1619
Canvas, 203 x 125 cm
Inscription: "1619"
Inv. 1166

Painted in 1619, this is one of the museum's few works of the Seville period, before Velázquez went to Court. It displays many features typical of that early period in his career and a number which were to be consistent throughout his life. Thus, his interest in chiaroscuro and the meticulous depiction of objects and textures is typical of the Seville years while his mastery as a portraitist, as seen in the faces of his subjects, is found in the whole of his production and, indeed, is one of his most unmistakable traits.

That realism in the faces of his subjects suggests that he worked with live models, which has given rise to the theory that this painting is not only a religious scene but also what has recently been called a "family portrait". When he painted this picture, Velázquez had been married for a year and it is thus very tempting to imagine that he wished to record the love and affection of his new environment in this painting of the Magi visiting the Holy Family. If such is the case, then the Virgin Mary would be Juana Pacheco, the painter's young wife, the features of the Child would be those of Francisca, their young daughter, the young king in the foreground would be a self-portrait, while the old king kneeling in the middle distance would be Francisco Pacheco, the artist's father-in-law. But the faces of the personages are not the only invitation to identification for we must bear in mind that it was common practice at that time to endow characters in biblical scenes with the recognizable features of the artist's contemporaries.

The nature of this painting can be associated not only with the artist's style at that time but also with the circumstances surrounding the commission for it and the building for which it was destined. This work is first mentioned in 1764 in connection with the Jesuit novitiate of San Luis in Seville and all evidence suggests that it was originally intended to be hung there. This view is supported not only by the painting's provenance but also by Pacheco's good relations with the Society of Jesus and by one apparently trivial iconographic detail: the hawthorn among the barren stones in the bottom right-hand corner of the painting is unequivocally an allusion (frequent in paintings of this kind) to the Passion of Christ. Nothing could be more fitting for a novitiate dedicated to the saintly King of France whose most treasured possession was one of the thorns from the crown of Christ.

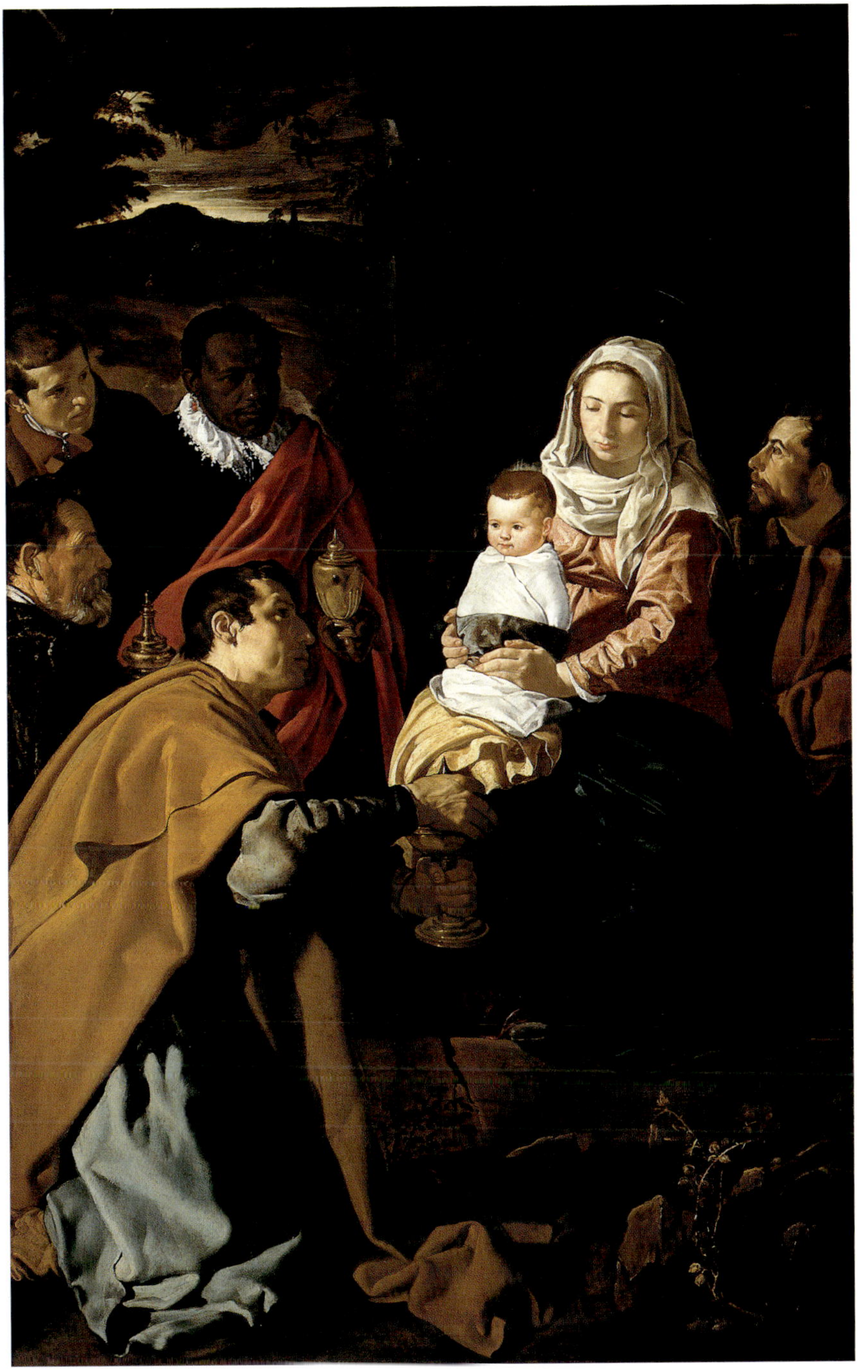

The relationship between the painting's original purpose and its destination also influenced its composition and style. By placing the group of figures very close to the spectator, limiting the number of allusions to the surroundings, and by concentrating expressive resources into the actions and features of the personages, Velázquez produced a "painting for meditation" whose content is conveyed immediately and directly. This coincides with the aesthetic theories of St Ignatius, the founder of the Society of Jesus, who encouraged artists to paint pictures of great communicative skill in consonance with "composition of place".

The influence of Pacheco, Velázquez's father-in-law, in this painting is multiple. As we have said, the features of the old king may well be his, but further influence can be seen in the actual composition of the picture, for Velázquez appears to have followed Pacheco's recommendations on iconography in *Arte de la Pintura* to the letter.

From the novitiate of San Luis, the painting came in 1767 into the possession of Francisco Bruna, a highly cultured politician and *Asistente* of Seville who possessed a magnificent library and a fine collection of paintings. After Bruna's death, his nephew Luis offered the picture to Ferdinand VII, who purchased it for the royal collections.

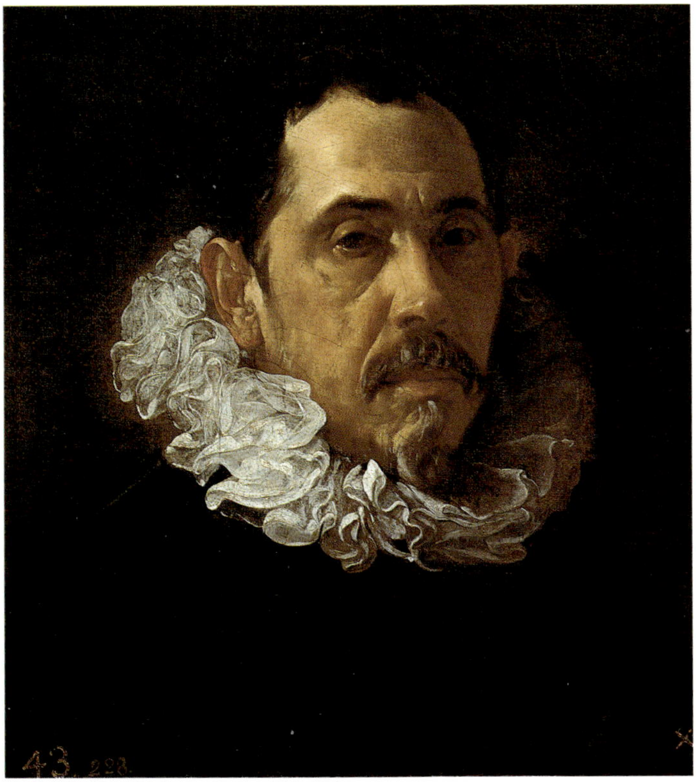

Francisco pacheco
c. 1620-1622
Canvas, 40 x 36 cm
Inv. 1209

Popular in Spain between the second half of the 16th century and the early decades of the 17th century was a type of male portrait, normally a bust against a neutral background and devoid of details denoting profession or identity. The black suit and ruff are also common features of these pictures and so help to place the subject socially as a member of the middle class or nobility. The lack of clues indicating social status or occupation make these works very interesting in that this means that they were private commissions from individuals or families. Thanks to this kind of approach the portrait ceased solely to serve the mainly public or representative purpose previously assigned to it to encompass the realm of private life. There are many fine examples of this type of picture in the Museo del Prado, some signed by El Greco, Tristán and Maino.

Although interesting in helping us to understand the development of the concept of the portrait, the relatively small amount of information these paintings provide makes identification of the models one of the most difficult tasks facing historians. One example is this portrait painted by Velázquez before January 1623, when this type of stiff collar was banned. Thus, from the collar and the model's brown skin tone, this picture is believed to have been painted around 1620. Its high quality and the extraordinary personality of the artist have led many people to wonder who the subject was. The name often associated with the picture is that of Francisco Pacheco, Velázquez's father-in-law, a painter himself and one of most influential men in the artistic and intellectual circles of the Seville of his age. This has been recently confirmed through a comparison of this portrait with Pacheco's self-portrait in the *Last Judgement* in the Museo de Castres, a painting whose existence was known of thanks to the writings of Pacheco but which was discovered only a few months prior to the publication of this book.

In any event, this work of noteworthy quality reveals the painter's knowledge not only of early 17th-century Spanish portraiture but also of Seville's artistic milieu, for it reflects the influence of Pacheco, Vázquez and Campaña. Furthermore, it bears witness to the social status of Velázquez's clientele and family and gives us an early intimation of his insuperable mastery of portrait painting.

First referred to in an inventory of Philip V's possessions at the Palace of La Granja in 1746, the painting was incorporated into the Museo del Prado's collection in 1819.

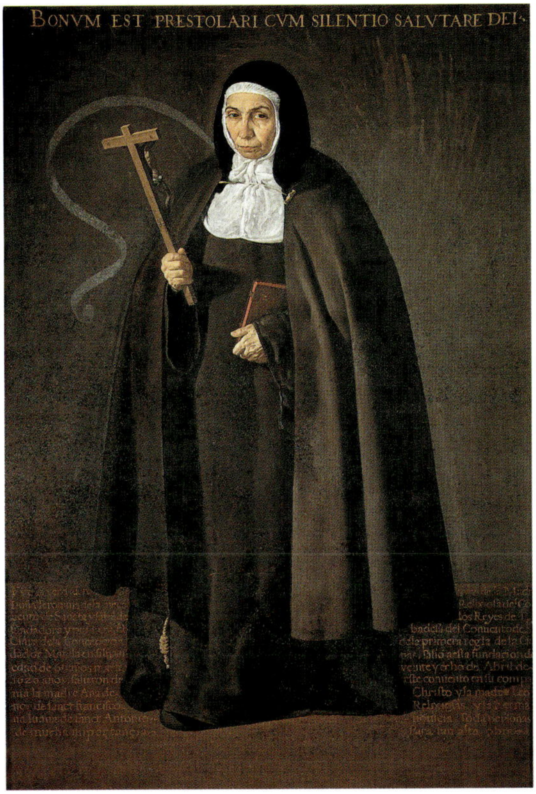

Mother Jerónima de la Fuente
1620
Canvas, 160 x 110 cm
Signed: "Diego Velázquez F. 1620".
Inv. 2873

Our general idea of the Spain of the Golden Age is one of kings active, capable or indolent to a greater or lesser degree, scheming favourites, powerful aristocrats, brilliant artists and prolific and witty writers... But our view of the "public" figures of that time would be very incomplete if we did not also include a large group of religious who, with their visions, miracles and in some cases their ploys to gain publicity, were of interest to people from all levels of society. Some, like Simón de Rojas, were among the greatest celebrities of the moment and were always capable of arousing the public's curiosity. Another exceptional person was Mother Jerónima de la Fuente, whose biography is paradigmatic of a group we might call the "professionals of saintliness" of the period. Born in Toledo into a "bourgeois" family (her father was a legal expert), by the time she was six years of age she was already disciplining herself and using hair-shirts, and at fifteen she entered the local convent of Poor Clares. She forged herself a highly distinguished career within her order and her reputation ultimately reached the Court, whither Queen Margaret of Inner Austria called her for consultation. Her firm, energetic and resolute character was ultimately reflected in her decision to take the Gospel to the Philippines.

When she set sail from Seville for the Pacific in 1620, she was 65 and therefore an old woman for those times. In Manila she founded the first convent in the Philippines and was so active in her evangelical work that a process of beatification was initiated. Between prayers she managed to find time to write a number of books including *Cartas de marear en el mar del mundo* (all now lost) and several poems, like the one below, which she dictated to a companion from her sickbed in 1626.

> "En medio del corazón / todo en su sangre bañado,
> muerto yace el buen Jesús / por los males que yo hago."

One of her principal devotions was the crucifixion, as Velázquez underlined in his painting and a biography mentioning her particular form of mortification reveals: "She had a great wooden cross fixed to the wall with three large nails; she would stand on a stool, grip the heads of the nails and mould her body to the cross, then she would push the stool away with her foot so that it would not support her weight, and she would hang in prayer on the cross in this most pitiful manner for two or three hours at a time".

Velázquez painted this portrait – one of the most impressive in the Spanish painting of that period – shortly before Mother Jerónima left Seville. The subject was the kind of person whose life fascinated people all over the country. Even if there were no information to tell us about Mother Jerónima's character, it would not matter, for Velázquez tells us everything there is to know about her in this painting: her energy, strength, determination, self-confidence, her total conviction of the importance of her mission are all revealed in this figure, in the hands firmly holding a book and virtually "brandishing" a crucifix, in the determined lips, and in that expression of one who has great experience in the wielding of power. At the same time as he depicted Mother Jerónima as an individual, Velázquez left us an accurate description of the "resolute religious" so typical of the Spain of those times.

The reason why this picture was painted lies in Mother Jerónima's already acclaimed reputation for saintliness, which must have prompted the nuns of her order or some other devout person to have her likeness painted. This would almost certainly account for the existence of a copy now belonging to a private collection which, like the painting in the Prado, came originally from the Convent of Santa Isabel la Real in Toledo.

The First Years at Court

A Young Man
Philip IV, Standing
Philip IV in Armour
The Infante Don Carlos
The Topers

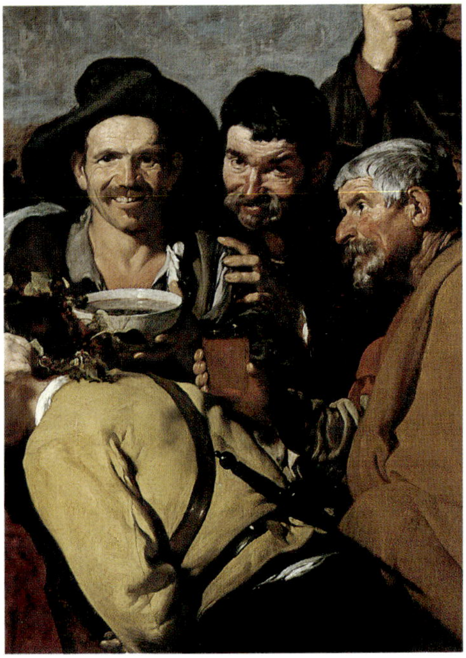

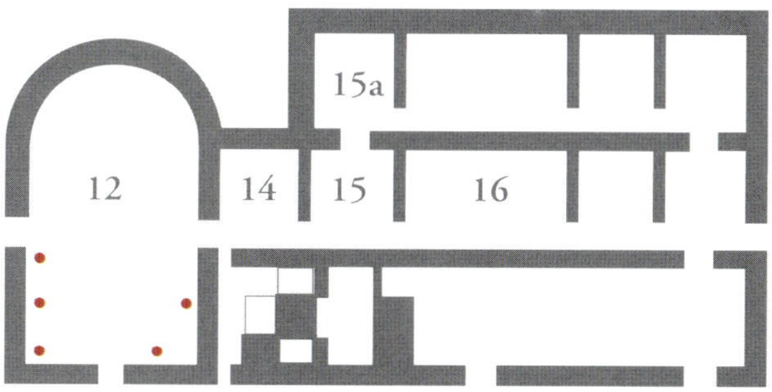

The First Years at Court

The great talent Velázquez displayed in Seville encouraged his father-in-law to send him to try his luck at Court in Madrid, a city rapidly displacing Seville as the main centre of power and culture in Spain. In 1622 the young painter spent some time there introducing himself to friends of Pacheco's who had influence at Court. One of these, Juan de Fonseca, used the recent death of the court painter Rodrigo de Villandrando and the influence of the Count-Duke of Olivares (a fellow Andalusian) to have Velázquez invited back to Madrid in August 1623. Velázquez immediately painted a portrait of Fonseca, who ensured that it reached the King. When Philip saw it he decided that he himself would be Velázquez's next model.

This decision was not only to affect Velázquez's life but also proved essential to history's view of the reign of Philip IV, who by then had been King for barely a year. The main effect on Velázquez was that for the rest of his career he lived in close proximity to the King, who was not only his most important client but also influenced the development of his style and the choice of most of his themes. A cultivated monarch, Philip was so fond of painting that he can be considered one of the greatest collectors of all time. Nor did he scorn the cultivation of other intellectual activities: he was a great music lover, the translator of a long historical work and a prolific letter-writer, and during his reign courtly theatre reached its greatest heights. With Philip the Spanish Court experienced a period of intense cultural activity and became fully aware that Spanish *fiestas*, theatre, poetry, painting, plastic arts, architecture and music were not simply trivial forms of entertainment but the best ways of supporting the King and the monarchy and projecting an image of prestige and splendour. Nor should we forget that when Velázquez met Philip IV, the King was one of the most powerful monarchs in Europe and held possessions all over the continent.

Thus, access to the King was essential for Velázquez. He found in Philip not only a life-long client but also an art lover capable of appreciating a kind of painting which, due to its novelty and unusual style, others might well have been unable to understand, Furthermore, Velázquez immediately identified his aims in life, which were not only to develop fully as an artist but also to initiate a prosperous career as a courtier, i.e. as a civil servant at the Spanish Court. Access to the royal palaces enabled him to see the extremely rich art collections which were to influence the development of his style and his artistic ideology. But his work as a painter and courtier was to have other effects on his art. Thus, although the bureaucratic tasks he was obliged to perform (above all at the end of his life) served to satisfy his social ambitions, they left him with little time to paint, which explains his relatively small *oeuvre*. Furthermore, the unique nature of his clientele compelled him to specialize in genres like portraiture and religious scenes and to explore realms which few of his Spanish colleagues had entered, such as that of the mythological theme. In many ways, Velázquez was a creation of Philip IV's.

The King liked the first portrait so much that he named Velázquez his painter (October 1623). From the professional point of view, the period between this and Velázquez's departure for Italy in 1629 was marked by a number of episodes which won him a preferential position as a Court painter. In Madrid he encountered a school whose work, although modest in quality, had won it a certain degree of social importance and influence. Its members included Vincenzo Carducci, Eugenio Caxés and Juan Van der Hamen, artists older than Velázquez whose style was a combination of Mannerism and naturalism. Cultivated painters, they were fully aware of their professional prestige and had managed to form an important pressure group whose members included such famous writers as Lope de Vega, Juan Pérez de Montalbán and Juan de Piña. The arrival at Court of a young Sevillian who immediately won the King's favour was at first frowned upon and a struggle arose between the older painters, endorsed by their prestige and the social circles they frequented, and Velázquez, whose most effective weapons were his artistic genius, the probable sympathy of the King, and the protection of the all-powerful Count-Duke of Olivares, an ally always ready to lend fellow Andalusians a helping hand. A number of *coups de théâtre*, like the public exhibition of his equestrian portrait of Philip IV (now lost) in 1626, also did a great deal to consolidate Velázquez's position.

The most famous episode in this confrontation took place in 1627, when, on the King's initiative, the principal artists in Madrid were invited to take part in a painting competition. The theme was the *Expulsion of the Moriscos* and the prize that the winning entry would be hung in the *Salón Nuevo* at the Alcázar. The judges, Juan Bautista Maino and Giovanni Battista Crescenzi, chose Velázquez's painting. The victory was a significant one as Velázquez's rivals retorted that he only knew how "to paint heads", i.e. that he was only proficient in portraiture, then regarded as a second-rate genre when compared with other more prestigious genres like "history". With his picture Velázquez demonstrated his mastery of a type of scene regarded as more "noble" and complex and requiring a greater knowledge of painting.

However, the Madrid painters were not completely wrong in claiming that the Sevillian devoted himself to portraits only. All his known works between the time of his establishment at Court and the competition (with the possible exception of *The Supper at Emmaus*) belong to this genre and are either of Philip IV, his brother Charles, the Count-Duke or some unknown sitter. However, as we shall see, *The Topers* may well have been another rejoinder by Velázquez to his critics.

Coinciding with the competition, in March 1627 Philip IV named the painter Usher of the Chamber, a fully bureaucratic position implying confirmation of the King's desire to have Velázquez close to him in his service both as a painter and as a member of the administrative organization at Court.

Velázquez was beginning not only to win small victories in Madrid but also to gain recognition as an artist with great prospects for the future when, in 1628 and at the best possible moment, an event essential to the subsequent development of his career took place. That year saw the arrival of Peter Paul Rubens, who at the age of fifty was one of the most important artists in Europe. Moreover, he came to Madrid not as a painter but as an ambassador to negotiate a peace between Spain and England. Velázquez found Rubens a highly cultivated artist, cosmopolitan, totally familiar with all the secrets of his trade, self-assured, fully aware of his own high standing and that of his art and a man of the highest social rank. The meeting of the two painters led to far-reaching consequences for the Sevillian. Rubens was the prime example of the socially successful artist and everything indicates, moreover, that he showed Velázquez how "to see" the paintings belonging to the royal collections, especially those of the Venetians, and taught him his own way of working (they shared a workshop). It is quite probable that it was Rubens who advised Velázquez to go to Italy – a journey which proved so important to his artistic maturity.

Paintings Exhibited

A young man

c. 1623
Canvas, 55.5 x 38 cm
Inv. 1224

The edict of January 1623 on attire (due to which it was possible to date the purported portrait of Pacheco) can also be used as a guide for this picture inasmuch as the subject wore the only kind of collar permitted after this date. The style of the painting, the dark, detailed brush-strokes, the rather harsh modelling and carefully focused light, also coincide with Velázquez's style of that time of transition between the last years in Seville and his definitive establishment at Court. Also common in the portraits of the 1620s is a very limited range of colours supported by various shades of black to depict male apparel, browns and pinks for faces, and greys and browns for backgrounds.

As with *Portrait of a Man with a Goatee* there has been a great deal of conjecture as to the sitter's identity and various writers have attempted to identify him as a member of the painter's family. His age, the way his head is turned towards the spectator, his fixed look and the similarity of his features with those of the main figure in *St John at Patmos* (National Gallery, London) have led some experts to state that it is a self-portrait, while others have suggested that the subject could be the painter's brother Juan. There is currently no conclusive proof of either of these theories, however.

The mystery surrounding the identity of the person portrayed also envelops the painting's provenance, for no reference to it can be found in any of the numerous inventories of the Royal Seats made in the 17th and 18th centuries. Nevertheless, it must have belonged to the royal collections at some point, as it was exhibited in the Museo del Prado from 1819.

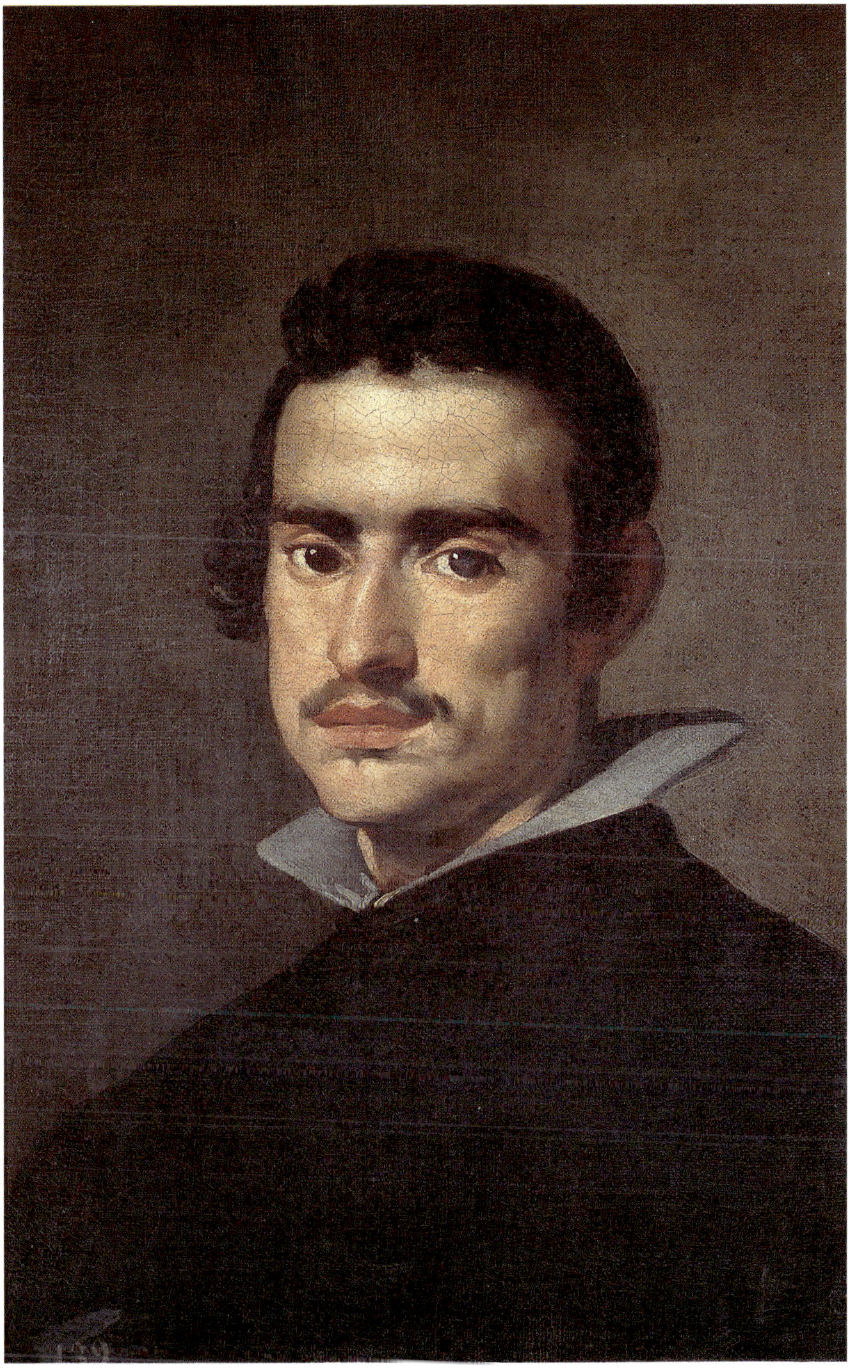

Philip IV, standing

1623-1628
Canvas, 198 x 101.5 cm
Inv. 1182

While it is true that Velázquez was in some respects a creation of Philip IV's, the opposite can also be said to be so. Or we can at least say that the idea we now have of Philip and his reign owes much to Velázquez's portraits. In spite of the fact that his career at the King's side was a long one (almost forty years), all the portraits of Philip have aspects in common which can also be appreciated in this painting: gravity, distance, impassiveness, allusions to his responsibilities as a governor – all characteristics contributing to the creation of an image of royal majesty. In this case the King stands commandingly, full-length, isolated in a neutral, indefinite space which serves to underline the corporal reality of his person, in a pose previously seen in Sánchez Coello's portraits and accompanied by references to his office and position – the insignia of the Order of the Golden Fleece around his neck, his left hand resting on the hilt of his sword, a paper in his right hand and his hat on a table. All these things tell us of his obligations to his kingdom – its administration and defence, the meting out of justice, etc.

Although there is doubt as to the date of the painting and the circumstances surrounding its execution, historians tend to believe that it dates from the end of 1623 and was based on the portrait of the King painted in August of that year which won Velázquez entry into the Court. Some years later (possibly around 1628) he made a great many changes to it, correcting the position of the legs (originally further apart) and the fullness of the cloak, and repainting the face, as the King had aged several years. These changes are confirmed by the copies made of the original portrait and recent X-ray analysis of the painting.

Records prove that this painting hung in the Buen Retiro Palace between 1701 and 1794, after which it was sent to the Palacio Nuevo. From there it reached the Academy of San Fernando in 1816, and finally the Museo del Prado in 1827.

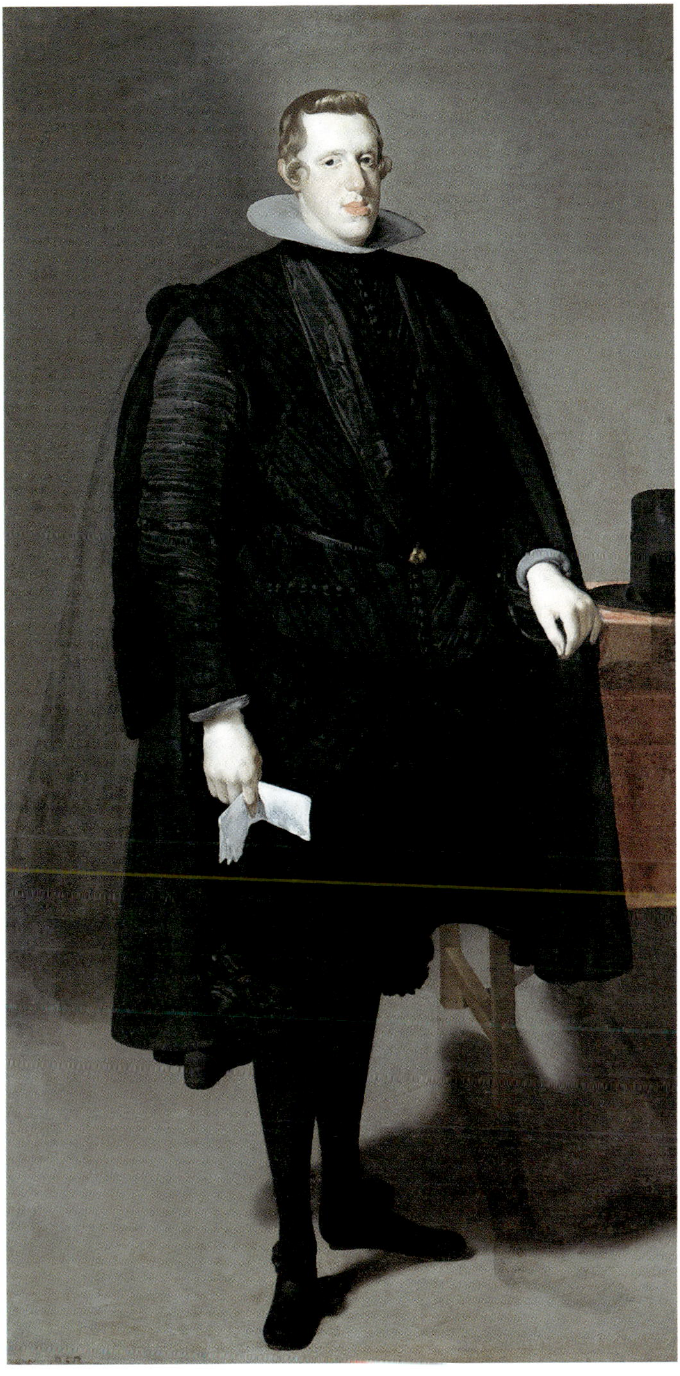

Philip IV in armour

c. 1626-1628
Canvas, 57 x 44 cm
Inv. 1183

In the 17th century, the life of a painting, especially a royal portrait, did not come to an end when the painter decided he had applied the last brush-stroke, for it was thereafter subject to various possible courses of action. The almost religious reverence we feel for art in this age of museums did not exist in Velázquez's times, for paintings were then regarded as multi-purpose objects. In this respect the works of Velázquez were no exception; given their function in the palace and the fact that they were always at hand, the painter could make changes to them at any time.

This painting of Philip IV is a good example of the eventful life of portraits which has given historians so much cause for conjecture. In the early decades of this century this canvas was proved to be no more than part of a larger one, prompting the suggestion that it might be what remained of the famous equestrian portrait exhibited in 1626. X-ray analysis has proved that changes were made at some time to the face, and the considerable differences in style between the head, the armour and the sash suggest that there were two different stages in its execution. It has even been suggested that it was the painting on which the Museo del Prado's portrait of the King standing (1182) was based and that further changes were made to it for its use as a model for the equestrian portrait. Experts tend to date this painting as between 1626 and 1628. It reached the Prado from the royal collections.

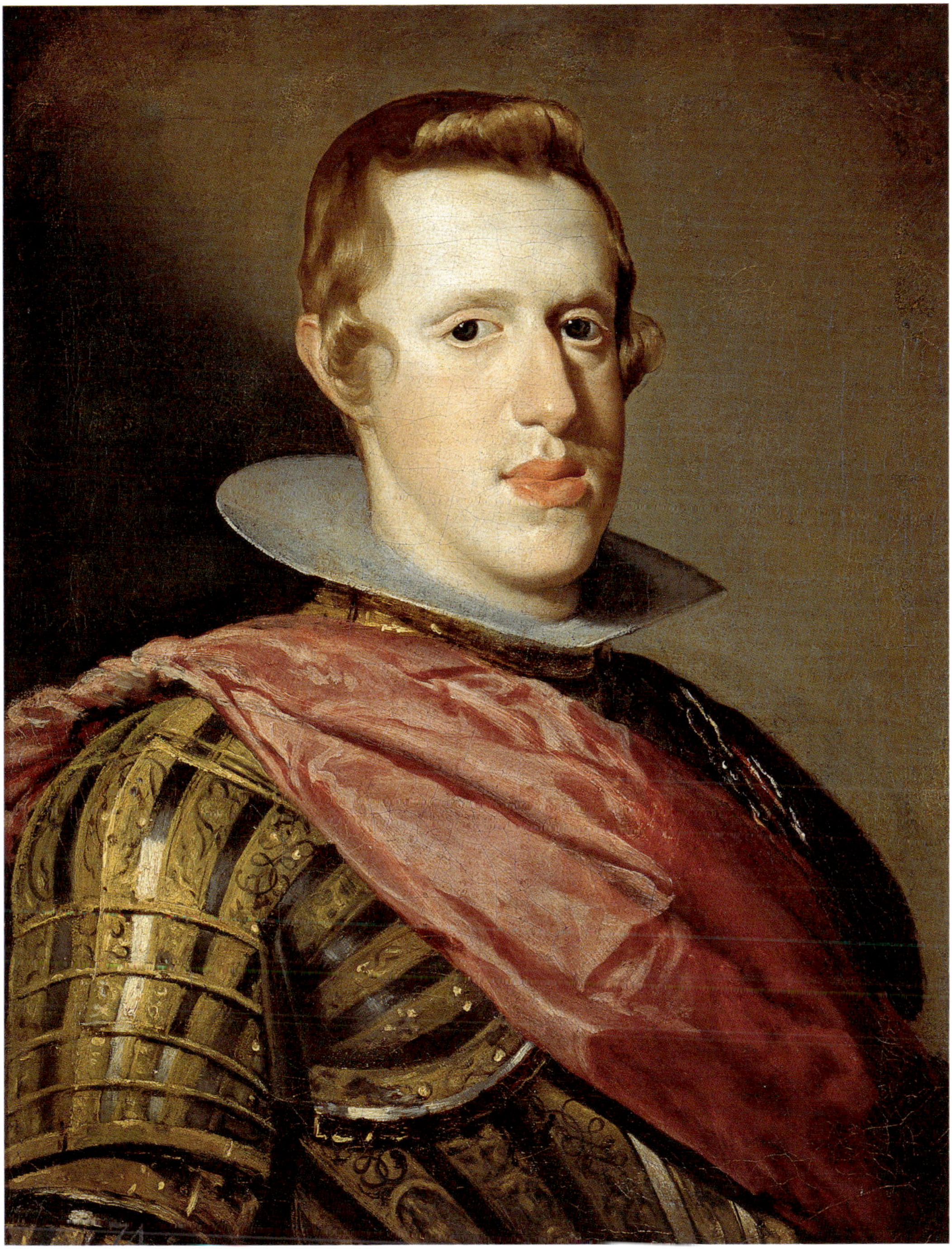

The infante don carlos

c. 1626
Canvas, 210.5 x 126.5 cm
Inv. 1188

Born in Madrid in 1607, Don Carlos was Philip's IV younger brother. He bore such a strong resemblance to the King that for many years this portrait was thought to be of Philip himself. The information available on Charles's character, his aspirations and even the most important events in his short life (he died in 1632) is ambiguous and in some cases contradictory and consequently confusing, but it seems that he was always overshadowed by his brother and did nothing exceptional in his lifetime. However, it is thanks to this portrait that we know of him today. One of the best paintings of Velázquez's early Court period, it is usually dated, despite a certain amount of disagreement among experts, around 1626 or 1627.

Through this painting Velázquez proved how the greatest possible elegance can be achieved with a wise choice of a small number of pictorial resources while avoiding ostentation and exercising moderation. In this case, the solemn figure of the Infante stands in a neutral space, depicted solely with gradations of grey and the black of his shadow on the floor. Velázquez included details which, although apparently trivial, endow the portrait with incomparable distinction – the right hand gripping the wide hat and above all the left hand barely holding a brilliantly executed glove.

The beauty of the detail in the hand and the glove (one famous painting by Titian includes the same detail) is unanimously acclaimed. Indeed, the poet Manuel Machado himself praised it in the final lines of a famous sonnet devoted to this portrait, then believed to be of Philip IV:

> "Y, en vez de cetro real, sostiene apenas
> con desmayo galán un guante de ante
> la blanca mano de azuladas venas".

The painting is first referred to in the Alcázar and, after the fire, in the Royal Palace. It was transferred to the Academy of San Fernando in 1816, reaching the Museo del Prado eleven years later.

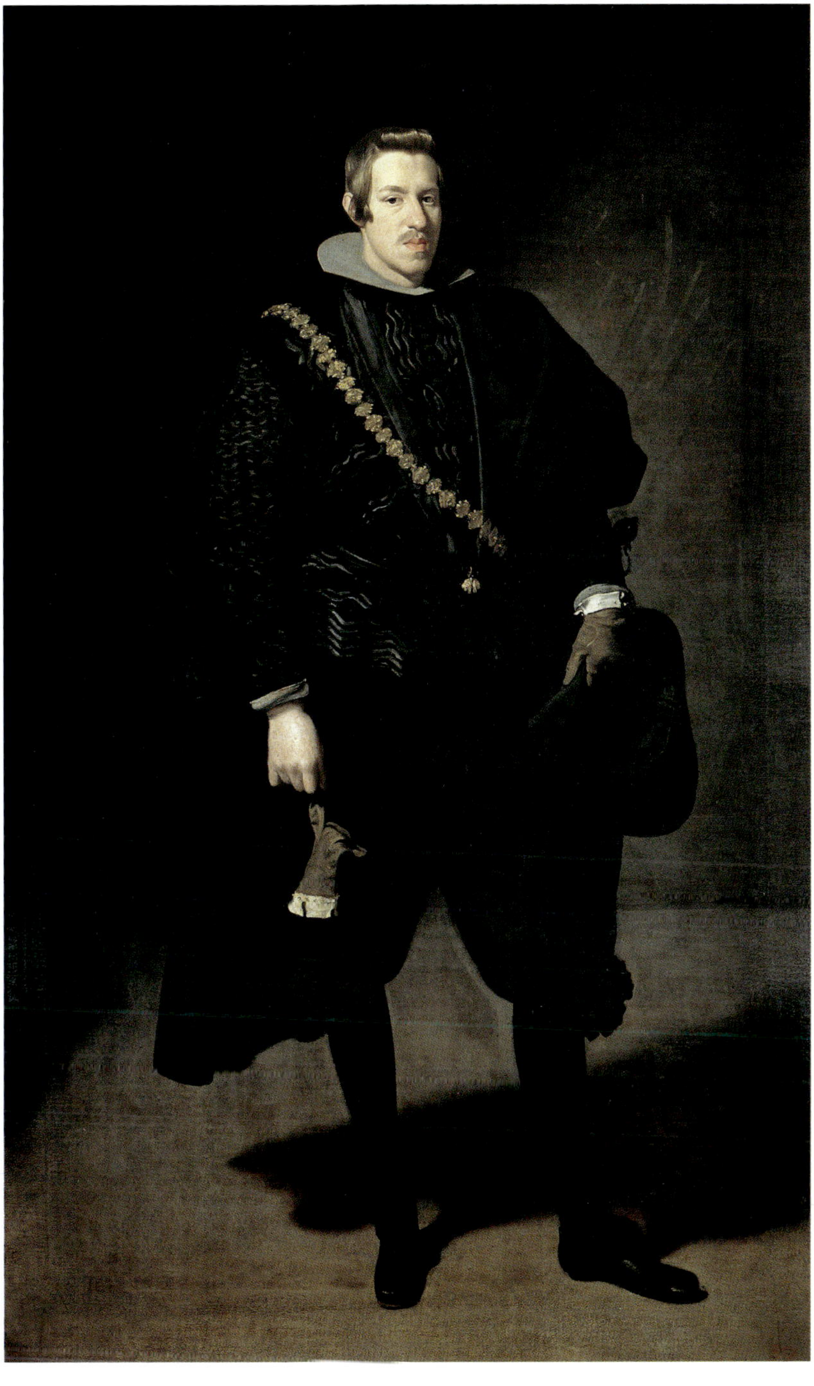

The topers

c. 1628-1629
Canvas, 165 x 188 cm
Inv. 1170

Of the factors that have made Velázquez one of the greatest figures in the history of painting, the one which has always been stressed above all others is his capacity to translate his own experience of reality into pictorial terms by means of a technique which, although highly personal, nevertheless reflects the influence of everyday life. But Velázquez was also a true innovator of many of the great genres in painting, including the portrait, the landscape and the historical scene. Another genre to which he brought innovation and a very personal approach – despite the fact that artists had been painting pictures of this kind for over a century – was that of the mythological painting.

Velázquez's approach to Classical legend had a number of points in common with that of certain Spanish writers and intellectuals of the Baroque period. As can be seen in *The Fable of Arachne*, he was always, on the one hand, fond of playing with the concepts of appearance and levels of reality with which legend provided him. On the other hand, like Cervantes, Quevedo and so many others, he viewed the gods and their troubles in human terms, literally bringing them down to earth from Olympus. One of the paintings which best reflects this is *The Topers*, its half-naked Bacchus in the foreground surrounded by a group of merry drinkers who, far from displaying idealized features, look as if they had come straight from the streets and taverns of Madrid.

From the narrative point of view the mixture of mythology and everyday life makes this painting very different from many of the usual representations of themes associated with Bacchus, and this has given rise to various interpretations of it. Some experts cite a number of similar Flemish masquerades as a precedent, but the fact is that in the Spanish literature and theatre and the festive depictions of the age there are many examples of this blend of contemporary life and mythological legend. All of which coincides with the attitude of detachment towards the Classical story typical throughout Velázquez's career which gave him the freedom to make a very personal reflection on mythology and the lessons to be drawn from it. In this case the painting is a proclamation of the virtues of wine and its capacity to console men in the face of life's hardships. The background is reminiscent of some of those in the biblical scenes he painted in Seville, e.g. *Christ in the House of Martha and Mary.*

A carefully composed work, this painting reveals a very patient, detailed study by the artist, who no doubt was fully aware that, although new for him, he was

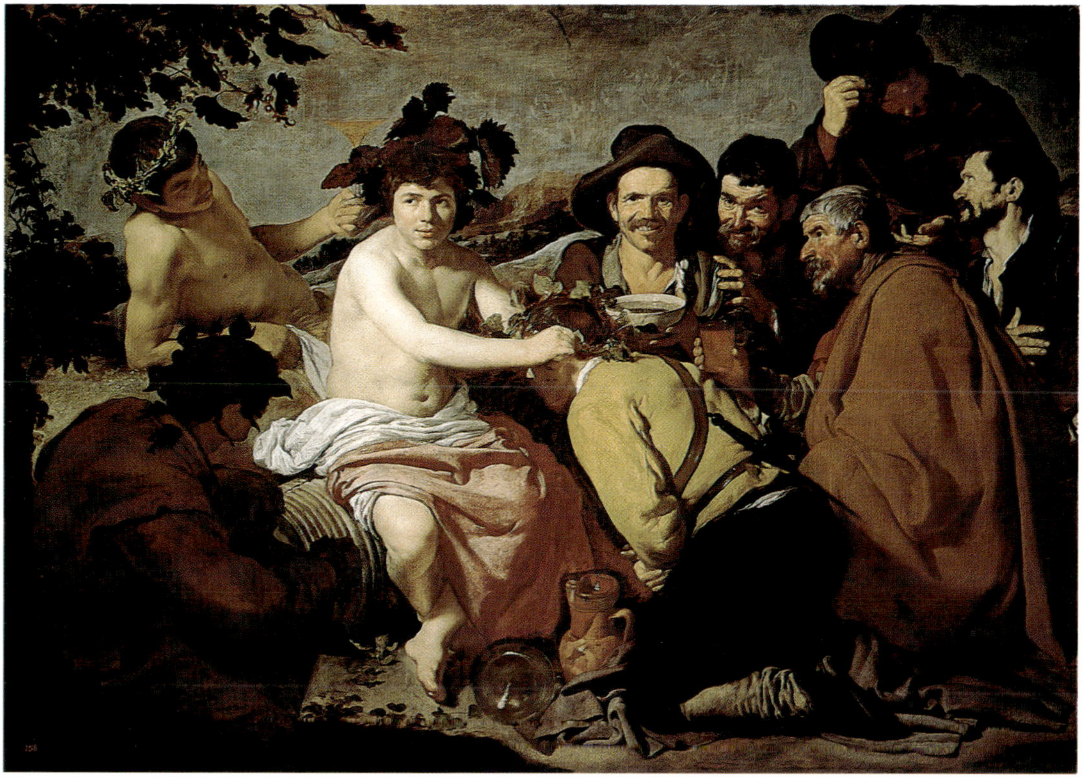

dealing with a genre with a noble, distinguished reputation. But instead of taking the safe course set by a tradition which ennobled Classical mythology – and which he could easily have studied through the paintings in the royal collections – Velázquez produced a painting which demonstrated his independence and self-confidence. He expressed his own ideas on the genre, as can be seen in his preference for earthy tones, weather-beaten faces, the garments worn by the common people, an interest in the narrative paradox, absolute proficiency (when he thought it necessary) in painting the human anatomy in accordance with academic conventions, while demonstrating his mastery in the rendering of facial expressions. And due to this it has been suggested – not without foundation – that this picture is actually a manifesto against those who scorned him for painting "only heads", for not knowing, they said, how to approach subjects requiring greater artistic inventiveness.

Although Philip IV paid for the picture in 1629, some critics believe that it was painted considerably earlier. Stylistically, however, it coincides with that year, a time when Velázquez continued to display the naturalist tendencies he had developed during the Seville years and was already familiar with the work of Rubens and the 16th-century Venetian painters. *The Topers* has been compared to a painting by Ribera of Bacchus (of which only three fragments have survived, two in the Prado) and Massimo Stanzione's *Sacrifice to the God Bacchus* (also in the Prado) in the belief that at some time the three formed part of a series.

A painting always highly valued by the kings who have owned it, it has belonged to the Prado since its inauguration in 1819.

The First Journey to Italy

The Forge of Vulcan
Infanta Doña María, Queen of Hungary
Villa Medici in Rome
Villa Medici in Rome

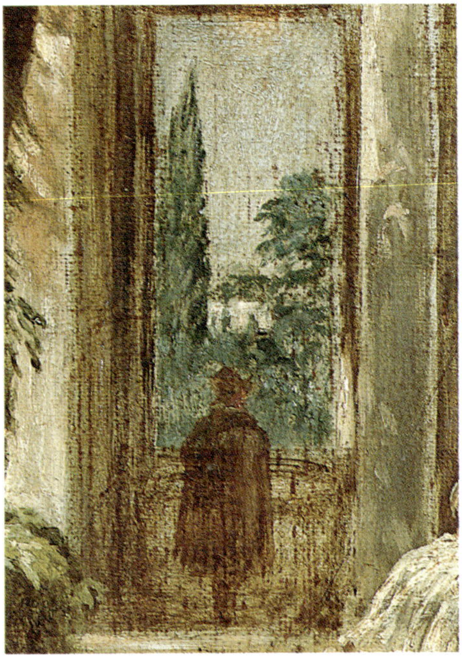

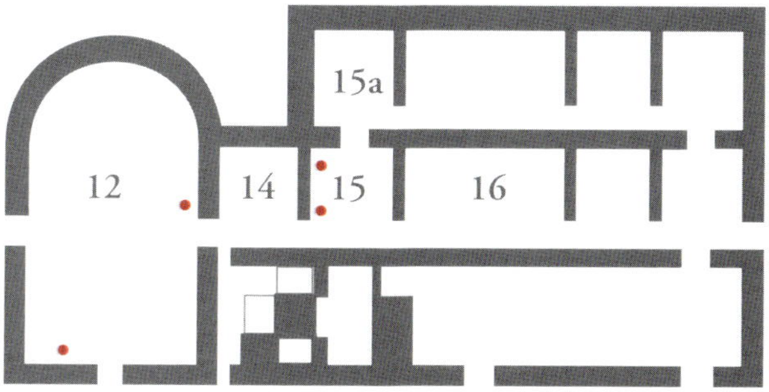

The First Journey to Italy

For Velázquez, contact with Rubens between 1628 and 1629 (referred to in the previous section) was to mean more than just discovering a court painter and intellectual on whom to model himself. In all likelihood it was the Flemish painter who opened Velázquez's eyes to the infinite possibilities offered for research into new styles by the magnificent paintings in the royal collections and encouraged him to travel to Italy. This country had been the fundamental frame of reference for Spanish art for over a century and indeed, many of the most important Spanish painters, sculptors and architects had gone there to study or work, with the result that Italian methods and techniques had entered Spain through paintings, sculptures and prints. However, these could not completely make up for first-hand experience, as most of the material available in Madrid dated from previous periods and current Italian art was poorly represented.

So it was that in June 1629 Velázquez obtained two years' leave of absence from Court, during which he was to continue to receive his salary as a royal civil servant. He took along letters of recommendation which would gain him admittance to otherwise inaccessible places in the Italian states – but also alarmed the various ambassadors in Madrid, some of whom wrote to warn their masters of a forthcoming visit by a painter-protégé of the King of Spain whose intentions were not completely clear.

Among the passengers on the ship which left Barcelona in August of that year and reached Genoa a month later was Ambrogio di Filippo Spinola, subsequently to be included in Velázquez's *The Surrender of Breda.* So began the first of the two long journeys through Italy which proved to be milestones in Velázquez's career. The first was of vital importance to the development of his style, and the second to his (always relative) establishment in the art circles of Rome. On this first journey he travelled the country from north to south, visiting some of the most important centres of artistic activity and taking in everything he saw. In the palaces and churches of Genoa he probably saw the work of Van Dyck, Rubens and Bernardo Strozzi and in Venice, after stopping over in Milan, reencountered old friends from the royal collections, including Titian. He was also able to increase his knowledge of Tintoretto, an artist less well represented in Madrid than Titian whose original style the Sevillian had studied in his copies of the Crucifixion and the Last Supper. The next destinations were Ferrara and Cento – the homeland of Guercino, an artist somewhat older than Velázquez and among the living painters to have the greatest influence on him during his Italian journey. After visiting Loreto he reached Rome, where he was assigned quarters in the Vatican and the Villa Medici, and stayed for about a year.

1630 was a crucial year, not only for Velázquez but also for art in general in the city on the Tiber. With the debate between classicists and naturalists – an issue which had kept the members of the local art circles occupied during the first two decades of the century – now over, the struggle began between the classicists (with their heirs) and the proponents of decorative Baroque. But this was also a period when foreign painters with new ideas – like Poussin and Claude Lorrain – were beginning to make names for themselves and paintings from the north of the country (such as Titian's "Andrians") were ushering in Neo-Venetian ways. This period also saw the appearance of masterpieces like

Guido Reni's *Rape of Helen*, Guercino's *Death of Dido* and Pietro da Cortona's *Rape of the Sabine Women* – outstanding examples of a vivifying moment of reflection on classicism expressed in new terms and removed from academic constraints. Velázquez was extraordinarily receptive to this climate and all his subsequent work was to be affected by this first experience in Rome; an experience which not only provided him with pictorial models but confirmed his view of painting as an intellectual activity, an idea he had become familiar with during his time at Pacheco's workshop.

The most immediate results of exposure to Italian art were the two great compositions he painted while in Italy: *Joseph's Bloody Coat Brought to Jacob* and *The Forge of Vulcan*, along the lines of the great "narrative" paintings to which works by Cortona, Reni and Guercino belong. In these pictures Velázquez not only shifted the narrative emphasis of his scenes but also changed his style; a style by now more confident, heralding what were to be the stylistic constants of his maturity. There was no hesitation of any kind in these compositions, he took greater interest in the depiction of human anatomy, and these paintings also revealingly reflect emphasis on the theory of gesture. All traces of the tenebrism of the previous period in Seville and Madrid disappeared, light began to model volumes directly and powerfully, and colour became lighter and richer. This change in style, however, was not only influenced by his knowledge of the painting then being produced in Rome but was also due to his studies of the great Italian masters of the Renaissance. In Rome, he was able to admire Michelangelo – from then on a constant point of reference in his paintings – at his leisure, and, as we have said, when in Venice he took in everything he saw. And this is evident in these two great works: while Velázquez's treatment of colour and insistence on atmospherical values in *Joseph's Bloody Coat Brought to Jacob* is comparable with the Venetian tradition, *The Forge of Vulcan* has been said to have more in common with the work of classicists like Guercino – another artist influenced by the paintings he saw in Venice. Artistically this was a particularly productive period not only in Rome but in Italy in general and there was a wide variety of pictorial alternatives, all of which encouraged Velázquez to seek his own expressive language. Without any doubt he found it, as these two paintings prove, and although comparable with other contemporary works, they bear no resemblance to them; or as the two views of the Villa Medici – if, as it seems, they were truly painted at that time – prove. As regards the two views, the fact that historians are now unsure whether they date from 1630 or twenty years later proves how highly developed was Velázquez's own, unmistakable style – a style equally distinguishable in the paintings immediately after his return from Italy – and how relatively early that development took place.

The last visit on his journey was to Naples, where he met up with Ribera and painted the portrait of the Infanta Maria Anna, who was on her way to join her new (and virtually unknown) husband, Ferdinand III of Hungary. From Naples he returned to Madrid, arriving there at the beginning of 1631, well ahead of schedule, as the King was impatient to have his painter near him again at Court.

Paintings Exhibited

The forge of Vulcan

1630
Canvas, 222 x 290 cm
Inv. 1171

As mentioned above, this picture was painted by Velázquez in Rome in 1630 during his first journey to Italy. Despite the difference in size between the two, many critics hold that it is the companion piece to *Joseph's Bloody Coat Brought to Jacob* (Monastery of El Escorial). Indeed, the two pictures are of the few which cannot be traced to a specific commission and it seems that Velázquez painted them on his own initiative and sold them to Philip IV in 1634. *The Forge of Vulcan* depicts the moment when Apollo – wearing a crown of laurels and an orange robe, his head surrounded by a halo – bursts into Vulcan's forge to tell him of his wife's (Venus) infidelity with Mars. Forever fond of turning myths upside down to exploit their more paradoxical possibilities, and instead of making a burlesque of the story (as was customary in the literature of the age), Velázquez painted a study of reactions such as surprise and incredulity. This work is a magnificent example of the painter's skill at composing a "story" not only from a group of individual actions but also from a coordinated repertoire of gestures and expressions.

The origin of the painting would seem to lie with a print on the same theme by the engraver Antonio Tempesta which served Velázquez as a starting point. But in addition to this iconographic debt, the painting reveals formal and stylistic influence stemming from the first-hand knowledge of Graeco-Roman sculpture Velázquez acquired in Rome and his study of some of the most important contemporary masters, including Guercino and above all Guido Reni, from whom the modelling of figures with their combination of structural power and expressive delicacy is derived. From the narrative and compositional point of view, this picture can be related to other works then being painted by some of the most important artists in Italy. These normally consisted of large-format canvases of mythological or biblical scenes displaying a special interest by the artist in the study of emotion and gesture, among the most important aspects of Baroque Classicism.

The key to an understanding of *The Forge of Vulcan* within the context of Velázquez's career is to compare it with *The Topers*: both depict mythological scenes in which there is a contrast between a main character with idealized features (in this case Apollo) and a number of highly realistic figures. But while in *The Topers* the characters are displayed as if in a frieze and the work is, first and foremost, a description of types painted according to a still very naturalistic technique, *The Forge of Vulcan* is a story based on action, gesture and expression told through a pictorial style devoid of all traces of tenebrism.

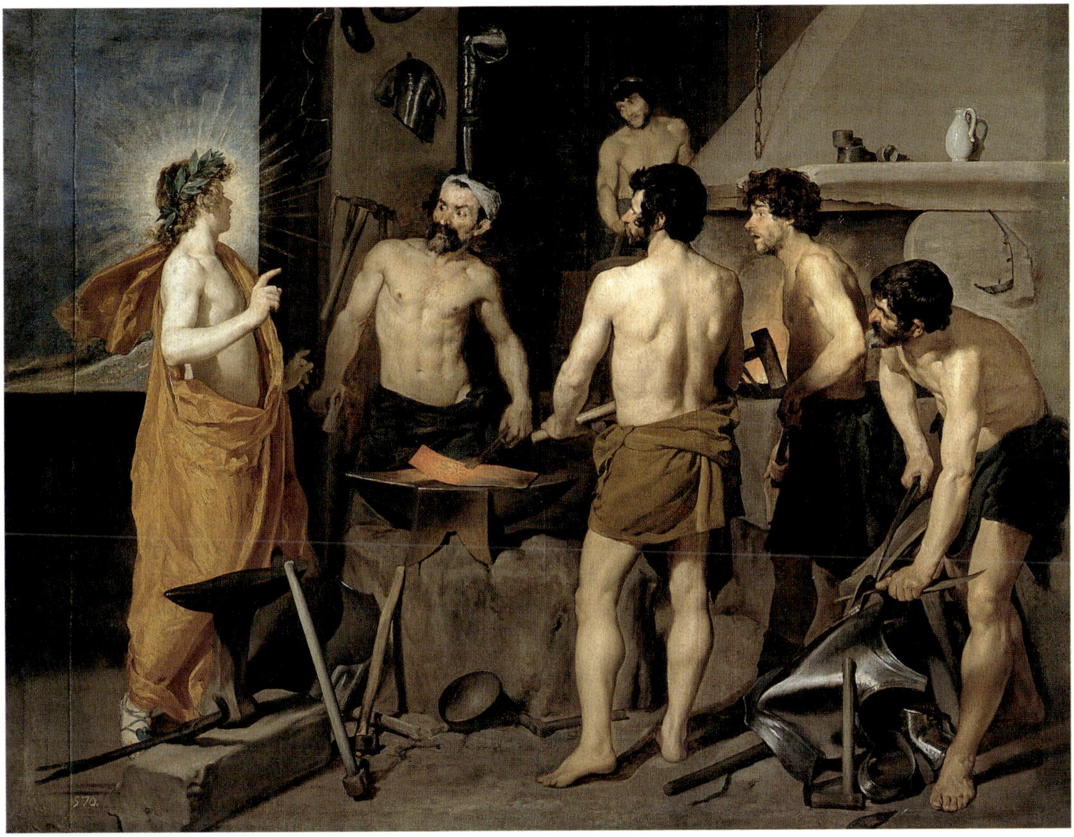

There has been a great deal of discussion on the true meaning of this painting. Some believe that it is an allegory on art: the shining figure of Apollo enters the workshop to illuminate the world of darkness with the light of the major arts. Following the same line of interpretation, yet others have pointed out the similarities between this work and *Joseph's Bloody Coat Brought to Jacob* – on account of their ambitious composition, the number of figures and the circumstances behind their execution – and suggest that the two paintings be interpreted together as the theme in both is the power of the word to influence the sentiments and conduct of human beings; this could then be interpreted as a statement on the superiority of the mind over manual labour.

First referred to in the Buen Retiro Palace in 1701, this painting appeared in various Royal Palace inventories before it reached the Museo del Prado in 1819.

Infanta doña maría, queen of hungary

Canvas, 59.5 x 44.5 cm
Inv. 1187

The sister of Philip IV, Maria Anna was born at El Escorial in 1606 and her fate, as corresponded with her royal blood, was to become another pawn in the game of matrimonial alliances then so popular at all the European Courts. As a marriageable Infanta, she was first considered as a means of improving diplomatic relations between Spain and England, which prompted the Prince of Wales's famous journey to Madrid in 1623. The Prince returned a bachelor and unbetrothed – but the proud owner of a magnificent painting presented to him by his would-have-been brother-in-law. With this marriage attempt thwarted by religious incompatibilities, Maria was betrothed some years later to her cousin Ferdinand of Habsburg, then King of Hungary and subsequently Emperor of Austria. They were married by proxy in Madrid in 1630, and four years later Maria made her own contribution to that long history of marriages between relatives by giving birth to a girl who would one day be her uncle Philip IV's wife.

For many years this painting was believed to be that referred to by Pacheco when he wrote that in Naples, on Velázquez's journey to Italy, his son-in-law had painted "a beautiful portrait of the Queen of Hungary, to bring it to His Majesty". This would date the picture between 13th August and 18th December 1630 and the painting would therefore be the result of the King's desire to have a likeness to remind him of the sister he knew he would never see again. In this respect it can be compared with many other portraits painted at European courts so that far-off relatives could follow the physical development of their loved ones.

However, the discovery of a document dated late October 1628 and referring to a commission for Velázquez to paint the portraits of several members of the royal family (including the Infanta Maria) casts doubt on the date of this painting. But this is still not confirmation that Velázquez actually painted the portraits, and historians, on considering both dates and analyzing the styles, are divided on the issue. Further doubts exist regarding the history of this painting in the royal collections. It is believed by some to be the picture referred to in Velázquez's chamber at the time of his death in 1660, but the absence of specific references to it in subsequent inventories before it reached the Museo del Prado makes it possible only to state that it came from the royal collections.

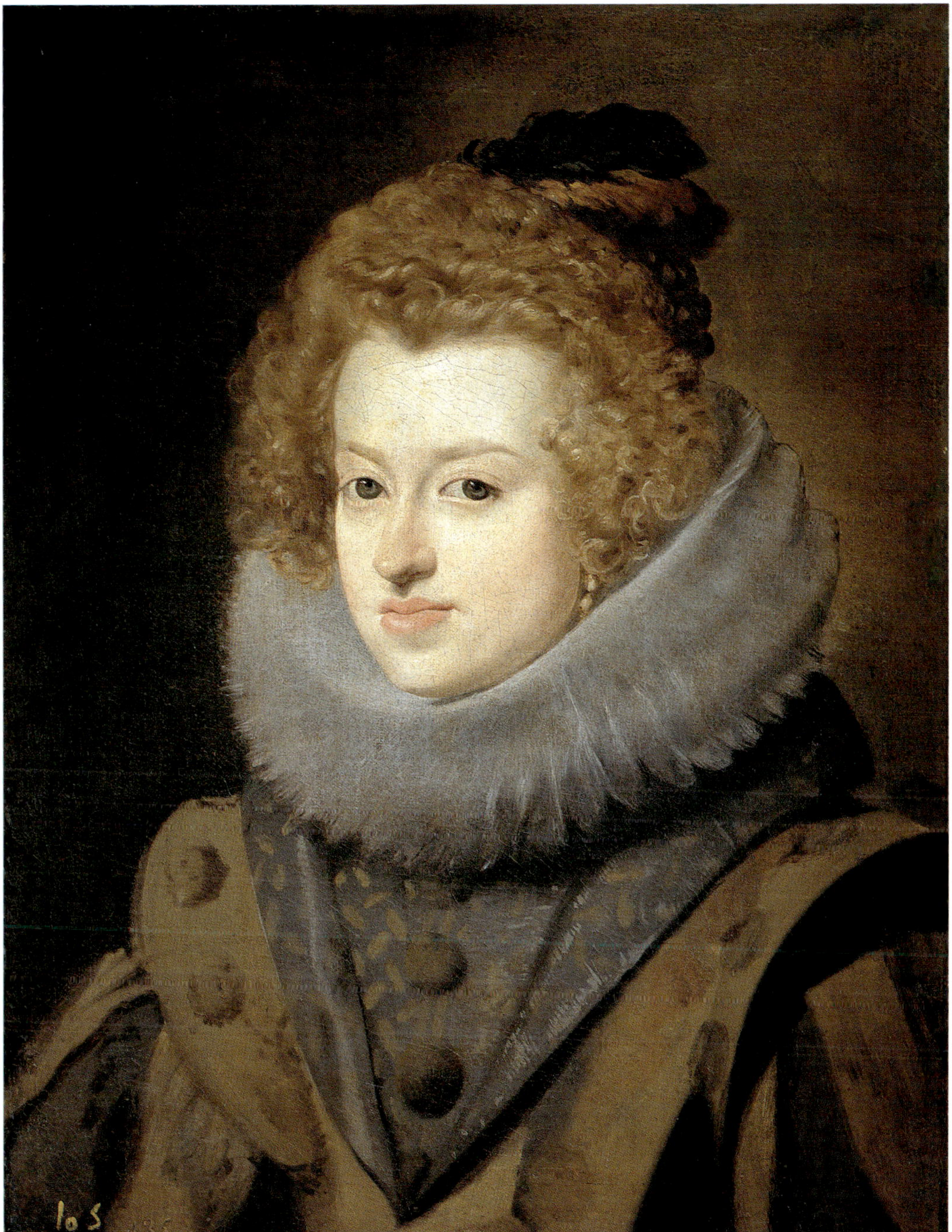

Villa medici in rome

Canvas, 48.5 x 43 cm
Inv. 1210

Villa medici in rome

Canvas, 44.5 x 38.5 cm
Inv. 1211

Due both to theme and pictorial technique, these two views of Rome are among Velázquez's most unique paintings and those which have made the greatest contribution to the painter's reputation as a precursor of later movements. The theme is a combination of architecture, plants, sculpture and people all naturally forming part of a garden area. As the critics never tire of repeating, the main components of these paintings are light and air. It has also been pointed out that the paintings reflect a specific moment, i.e. that they depict specific "atmospheric circumstances", and this has led to the theory that they represent "evening" and "noon" – thus anticipating Monet's famous Rouen Cathedral series by more than two hundred years. As a motif common to both paintings, Velázquez used a *serliana* – an architectural structure consisting of an opening that is flanked by two lintelled spaces and has a semi-circular arch above it. In one the *serliana* is open with the sky and the light entering the scene through it, while in the other it is closed and acts as an opaque wall.

The two paintings faithfully reproduce nooks in the Villa Medici, one of the greatest palaces in Rome. However, they appear to depict no recognizable theme, as the figures seem to wander around the garden without telling any particular story. In the first, the figure of what is believed to be a washer woman seems to be hanging a sheet over the balustrade, while two men below are perhaps discussing the architectural structure before them. To one side, a Classical bust (probably a herm) is visible behind a hedge and in the wall a sculpture recalls the prestige of this palace as the home of a splendid collection of ancient sculpture. In the other canvas, a servant or gardener stands in the foreground talking to a gentleman, while in the background a man in a cloak – anticipating the delicate, contemplative figures popularized by Northern European Romanticism – looks through the opening to admire the splendid view of cypresses, sky and buildings. To his right a marble Ariadne sleeps.

Two factors (in addition to their exceptionally high quality) set these works apart from others of the times. First, the absence of a story. In the 17th century

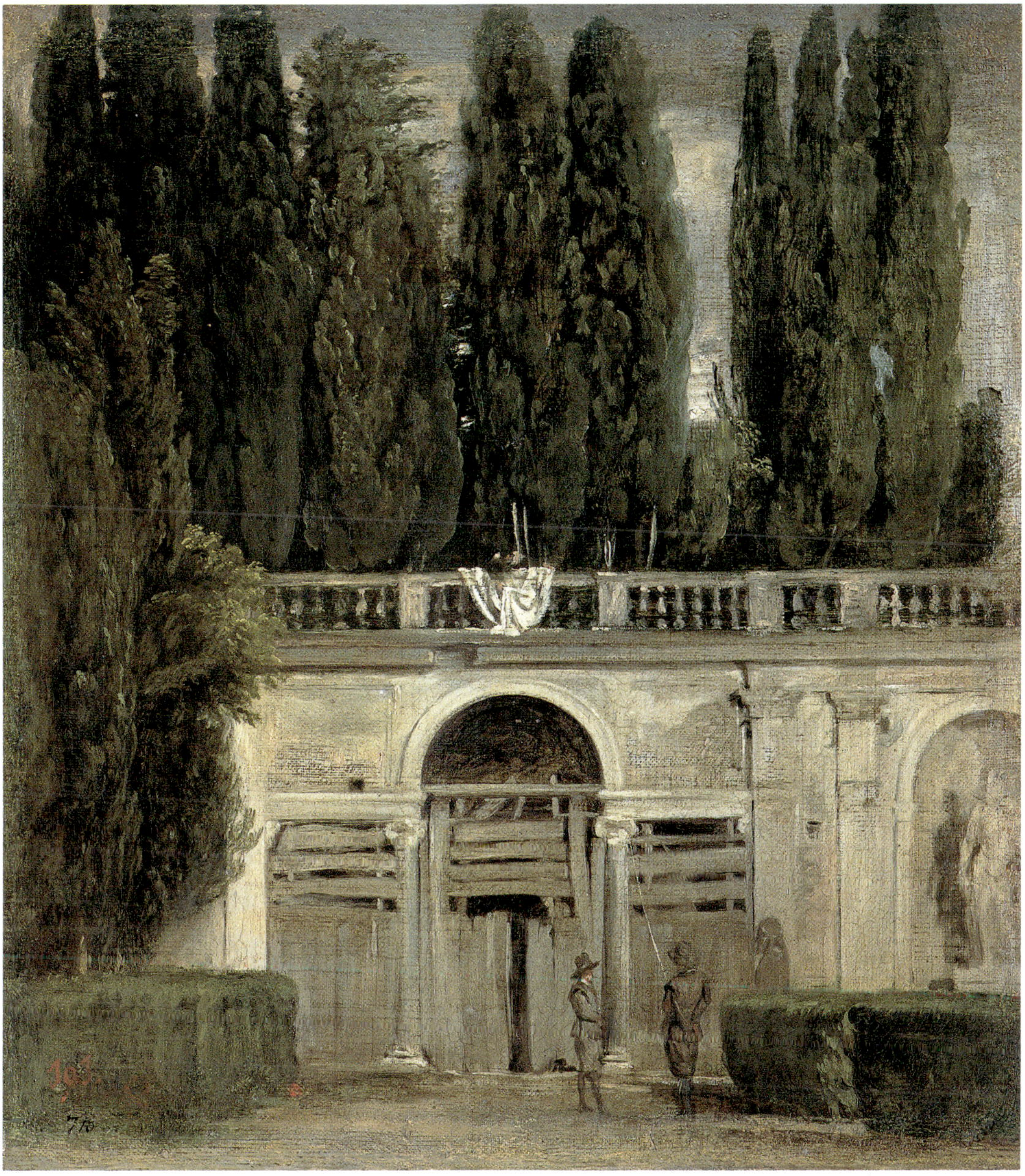

landscape became a relatively important genre, as the splendid French, Flemish and even Spanish collections in the Museo del Prado prove. However, very rarely was nature *per se* depicted on canvas (the same cannot be said of the drawing or gouache), as some kind of mythological or biblical "story" was usually considered necessary to justify the painting; landscape in itself was not considered worthy of depiction unless endorsed by a narrative or a view of a building or town. There were exceptions of course (in Italy and Flanders) and of these Velázquez's two views convey the most direct interpretation of the experience of nature. This is contributed to by the second of the two factors which make these paintings so extraordinary: although a small number of artists, Claude Lorrain being one example, went out into the country to sketch directly from nature, it was extremely unusual for a painter to stand with the tools of his trade before his subject and render it directly onto the canvas. And that is precisely what Velázquez did in these two pictures.

Also unusual in these paintings is the impression of nature the artist wished to convey. These are not timeless, immutable views of one part of a garden; rather, Velázquez seems to have wished to capture the experience of a single moment. And he did not avoid the difficulties inherent in this extremely complicated task for he composed two works which displayed his great skill. In the second view, for example, he used the very difficult contrast between a background acting as a focus of light and a foreground shaded by trees in order to augment the interplay of light and shade and create an unparalleled sensation of life and animation. However, being a lover of paradox and saying things by halves, he also included the contrast between the two men in the foreground frozen in a moment in time and – contrasting with such fleetingness – the man admiring the view and the sleeping statue.

Very little information is available on these two paintings, and although their very existence and exquisite beauty should suffice, experts have been theorizing on them for decades. The first problem regards their nature or function as paintings. Some experts once believed that they were studies made with a view to being used later in more detailed compositions but they now tend to be regarded as complete paintings. There is greater discrepancy over dates, however. As it is clear that they were painted during one of the two journeys to Rome, there are three possibilities: they both date from the first journey; they date from the second; the "evening" picture dates from the first journey and the "noon" from the second.

Those who believe that they date from the first journey point out: that the painter resided at the Villa Medici for two months, drawn to it by its healthy, open-air location and by the opportunity it gave him to study its ancient statues; and that

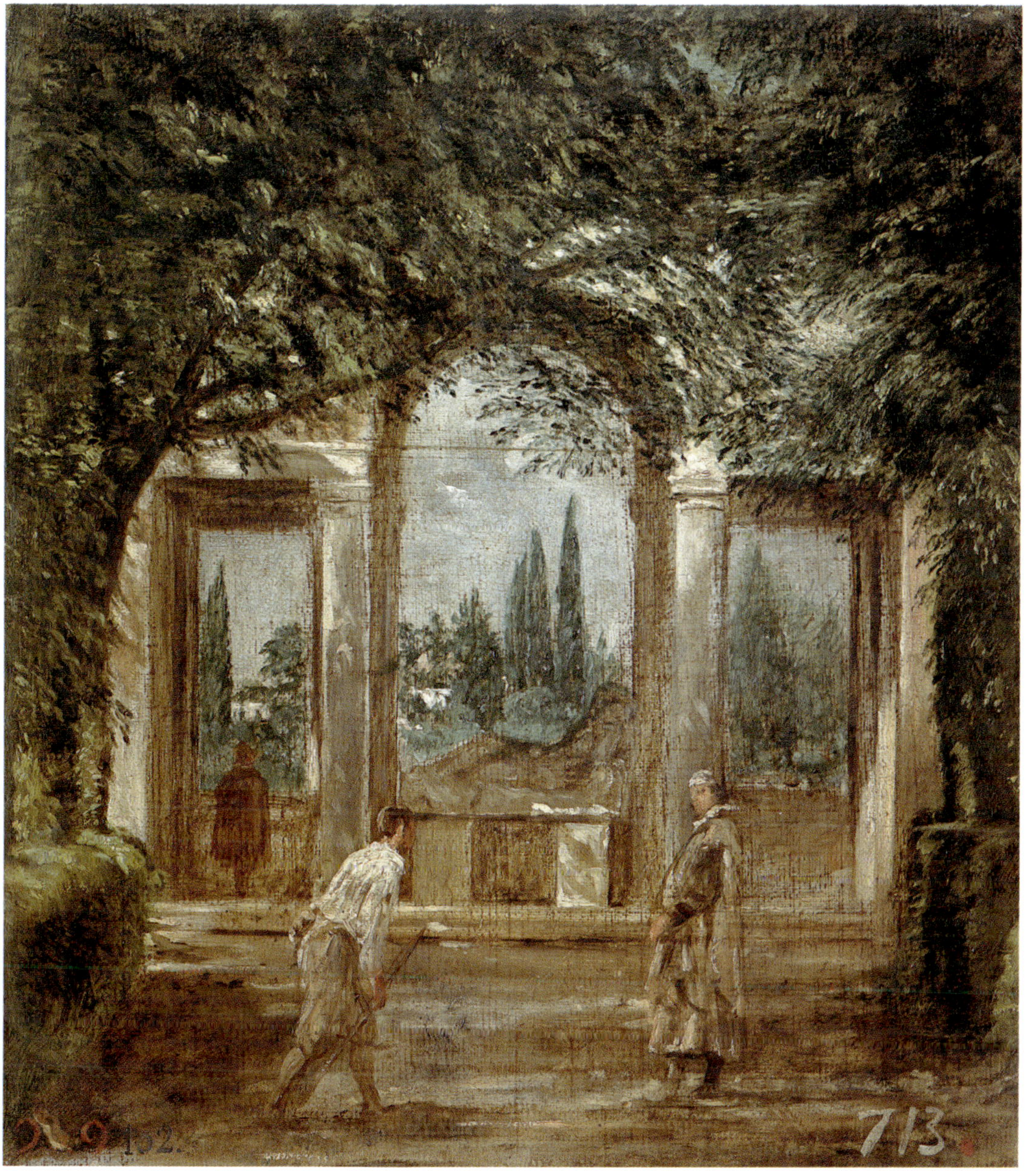
713.

Velázquez painted them over a preparation of pigment called *tierra de Sevilla* (common practice in his early career as an artist) and that stylistically they display a maturity similar to that observed in paintings from the same period such as *Joseph's Bloody Coat Brought to Jacob* – also painted in Italy and displaying great freedom of brushwork and a similar interest in light and atmospheric effects. They also refer to a document of 1634 in which the protonotary Jerónimo de Villanueva purchased "four small landscapes" from the painter for Philip IV. These pictures would not have been so exceptional in Rome in 1630, where a certain tradition in landscape painting already existed (led by artists such as Paul Brill) and a number of artists, e.g. Agostino Tassi with his Quirinal Palace frescoes, had painted pictures in some ways similar to these by Velázquez.

Those who argue that the views were painted during the second visit point to certain stylistic aspects which they believe to be more in line with the last phase in Velázquez's development and to denote a stage in his style subsequent to the backgrounds of his portraits of huntsmen. Furthermore, some records from that time refer to alterations made to the artificial grotto featured in the canvas in which the entrance is covered with boards.

Whatever the case, these are two masterpieces of Western landscape painting. Masterpieces which anticipate certain 19th-century art movements, although naturally their importance does not lie there but in their being works of art in which the painter, in an original and highly personal way, expressed his conception of landscape as a motif modelled by light, colour, air, space and time rather than as simply a setting to a story. They are paintings regarded as among the most unique in a museum full of outstanding works; paintings which Eugenio d'Ors so rightly referred to as those which "all of us have come to love so much".

The Religious Compositions

Christ Crucified

Christ on the Cross

St Anthony Abbot and St Paul the Hermit

The Coronation of the Virgin

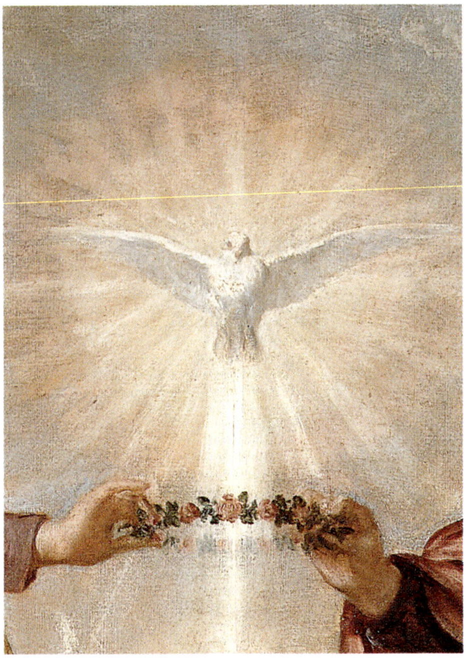

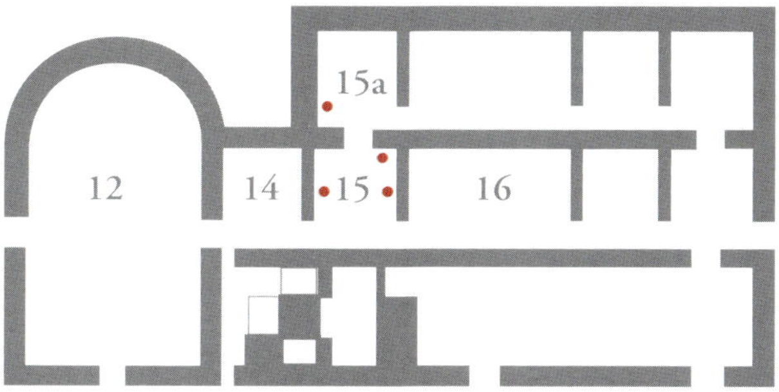

The Religious Compositions

Apart from certain painters of *bodegones*, Velázquez is without any doubt the Spanish artist of his age who painted the fewest pictures with religious themes. Indeed this statement could be extended to painters then working in Italy, Belgium and France. This is especially surprising if we recall that the Church was the most important client of most of the artists of the age and the Bible and hagiographic writings the inspiration for the vast majority of their paintings. The reasons, however, are obvious and connected with the source of the commissions Velázquez received – the royal family and a small number of nobles interested almost exclusively in portraits – although like all other artists, in the Seville years he had spent most of his time working for a market mainly requiring religious scenes.

Once at Court, he specialized in other themes, painting religious pictures only when the King and his immediate circle asked him to do so. The Museo del Prado possesses four compositions of this type from the stage subsequent to his establishment at Court, three of which were royal assignments, while the provenance of the fourth is doubtful and its attribution problematic. The origin of a fifth great religious work – *The Temptation of St Thomas* in the Diocesan Museum of Orihuela – may lie with an influential monk at Court, Friar Antonio de Sotomayor.

Although this paucity of religious works has sometimes been used to argue in favour of a certain indifference to religion on Velázquez's part (substantiated by the small number of books on religion in his library) there is, in fact, no real proof that this was so. Moreover, it is very hard to find evidence of unbelief in the Spanish society of those times, despite many references to heterodoxy. The subject is therefore an ambiguous one which lends itself to a number of interpretations. Thus, while some doubt the sincerity of Velázquez's religious feeling, others, contemplating works like *Christ Crucified*, have claimed that Velázquez was one of the artists most capable of conveying both categorically and convincingly the very deepest sense of religious devotion.

& Paintings Exhibited &

Christ crucified

c. 1631-1632
Canvas, 248 x 169 cm
Inv. 1167

This is not only one of the Museo del Prado's most widely reproduced possessions but also the painting that has given rise to the largest number of commentaries and best illustrates the change in status some pictures undergo once they enter this type of institution. For Spaniards, the serene, half-hidden face of this Christ is an extremely familiar image, for they have seen it constantly reproduced in notices of death and presiding over many of their classrooms. Such wide iconographic diffusion has been accompanied by enormous literary prestige, for on contemplating this painting many famous writers have reflected not only on the painter himself but also on the religious and human condition. Of these, the writer who did so in the most beautiful, intense and profound manner was Miguel de Unamuno, whose *El Cristo de Velázquez* (Madrid, 1920) is one of the landmarks of 20th-century Spanish poetry. The painting's status as a "national icon" has also been used by painters like Antonio Saura, who recreated the image in several of his canvases. Although it is often said that the appearance of museums in Europe changed the function of many of the works they contained by turning what were instruments of devotion into objects of aesthetic contemplation, this and other paintings in the Prado (like those by Murillo) prove that on occasions the fame and dissemination provided by a museum has served precisely to intensify the religious and devotional prestige of those works.

This painting was intended for the Convent of Benedictinas de San Plácido, which still stands in the Calle San Roque in Madrid. According to popular belief, it was painted for Philip IV, who wished to atone for having fallen in love with one of the nuns there. It has also been suggested that it was commissioned by the protonotary Jerónimo de Villanueva, who lived in that area at the time. Whatever the case, the painting remained in the convent until the beginning of the 19th century, when it came into the possession of Godoy. When his wife, the Countess of Chinchón, died, his son-in-law chose this work as part of his legacy from among her possessions and in 1829 presented it to Ferdinand VII, who immediately had it reserved for the Museo del Prado.

It would be pointless to discuss why this work is so famous for it is immediately obvious to anyone who contemplates it. Never has a crucified Christ been painted with such geometric rigour as that produced by the double triangle forming the cross and the figure. As regards the anatomy of the figure, the careful study of

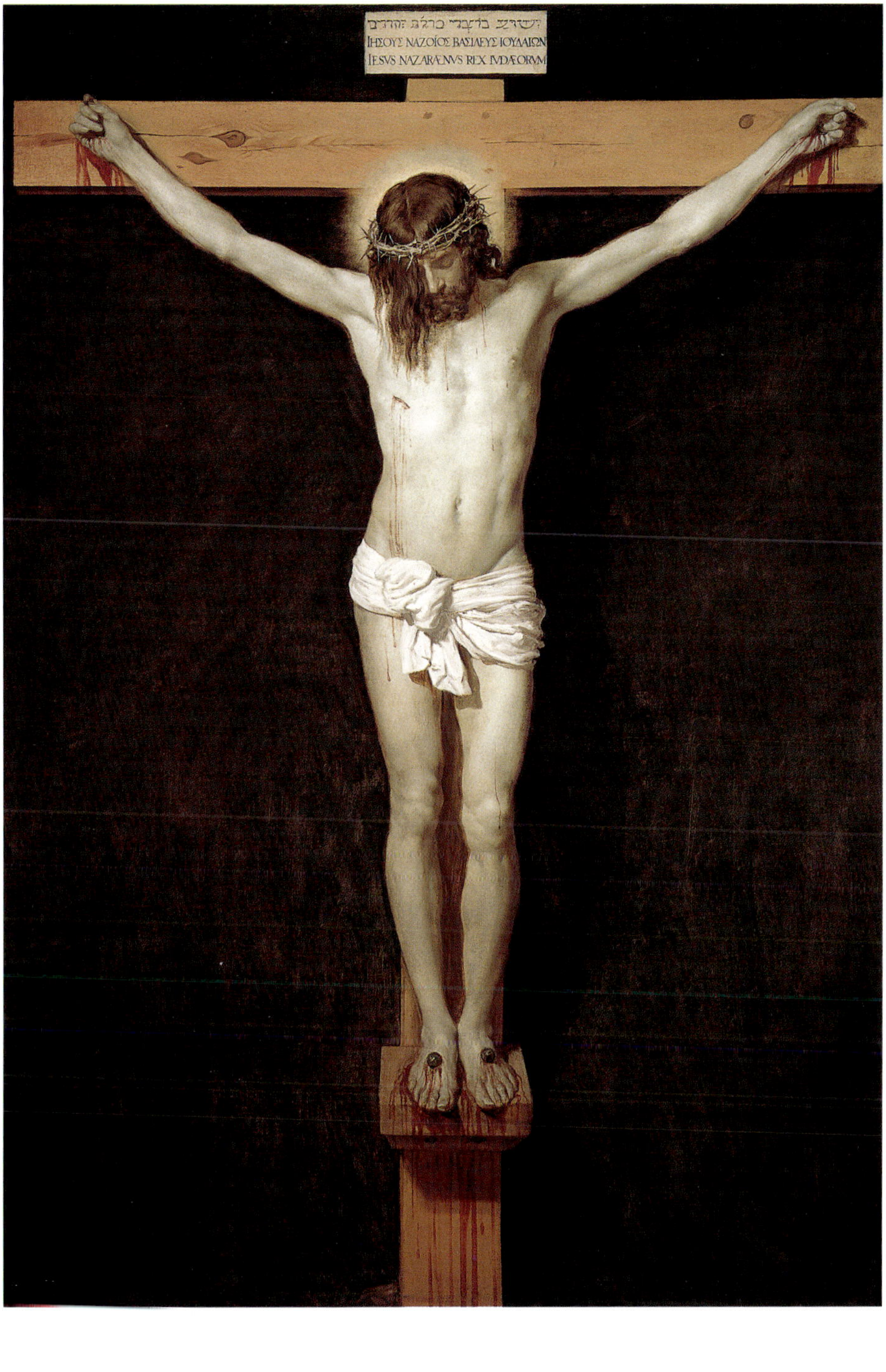
IHSOYS NAZOÍOS BASIAEYS IOYAAIΩN
IESVS NAZARAENVS REX IVDAEORVM

proportion reminds us that for Western painting the human body has always been the model by which the whole of nature must be measured. Furthermore, with the limbs gently modelled by the subtle lighting, this is one of the most beautiful and accomplished renditions of human anatomy in the history of painting. For some months this painting hung together with the *Venus at Her Mirror* in the Godoy collection and it is very attractive to imagine the two masterpieces side by side. Two examples of an ideal of beauty: in one the flesh illustrates an erotic scene; in the other it is the subject of religious sublimation.

As opposed to the many conventional versions of the crucified Christ which express the extreme drama of martyrdom and sacrifice, in his painting Velázquez sought to depict concentration, silence and a sense of forsakenness through a lifeless, noble Christ, Apollonian in proportion and nailed to a cross of extraordinary smoothness standing out against the nothingness of a dark background. The only element to break this rhetoric of quietude and silence is the luminous halo surrounding the face, unforgettably hidden by the long hair and beard. Similar serenity and equilibrium can be seen in the work of the Seville sculptors of that time, such as Martínez Montañés, as heightened by Christ nailed to the cross with four nails – an iconographic feature already found in Dürer's work and encouraged by Francisco Pacheco, the painter's father-in-law and the driving force behind a veritable campaign promoting this form of representation.

As regards dates, many experts believe that it was painted between 1628 and 1635, most preferring the period between 1631 and 1632 due to similarities with the anatomy in *The Forge of Vulcan.*

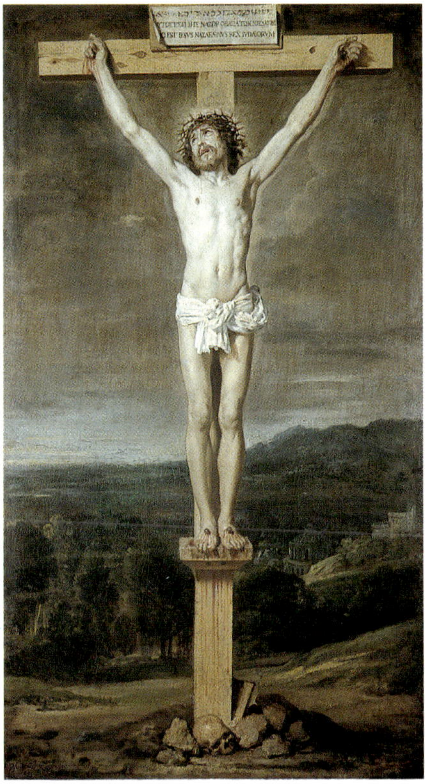

Christ on the cross

1631
Canvas, 102 x 57 cm
Signed: "D°. Velázquez fa. 1631".
Inv. 2903

One of the last paintings attributed to Velázquez and incorporated into the Prado collection, *Christ on the Cross* belonged to the Convent of Las Bernardas del Santísimo Sacramento in Madrid until 1946, when it was donated to the Spanish state by the nuns in gratitude for the reconstruction of their church.

In contrast with the unanimity regarding the authorship and extraordinary quality of the San Plácido *Christ Crucified*, this picture has greatly divided historians, some of whom do not believe it was painted by Velázquez at all. Among the arguments supporting the claim that Velázquez did paint it is the existence of the signature, although it is indeed strange that a painter apparently not overfond of leaving his name on his paintings should have wished to do so in this case. Another argument points to its anatomical similarities to the San Plácido Christ and the inclusion of the four nails in the painting – an iconographically unique feature associated with the artists of Pacheco's circle, including Velázquez himself and Alonso Cano. Yet others have found similarities in the use of colour to *Joseph's Bloody Coat Brought to Jacob* and *The Forge of Vulcan*, which were painted at around the same time.

Yet others believe that its only association with Velázquez is that it came from his workshop, as with its somewhat rudimentary background this picture falls far short of the painter's capabilities. Furthermore, the results of recent analysis have prompted scepticism as to Velázquez's full authorship of this painting.

St anthony abbot and st paul the hermit

Canvas, 261 x 192.5 cm
Inv. 1169

The Buen Retiro Palace was designed as a suburban villa abounding in allusions to nature expressed in some cases through splendid series of classicistic landscapes by Claude Lorrain, Poussin and Dughet, etc. and in others through the large gardens surrounding it, most of which still exist. The gardens could not lack references to religion, and so hermitages were placed at various points in them. A commonplace of the Spanish culture of the age, allusions to hermitical life were used to extol the virtues of close contact with nature and an aspiration to a quiet life devoid of earthly ambitions. In a sense this was the Catholic reply to Horace's *beatus ille.* Although cases of practitioners of hermitical life were rare (one exception being the soldier Alonso de Contreras), Court society liked to be reminded of the subject through literature, iconographic series and an occasional visit to such places.

For the Hermitage of San Pablo Velázquez painted this magnificent canvas which depicts better than any other the combination of nature, stoicism and hermitical life so popular with the society of his times. It takes the form of an account of various episodes in the life of saints Anthony Abbot and Paul the Hermit: Anthony's search for Paul, guided by a centaur and a satyr; his insistent knocking on the door to Paul's cave; their meeting, with the miraculous transportation of the double portion of food by a raven; and Anthony's prayer before the body of his companion in saintliness. This conjunction of actions in a single scene breaks the basic rules of Classical composition, but the narrative subtlety with which they are woven together fills the work with freshness. The painter stressed the relationship between nature and hermitical life, concentrating on the former in the composition. However, it should not be said – although it often is – that this is simply a landscape painted with a narrative pretext. If the personages were not included, the result would be a painting with a very different meaning, for the subtle reference to nature as the most suitable background to the quiet, meditative, true way of life would have disappeared.

The story depicted in the painting has often been cited in hagiographic accounts. Thus, the *Golden Legend*, for example, tells that: "At the meal time a crow appeared in the cell carrying in its beak a portion twice as large as the normal. Paul explained to his surprised companion that every day God sent him a loaf of bread by that crow, but on that occasion He had sent two portions because there were two at table".

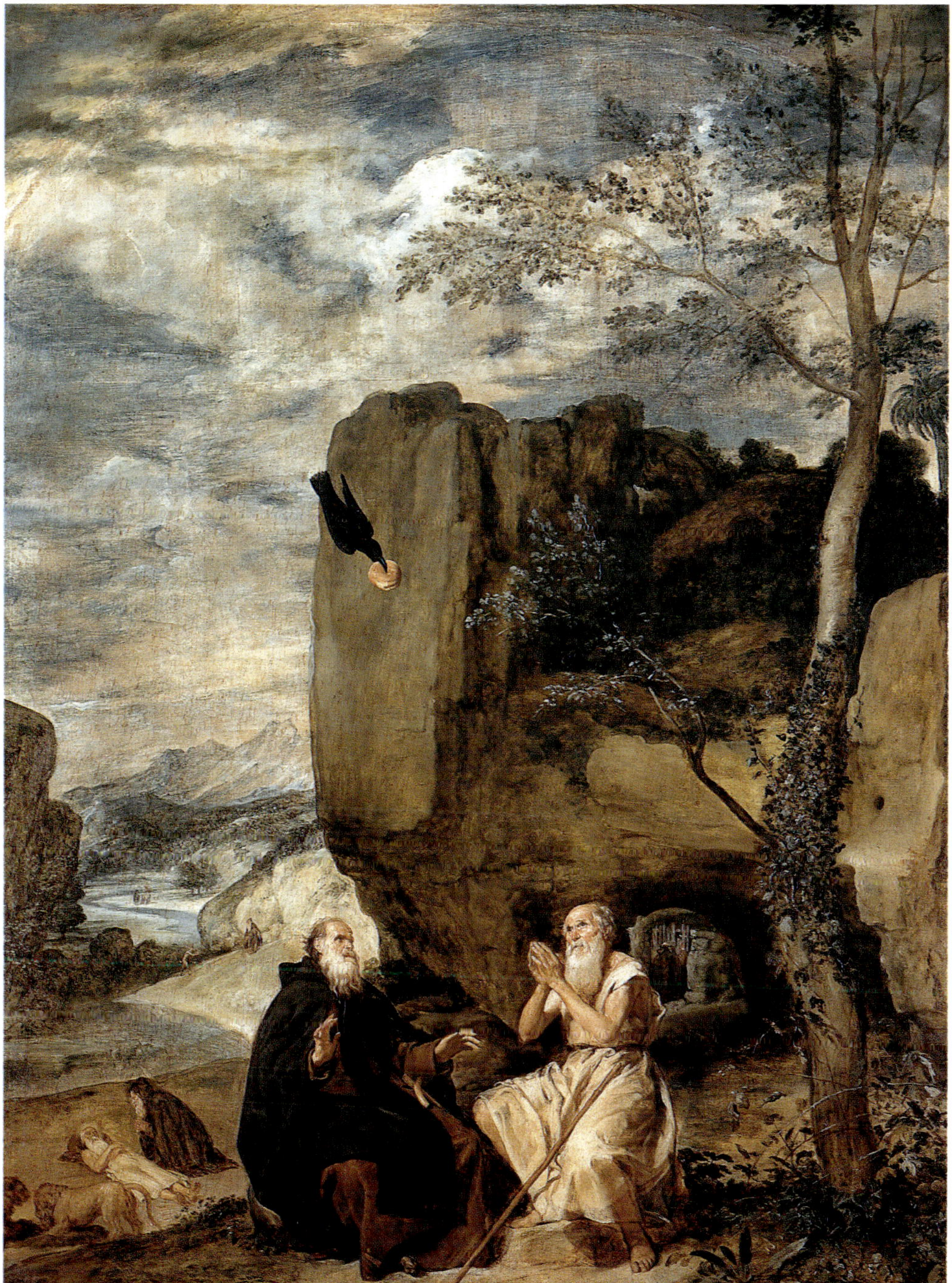

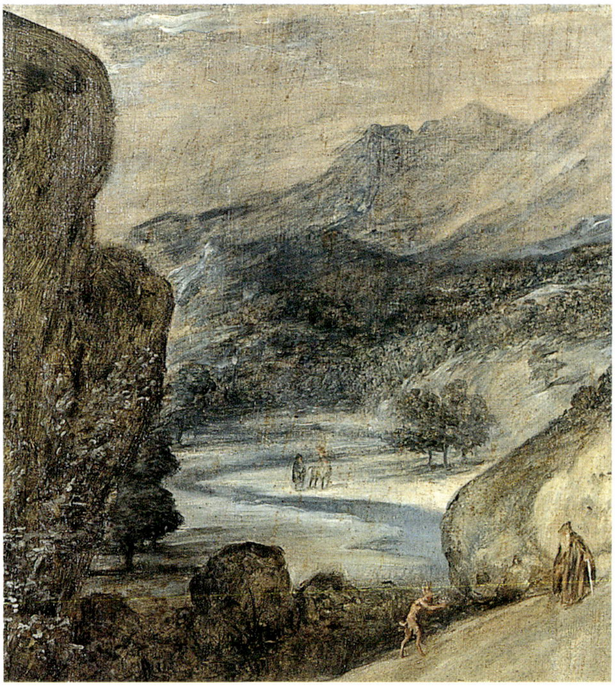

This work of extraordinary freshness and boldness reveals such self-confidence on the part of the painter that for many years it was considered his last painting, the kind of work that is the culmination of a whole career dedicated to the investigation of how best to infuse a piece of canvas with light, air and life. However, the present tendency is to date it in the years immediately subsequent to 1634, when the Hermitage of San Pablo was being refurnished. By then Velázquez had probably painted the views of the Villa Medici and the landscape background of *Joseph's Bloody Coat Brought to Jacob*, expressing in all a conception of landscape similar to that in this painting. However, while the Medici Views were painted directly from life, this is a studio painting owing much to the prints and paintings of other masters. It has therefore been associated with the work of Dürer and Patinir, among others, and also with a fresco on the same theme in Santa Maria dell'Orazione, Rome, painted by Lanfranco.

The artist made use of all such influences, blending them together to create an unmistakably personal painting in which objects and personages are enveloped in life-giving light. The Scottish painter David Wilkie said that in this picture it is the

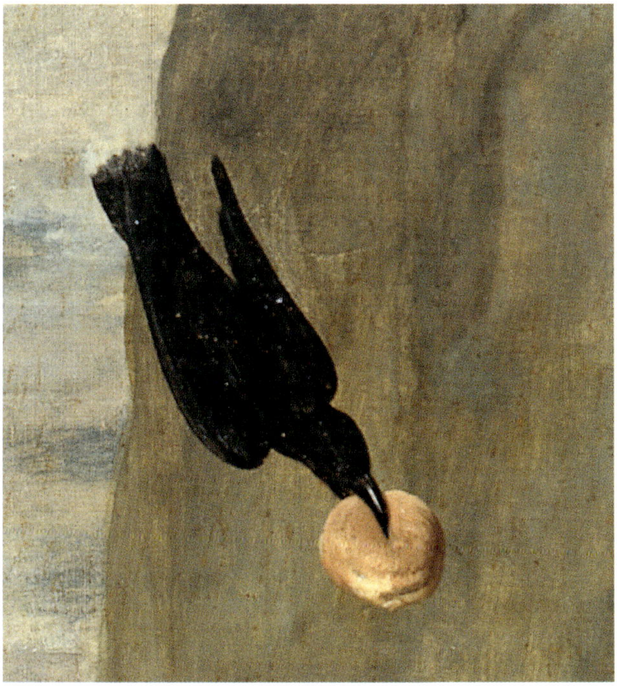

very sun we see and the very air we breathe, and the true spirit of nature. Since the Seville years, Velázquez had been a master in exploiting the infinite possibilities of a small range of colours. In this case, he limited his palette to greens, blues and greys with touches of black in order to transmit most faithfully the experience of landscape.

This work is first referred to at the Hermitage of San Antonio de los Portugueses, also in the Buen Retiro Palace, *c.* 1660. By 1772 it had reached the Palacio Nuevo in Madrid, from where it entered the Museo del Prado in 1819.

The coronation of the virgin

Canvas, 178.5 x 134.5 cm
Inv. 1168

Antonio Palomino, one of Velázquez's first biographers, referred to this picture in 1724, stating that it had been painted for the oratory in the Queen's Room at the Alcázar in Madrid around the same time as *The Surrender of Breda.* Although the painting is not mentioned in any known inventory of the palace until 1734, the information supplied by Palomino on its first destination is generally regarded as valid. But as always the experts cannot agree on the date, not necessarily because of any disparity of criteria, but because it is impossible to view Velázquez's works in what today is referred to as "evolutionary" terms. Some believe it to be among his last works, while others – basing their opinion on the fact that the Saragossa artist Jusepe Martínez painted a picture apparently inspired by this one in 1644 – date it as the early 1640s. On account of certain similarities with *The Fable of Arachne* and *Venus at Her Mirror*, yet others date it *c.* 1645-1648.

As formal precedents to *The Coronation of the Virgin*, references have been made to paintings and prints by various artists, including El Greco, Dürer, Maarten de Vos and even Rubens. As regards El Greco, similar compositions now in the Museo del Prado, the Hospital de la Caridad de Illescas (Toledo) and the Chapel of San José, Toledo, have been cited, and as regards Dürer, the model referred to is one of his prints (which also influenced other works by Velázquez). As for Maarten de Vos, a painting with a similar composition was reproduced in a print by Jan Sadeler and Karel de Mallery. But as is always the case with Velázquez, this type of association can ultimately only prompt admiration for the very personal manner in which he went on to transform the models of others. The theme, which required a dynamic treatment of the composition, is nevertheless presented in an extraordinarily peaceful manner – a factor contributed to by the geometric rigour in the arrangement of the figures, by their attitudes and by the unitary sense bestowed on the painting by the preponderance of reds and ochres. One of Velázquez's most serene and well-balanced paintings, it is comparable with some of his best religious works reflecting quiet, private meditation. In this respect, it is the best possible companion to the *Christ Crucified.*

It has been pointed out very perceptively that this picture may contain a subtle allusion to the Heart of Mary, a devotion in vogue during the period when it was painted, and indeed, the manner in which the holy figures are arranged plus the

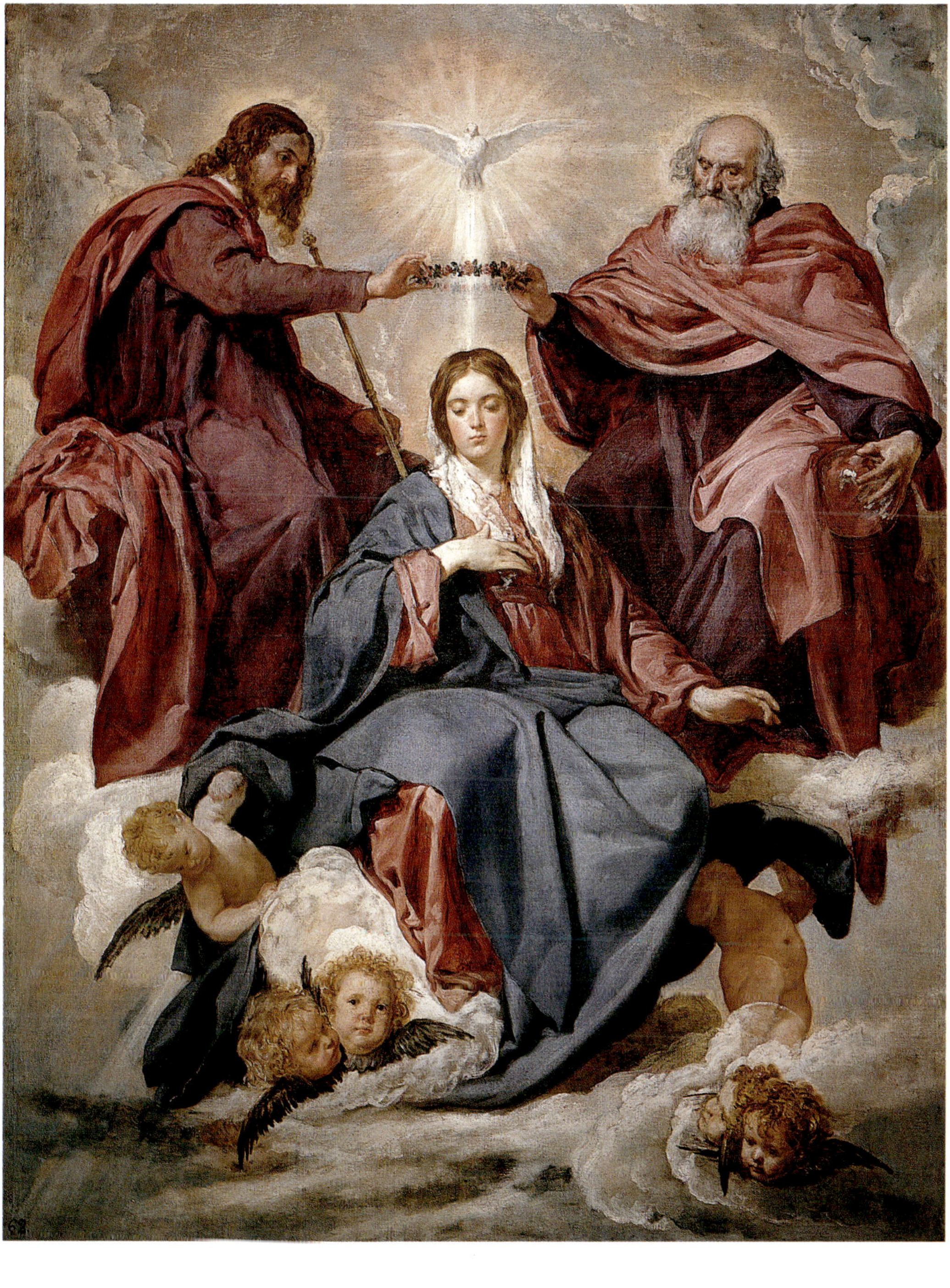

reddish tones of their garments do evoke the human heart. This interpretation is supported by that fact that the Virgin's right hand is raised to her breast.

After the fire in the Alcázar in 1734 the painting was transferred to the Convent of San Gil, from there to the Palacio Nuevo, and finally to the Museo del Prado in 1819.

Portraits of Courtiers, Artists and Others

Don Diego del Corral y Arellano
Doña Antonia de Ipeñarrieta y Galdós with One of Her Sons
The Sculptor Martínez Montañés
A Sibyl (Portrait of Juana Pacheco?)
Count-Duke of Olivares on Horseback

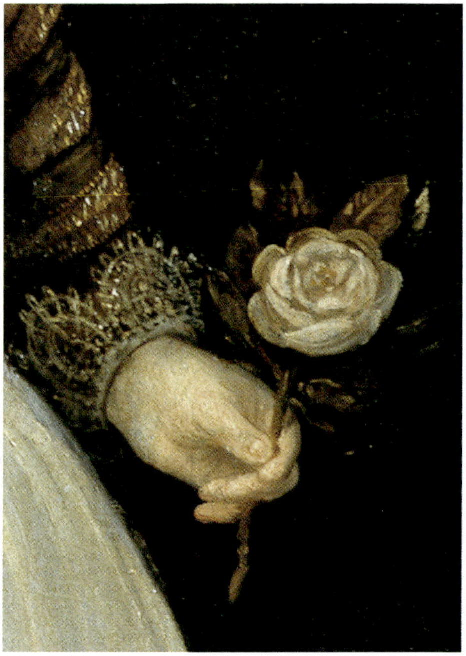

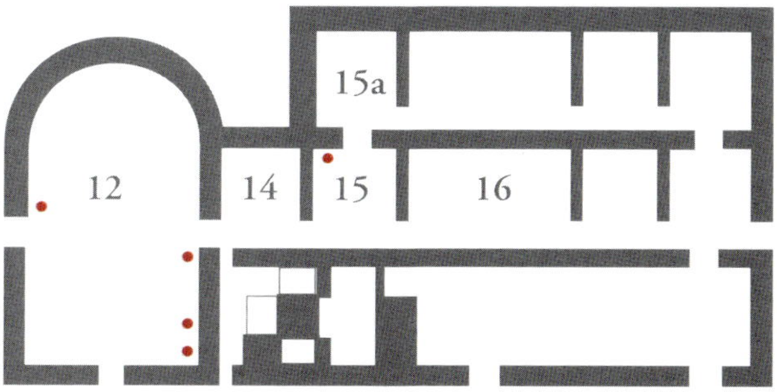

Portraits of Courtiers, Artists and Others

Although Velázquez painted mainly for the King – the majority of his works were intended for Philip after his establishment at Court in Madrid – part of his production was intended for clients whom we might term "private" and who all belonged to Court circles. For certain powerful aristocrats Velázquez painted ambitious compositions of mythological subjects like *The Fable of Arachne* and *Venus at Her Mirror*, but the greater part of his private commissions were portraits, a genre in which he specialized. During this period there was a growing demand within Spanish urban society for this type of painting, for in imitation of the kings, people developed a taste for pictures enabling them to leave testimony of their physical appearance and social position. Novels and plays of the age are full of references proving to what extent portraits were items of everyday life to Spanish city-dwellers, who viewed them as a way to winning greater prestige.

For would-be clients Velázquez's position in the King's service was a guarantee of excellence in itself and many must have wished to have their likeness painted by the very artist the King posed for. However, few records referring to this fact exist. Here Velázquez's style should be taken into account, for although it inspires universal admiration today and was greatly appreciated by Philip IV, not everyone understood it then, as a well-known anecdote told by the writer Jusepe Martínez of an Aragonese lady's displeasure with her portrait, proves. Even Cassiano del Pozzo, one of the most influential Roman intellectuals in the first half of the 17th century and a patron of artists expressed a preference for the dry, "proper" portraits of Juan Van der Hamen and little appreciation of Velázquez's. What is interesting is that, far from having only the most important members of the King's circle as models, Velázquez's portraits of courtiers present a curious variety with respect to the social level of the sitters. Although it is true that his sitters included none other than the King's favourite, the Count-Duke of Olivares (of whom various portraits still exist) or princes like Francesco d'Este, Duke of Modena (who had Velázquez paint him during a visit to Madrid), others belonged to a group consisting of member of the lower and middle nobility whom we might call "senior officials". This group included: Don Antonio Corral and his wife; Juan Mateos; Pedro de Berberana; the anonymous Knight of the Order of St James (Dresden Museum); and Francisco Bandrés de Abarca, also a Knight of the Order of St James and a member of the Cardinal Infante Ferdinand's household. Nor is there any lack of portraits of fellow artists painted by Velázquez during their visits to the Court, one example being the Andalusian sculptor Martínez Montañés. There are also a number of portraits of ladies whose name and rank are unknown, such as the *Lady with a Fan.*

To sum up, although Velázquez painted the most complete and accurate image of two of the most important sections of Court society in the times of Philip IV (the royal family and the buffoons), it is to be regretted that his administrative duties and a lack of interest on the part of would-be clients prevented him from doing so in the case of many of the other social groups.

PAINTINGS EXHIBITED

Don diego del corral y arellano

c. 1631
Canvas, 205 x 116 cm
Inv. 1195

Doña antonia de ipeñarrieta y galdós with one of her sons

c. 1631
Canvas, 205 x 115 cm
Inv. 1196

Many of the people Velázquez had daily dealings with in the performance of his palace duties were senior officials and qualified Court servants. Indeed, he himself set his own social sights on membership of this professional group and finally succeeded in gaining admission into it. He left us paintings of some of the members of that group, including the Museo del Prado's portraits of Diego del Corral and his wife Antonia de Ipeñarrieta. Don Diego was born in Silos in 1570 and died in Madrid in May 1632, having held important posts in jurisprudence. A magistrate at the Court of Castile and a Professor at Salamanca University, he took part in a number of important trials, including the one at which Don Rodrigo Calderón was sent to the gallows. In 1627 he married Antonia de Ipeñarrieta, born in Madrid between 1599 and 1603 and widow of another lawyer. In the palace hierarchy, Doña Antonia served Prince Baltasar Carlos.

Even if we could not identify the subjects of these portraits, the information provided by Velázquez is enough for us to place them on the social scale with a certain degree of accuracy. The Cross of St James on Don Diego's chest indicates his noble origin, while the bureau, the magistrate's robe and the papers in his hands reveal his position as a servant of the law. Nothing is gratuitous in this type of portrait, and all the elements in it provide us with information, if not on the model's character then at least on his or her social status. As Don Diego was a member of so hierarchic a society as that in Spain, a society ordered according to a complex system of privileges, it is natural that references to those privileges should appear for they were absolute symbols of integration in the social order. Thus, the tall hat resting on the table alludes to the fact that Don Diego may have had to cover his head at any moment, and regarding his wife, the fact that she rests her left hand on a chair is far from a gratuitous detail or a simple compositional resource, for it is an allusion to the fact that she had the right to sit down.

In these two high-quality portraits the painter demonstrated his skill at taking the fullest advantage of a very limited range of colours and compositional resources.

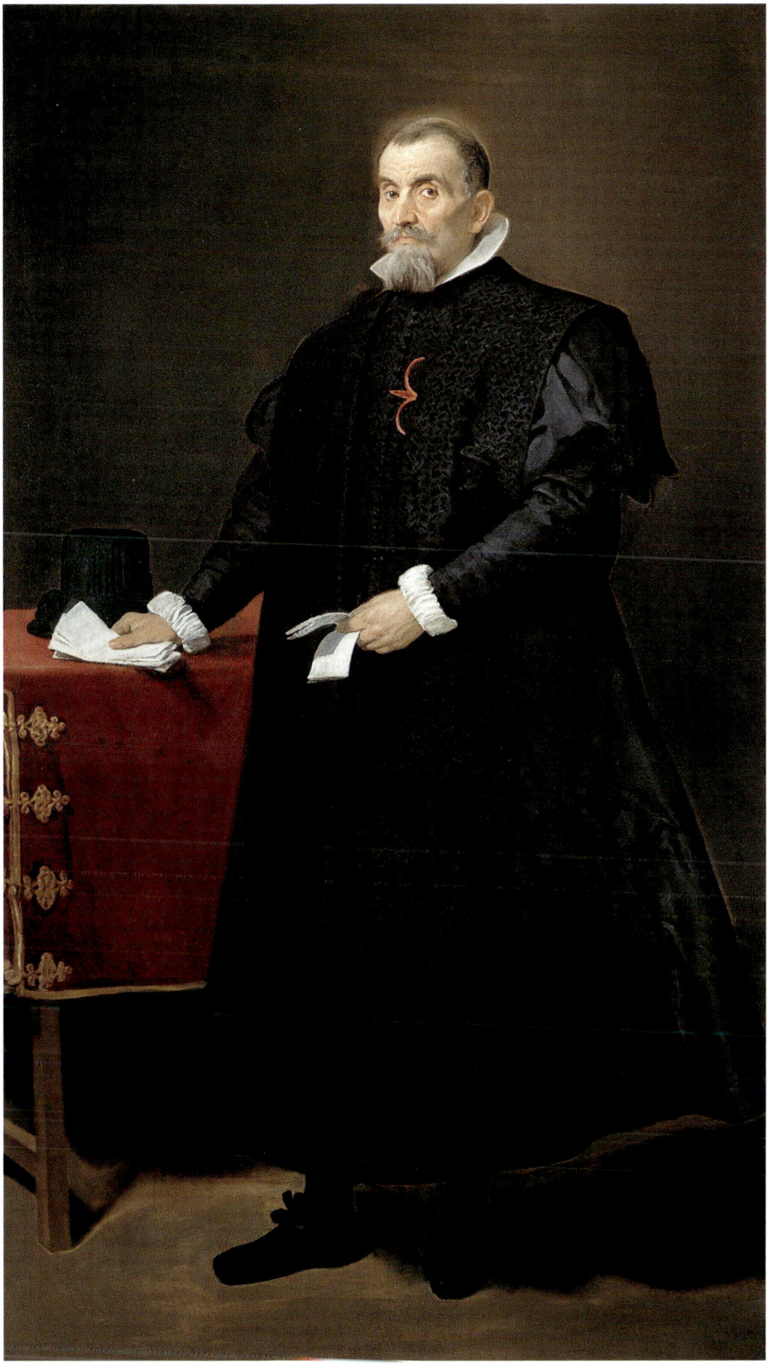

The simple figures are well situated in an indefinite area by means of the conical structure of the bodies, and are accompanied by the essential rhetorical elements. Their communicative efficiency is based on the contrast between the sober general surroundings and the focuses of light and expressiveness formed by the face and hands.

Various technical, iconographic and chronological questions remain unanswered about these two paintings. The existence of a receipt dated 1624 through which Doña Antonia commissioned the portraits of the King, the Count-Duke of Olivares and her first husband plus the fact that the latter had also been a jurisconsult and a Knight of the Order of St James, have led some to claim that this is actually a portrait painted that same year but that changes were subsequently made to the face so that it would depict the second husband. However, analysis of the style seems to contradict this hypothesis, inasmuch as it reveals a technique similar to that found in Velázquez's work of the early 1630s. In any event, it must date from before 20th May 1632 – the date of the subject's death – as it is extremely unlikely that this is a posthumous portrait.

Regarding its companion, there is some doubt as to the identity of the child. As we have said, Doña Antonia served in Prince Baltasar Carlos's household and, like most of the servants, was forbidden to hold the child's hand, which has prompted the theory that this is a portrait of the prince. However, records from 1688 of the possessions of two of the couple's children prove that this is Luis, one of the two brothers who bore that name.

Both paintings are referred to at the Corral mansion in Zarauz, Guipúzcoa, where they remained until they were sent to Madrid in the mid-19th century. As they were then inherited by the Duchess of Villahermosa, who, in 1905 bequeathed them to the Museo del Prado, they are two of the very small number of Velázquez paintings that have not come to the museum from the royal collections.

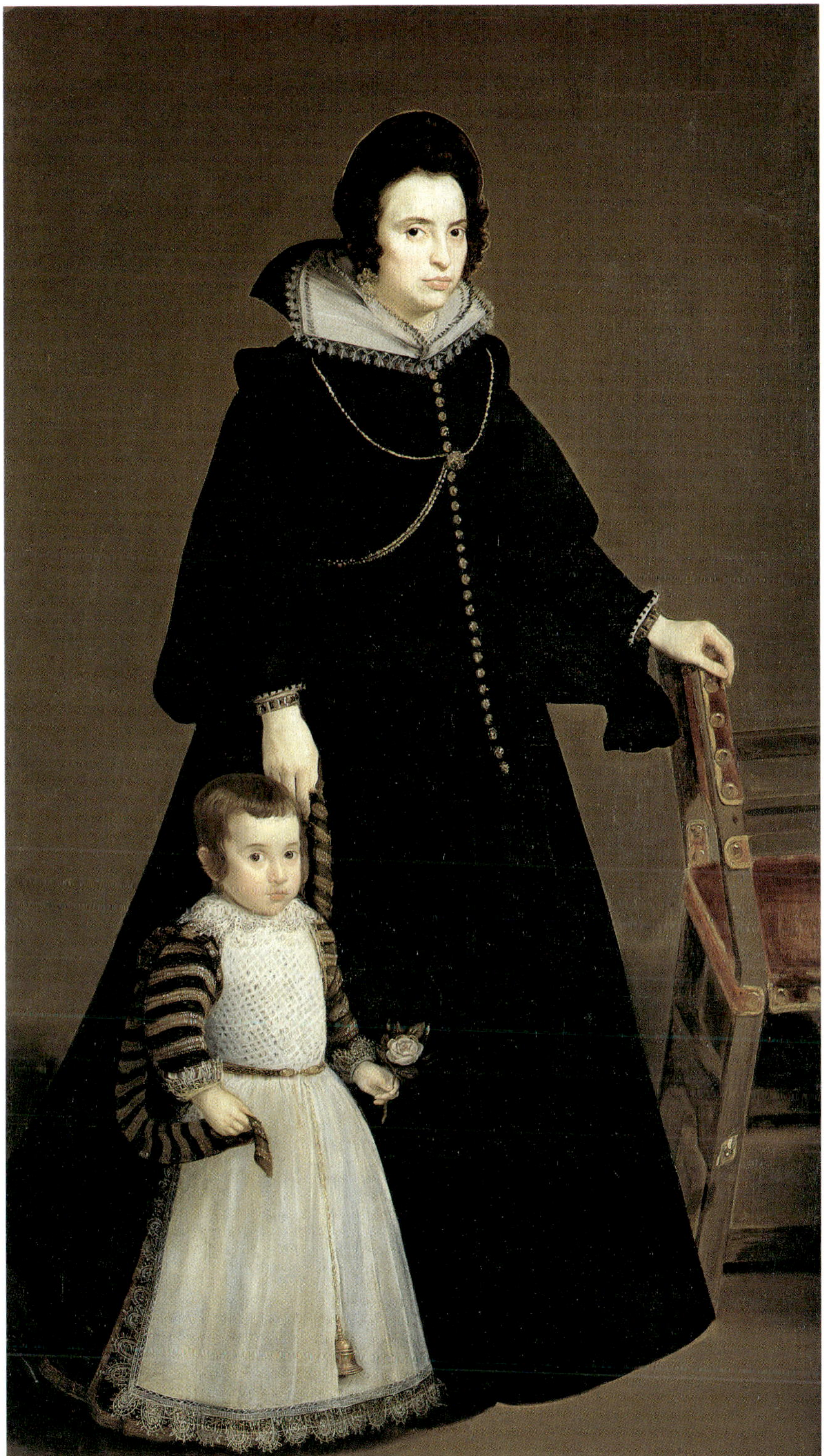

The sculptor Martínez Montañés

1635-1636
Canvas, 109 x 107 cm
Inv. 1194

This painting reached the Museo del Prado from the royal collections it the late 18th century. It shows a sculptor modelling (it has been suggested in wax) a head of Philip IV, and is one of the most important portraits of 17th-century Spanish painting, for apart from its high quality, it is a veritable manifesto on the image craftsmen wished to project of themselves. As the sculptor stares out at the spectator, we see that his expression and face (wherein lies the Idea) are more important than the manual work he is doing; furthermore, his attire refutes all ideas of the "craftsman" and he is engaged in one of the most useful social activities an artist could be employed in – that of making a likeness of the King and thus performing an important service in the projection of the royal image. Here we must remember that the status of the artist in 17th-century Spanish society was still an ambiguous one and that painters and sculptors were constantly striving to win the social recognition often denied them. This issue, which underlies Velázquez's finest pictorial work, including *Las Meninas* and, according to some, *The Fable of Arachne*, gave rise to a great deal of literature by art theoreticians, poets, playwrights, etc.

There has been much discussion over the subject's identity. From time to time some art historian will assert that it was Alonso Cano, arguing that the clothing is similar to that worn at the time by the clergy and that Cano was ordained priest in the 1650s. If this is the case, then the painting must date from around 1658, when Cano travelled to Madrid. However, many experts believe that it is Juan Martínez Montañés, one of the most important sculptors of the generation previous to Velázquez's. This is supported by the similarity between this painting and two portraits of Martínez Montañés, one definitely and the other supposedly painted by Velázquez and, above all, by the fact that the sculptor was called to Court to make a bust of the King from which Tacca in Florence was to cast the equestrian statue which today stands in the Plaza de Oriente, Madrid. If such is the case (and it is very likely) then the painting would date from between June 1635 and January 1636. In any event, both Cano and Martínez Montañés, who were extremely conscious of their intellectual dignity, left us many examples of their professional pride which match the image of the self-sufficient artist conveyed by Velázquez in this canvas.

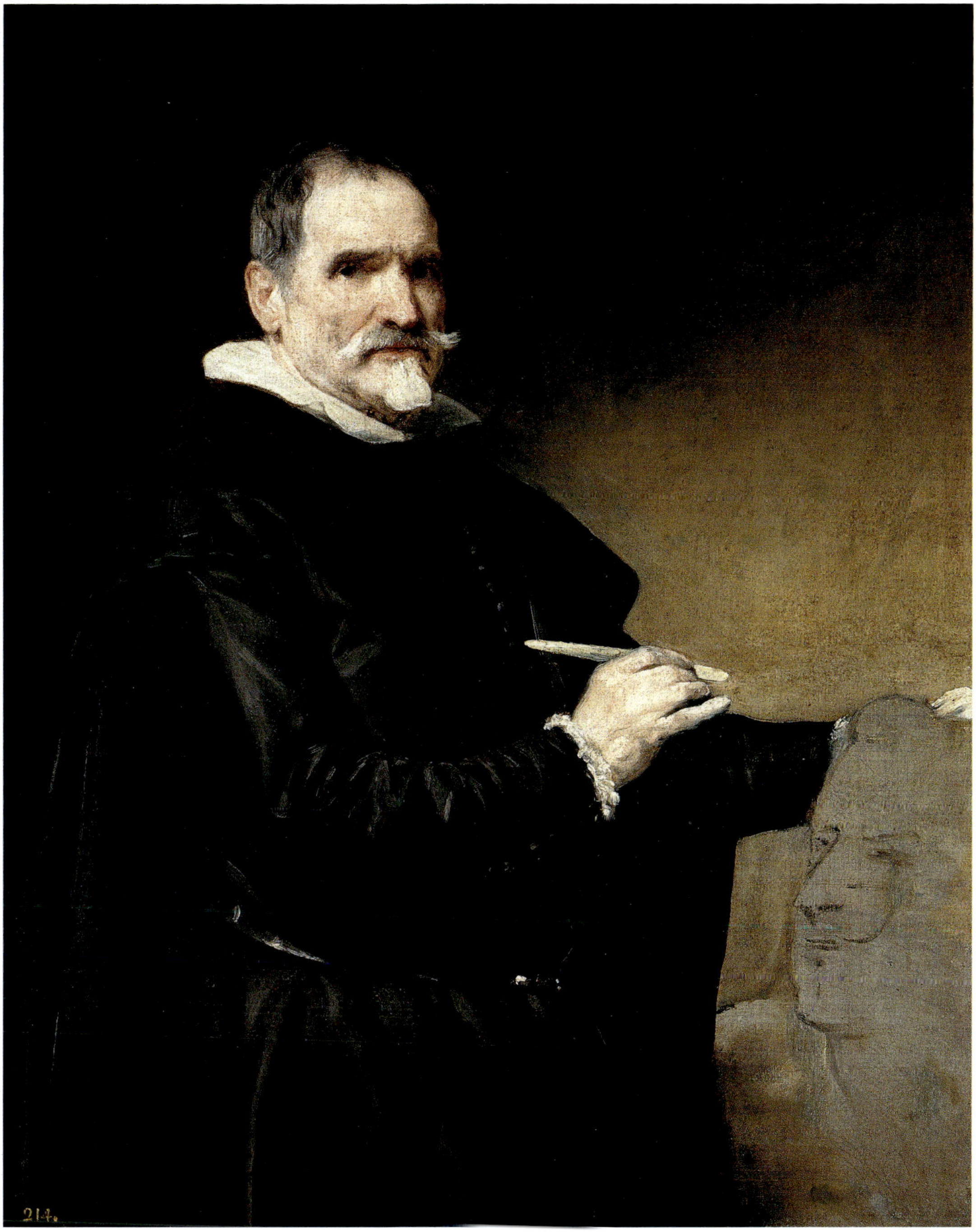

A sibyl (portrait of Juana Pacheco?)

c. 1631-1632
Canvas, 62 x 50 cm
Inv. 1197

Due to the insistence of some art critics and historians on putting a name to the sitters for Velázquez's paintings and whenever possible associating them with his family, this picture was described in an inventory of 1746 as "of Velázquez's wife". Since then a number of writers have given credit to this theory and set out to prove it, their main argument (apart from the 18th-century precedent) being based on the model's features, which they have taken as an invitation to regard the picture as a portrait. It has also been pointed out that the subject bears a resemblance to other figures in Velázquez's paintings, such as one of the angels in the upper half of *St Ildephonsus Receiving the Chasuble from the Virgin* (Seville City Council). Nevertheless, no conclusive evidence exists to endorse this theory; a theory in any case contradicted by the fact that in 1631-1632 (when the picture was supposedly painted) Juana Pacheco would have been 28 years old – the age, in those times, of a mature adult.

Neither is there agreement as to the theme depicted. Some experts have claimed that it is a sibyl because her left hand holds what is thought to be a tablet on which she would have written premonitions of the New Testament. Furthermore, she is depicted in a manner common to this kind of theme, gazing into the distance in search of inspiration. Others, however, believe that it is a rendering of Clio, the Muse of History, or even an allegory of painting.

Due to the theme and technique, this painting can be associated with Velázquez's works of the early 1630s, e.g. *Joseph's Bloody Coat Brought to Jacob*, as it is one of the many examples of the painter's predilection for including references to everyday life (in this case the face of a recognizable woman) in allegorical or historical works.

The painting was acquired by Isabella Farnese after 1714 and is referred to at La Granja between 1746 and 1794. It had reached the Royal Palace in Madrid by 1814 and the Museo del Prado by 1843.

116

Count-duke of olivares on horseback

Canvas, 314 x 240 cm
Inv. 1181

The Count-Duke of Olivares (Rome, 1587 – Toro, 1645) was the most influential man in Spain during the first part of Philip IV's reign. Eighteen years his junior, the King made him his favourite immediately on his accession to the throne in 1621. Highly intelligent, tenacious and a shrewd politician, Olivares managed to hold the reins of government for two decades while keeping the King occupied in matters often having little to do with his duties as a statesman. In this way he became the most powerful man in Spain until he fell from favour in 1643 in the wake of the severe political crisis into which the nation was plunged.

Olivares is one of the most important figures in any biography on Velázquez inasmuch as it was almost certainly he who introduced the painter to the Court and gave him his constant protection. It has been said that one of the reasons for this was that the Count-Duke liked surrounding himself with fellow Andalusians. Several portraits bear witness to his relationship with the painter, particularly those of the Count-Duke standing (mid-1620s) and this equestrian painting. All have points in common with the portraits of Philip IV: the first with the Museo del Prado's portrait of the King (1182) standing next to a table in an undefined space and displaying attributes of his power and position, and this one with the equestrian portrait of the King painted for the *Salón de Reinos.*

In the equestrian portraits, both the King and his favourite appear "in a curvet", i.e. with their steeds standing on hind legs only – the same position as that in Tacca's equestrian statue of Philip IV. This is not just a compositional formula, however, for the position is full of deep significance. As is explained in books of insignia and other types of literature, the position represented the highest possible expression of command and power, and not only where military might was concerned, for inherent also were moral and political considerations, including the capacity to govern oneself. Unlike the portrait of Philip IV in which the King advances majestically and serenely, this one shows the favourite as haughty and impetuous, an impression heightened by the rather oblique position of horse and rider and the variety of colours used. The very existence of this portrait is proof of the Count-Duke's power inasmuch as only a man who had achieved such a privileged position at Court would have dared to have himself painted in a similar manner to the King, controlling a horse in a curvet.

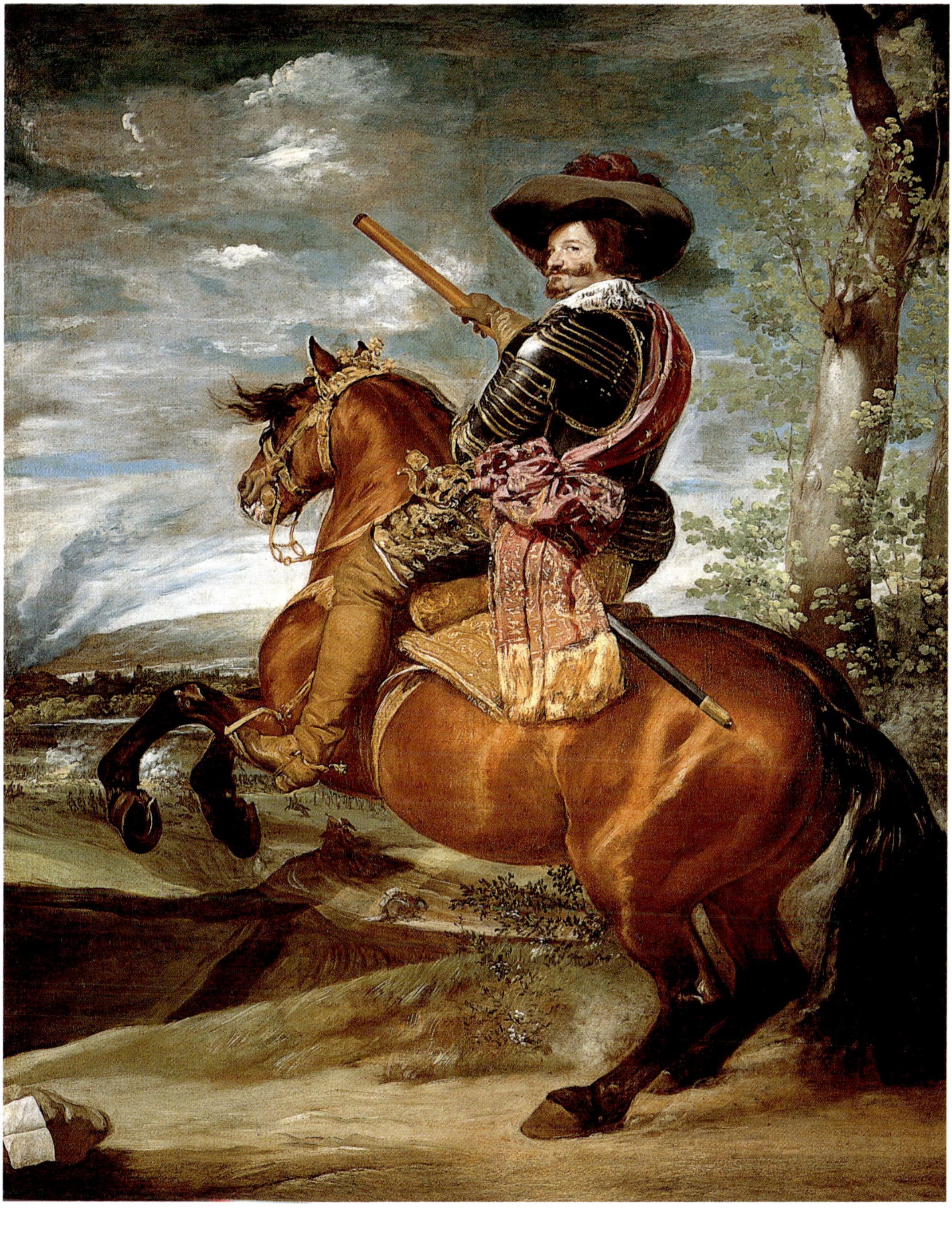

There has been much discussion as to the date of this painting. Those who believe that the battle scene in the background is the Battle of Fuenterrabía – an event at which Olivares, incidentally, was not present – date it after 1638, while many others claim that the smoke and the battle are simply an allusion to the Count-Duke's rank as a general, as is also conveyed in the sash and staff of command. Those who uphold this second view believe it was painted around 1634, that is at the time when work was under way on the *Salón de Reinos* in the Buen Retiro. In this respect, the many similarities between the figure in this composition and that of the general in the foreground of Jusepe Leonardo's *The Taking of Brisach* have been cited to argue that one painting was a result of the other or that the two were after a print by Tempesta.

The painting belonged to the Count-Duke and his descendants until the mid-18th century, after which it is referred to in the residence of the Marquis of La Ensenada, from whom Charles III purchased it in 1769. From then on it remained in the Royal Palace until it entered the Museo del Prado in 1819.

THE *SALÓN DE REINOS*

The Surrender of Breda
Philip III on Horseback
Queen Margarita on Horseback
Philip IV on Horseback
Queen Isabel on Horseback
Prince Baltasar Carlos on Horseback

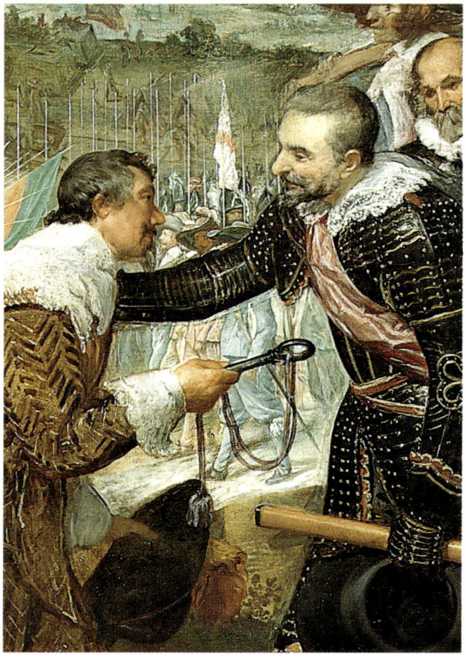

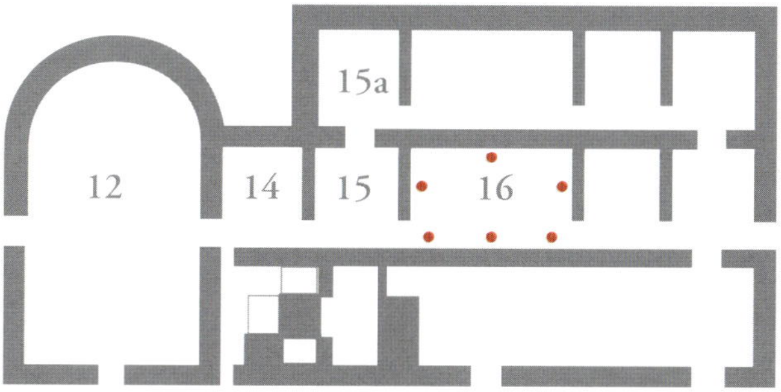

℣ The *Salón de Reinos* ℣

One of the most important events arising out of the great artistic activity generated by the Spanish Court in the 1630s was the construction and decoration of the Buen Retiro Palace, a suburban villa intended as a place of relaxation and leisure for the King and his entourage. Built by the Count-Duke of Olivares as a distraction for the King and to allow himself to hold the reins of government with greater freedom, it was begun in 1629 on land adjacent to the Monastery of San Jerónimo el Real. The complex abounded in gardens, ponds, hermitages and squares where lavish celebrations were held, and although the architecture was rather mediocre (not surprisingly, given the haste with which it was built) it was adorned with an extremely impressive collection of paintings, generally arranged in series. It contained not only landscape galleries, a coliseum for the staging of plays, and other areas for the

King and Court's leisure and pleasure, but also one of the halls of the greatest ceremonial and political importance to be found in royal palaces anywhere. This was the *Salón de Reinos* ("Hall of Kingdoms"), a huge room 34 X 10 X 8 metres situated at the centre of the palace's north wing. It presently houses part of the Army Museum and in a few years' time will become part of the Museo del Prado.

The adornment of the *Salón* took the form of a pictorial discourse on the Spanish monarchy. In addition to a number of mural paintings (noteworthy among these being the coats of arms of the various kingdoms possessed by the Spanish monarchy – hence the room's name) were paintings arranged in series according to theme. Thus, on the shorter walls of the rectangle formed by the hall were the equestrian portraits of Philip III, Margaret of Inner Austria, Philip IV, Elizabeth of France and Prince Baltasar Carlos, all painted by Velázquez. In this way the concept of dynastic continuity was asserted through the portraits of the current kings, their immediate predecessors and the heir. The other walls displayed twelve great paintings of battles, all by artists currently working in Spain, including Juan Bautista Maino, Eugenio Caxés, Vincenzo Carducci, Jusepe Leonardo, Antonio de Pereda, Francisco Zurbarán – and also Diego Velázquez, who was represented by *The Surrender of Breda*. The eleven surviving pictures now belong to the Museo del Prado and were painted between 1633 and 1635. All have in common the fact that they depict events connected with more or less contemporary battles – two in 1622, five in 1625, one in 1629 and five more in 1633 – and are characterized by the use of a narrative language shunning allegory and striving for historical accuracy. This was one way of reaffirming graphically the military power still held by a Spanish monarchy on the eve of a decade that was to prove disastrous in this respect. However, the battle scenes were not only intended as an assertion of Spain's military might but also as an image of Spain as a "just" power capable of showing clemency to those it defeated. The coats of arms, royal portraits and victorious battles were complemented by ten pictures of the "labours" of Hercules painted by Zurbarán around 1634 and placed (although historians disagree on the specific position of each one) between the battle scenes.

Such a reiterated reference to the mythological hero in the *Salón de Reinos* is explained by the fact that Hercules was regarded as the founder of the Spanish monarchy; indeed, the famous motto "Non plus ultra" on the Spanish coat of arms is an allusion to him. The paintings of Hercules were not only a perfect conclusion to the genealogical discourse formed by the equestrian portraits but a way of depicting the virtues which were supposed to govern a Prince's conduct. In this respect according to the political theory of the times, kingship not only involved a great many privileges but also specific responsibilities towards one's subjects. Thus the majority of the allegorical iconographic discourses on the Spanish monarchy contained allusions to those virtues essential to the possession of power, such allusions frequently being made through the mythological hero par excellence – Hercules – whose "labours" exemplified the virtues of shrewdness, prudence, loyalty, a sense of duty, self-denial, etc.

The *Salón de Reinos* was the most important decorative project of political exaltation to be implemented during the reign of Philip IV and most of the effectiveness of its discourse was due to its having been conceived as a whole and simultaneously. However, its fundamental role in the establishment of a national historical "record" does not lie so much in its iconographic consistency but rather in Velázquez's part in it, for in addition to the five great equestrian portraits of the royal family for the *Salón de Reinos* the Sevillian also painted what can be considered one of Spain's national "symbols": *The Surrender of Breda,* which for many years represented the official version of Spanish military hegemony in Europe.

Paintings Exhibited

The surrender of breda

1634-1635
Canvas, 307 x 367 cm
Inv. 1172

One of Velázquez's most famous paintings, *The Surrender of Breda* depicts the moment when Ambrogio di Filippo Spinola, the Genoese General and commander-in-chief of the infantry regiments in Flanders, received the keys of the city of Breda from the Dutch governor, Justin of Nassau, after a long siege. The event, which took place on 5th June 1625, was considered a key episode in the long war waged by Spain to impede Dutch independence.

Painted before the end of April 1635, the picture not only depicts one of the most important historical events reproduced in the *Salón de Reinos* but is also the painting in which Velázquez most clearly revealed his personal attitude towards historical narrative. The importance of the event had given rise to a large number of laudatory artistic and literary works in a propaganda campaign which showed to what extent the Spanish monarchy was still capable of setting in motion the machinery of self-exaltation. Indeed, the theme was the subject of noteworthy prints by Callot, various paintings by Pieter Snayers (Museo del Prado), a magnificent historical narrative by the Jesuit Hermann Hugo (*Obsidio bredana*) illustrated with several engravings, and a play by Pedro Calderón de la Barca, *The Siege of Breda.*

Calderón's play and Velázquez's painting have much in common, not only because the latter took inspiration from some of the scenes in the former but also because both reflect an attitude and ideology which set them apart from other literary and pictorial narratives of battles. Unlike the majority of battle scenes then painted (including many of those in the Buen Retiro Palace), Velázquez's picture does not gloat over victory nor is it a panegyric interpretation of the events. There are no triumphant generals or humiliated armies, although Velázquez did not ignore facts, for he shows us a smoke-filled background redolent of war, death and destruction. However, he also draws our attention to a foreground containing not the end of war but the beginning of peace. The victorious general receives his vanquished counterpart attentively, all is expressed in "realistic" or objective terms, while the triumphal allegory so frequent in paintings of this kind is totally absent.

The same attitude predominates in *The Siege of Breda*, first performed a few months after the surrender of the city. Calderón shunned the use of melodrama and concentrated on the episodes which best demonstrated the moral grace of the victors, expressing it in the following lines:

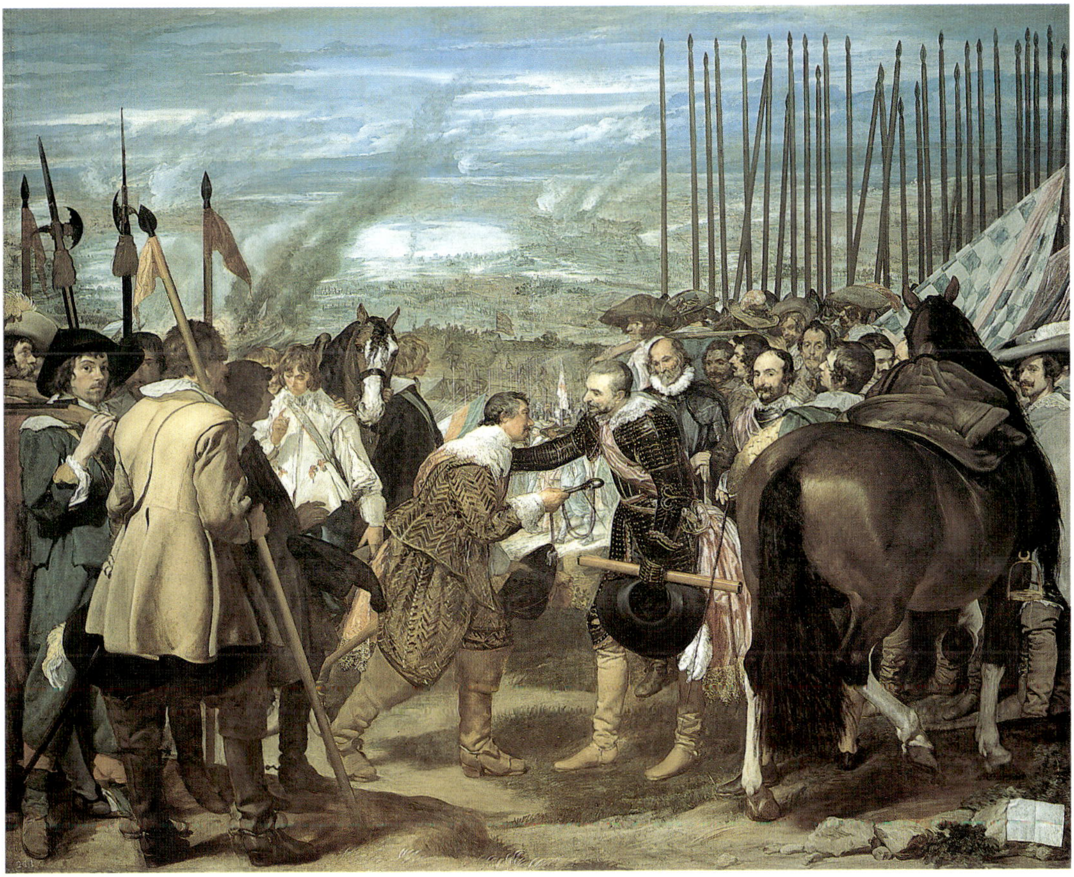

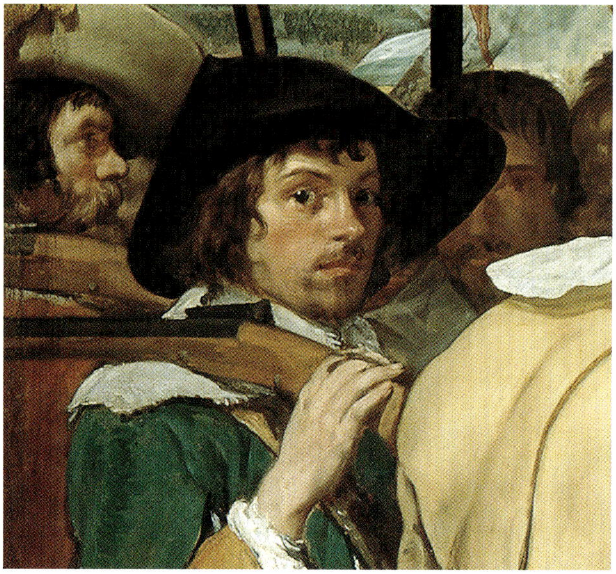

"Honrar al vencido es
una acción que dignamente
el que es noble vencedor
al que es vencido le debe.
Ser vencido no es afrenta".

In a similar vein, General Spinola later says:

"Que el valor del vencido
hace famoso al que vence".

Both the playwright and the artist concentrated on the idea of "clemency" which in warlike or political contexts has precedents in ancient tales of the Roman emperor Augustus. It is also an idea consonant with the image which some thinkers wished to project of the Spanish monarchy's attitude in issues of this kind and by so doing make it the champion of humanistic principles.

Although this painting does not contain the customary rhetoric on victory and symbolic elements are apparently absent from it, rarely has a painting of historical events succeeded in conveying a specific message so precisely, clearly and effectively

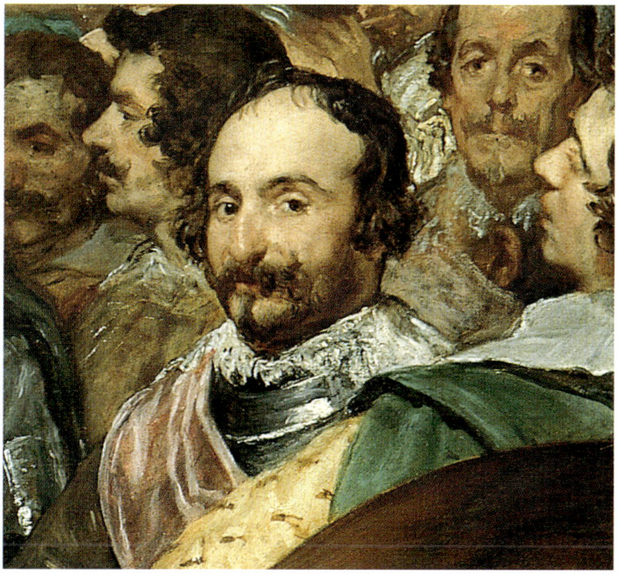

– due mainly to that very lack of rhetoric. Indeed, simple gesture and compositional skill were enough for the painter to convey his view of war. On the right-hand side, the magnificent horse and the group of Spanish soldiers form a kind of horse-shoe that is mirrored by the other horse and Dutch soldiers on the left, while between the two is the main focus of action – the beginning of the respective leaders' embrace. Here Velázquez used the extraordinary communicative capacity of the gesture of Spinola receiving Nassau to state that in a just war the vanquished must be treated with clemency. Significantly, researchers who have attempted to find previous examples of this gesture have managed to do so mainly in religious and similar scenes.

All of this could only have been expressed with such clarity and power through Velázquez's compositional skill, as seen here in his control of all the pictorial resources: his ability to infuse his paintings with air, light and landscape, his mastery of portraiture, his extraordinary knowledge of perspective, etc. However, he did not lack a starting point and it was pointed out long ago that, where composition and detail are concerned, this picture is indebted to numerous paintings and prints.

The painting remained in the *Salón de Reinos* until well into the 18th century. It is known to have been at the Royal Palace in 1772 and 1794 and it entered the Museo del Prado in 1819.

Philip III on horseback
Canvas, 300 x 314 cm
Inv. 1176

Queen Margarita on horseback
Canvas, 297 x 309 cm
Inv. 1177

These two paintings hung on one of the shorter walls of the *Salón de Reinos* and depicted Philip IV's parents in a reference to the King's immediate predecessors in the line of royal succession. It seems that their provenance does not lie with the Buen Retiro Palace, as everything indicates that they were adaptations of previous portraits made specially for their new purpose in the *Salón.* Even Velázquez's part in their painting was sporadic and it has been suggested that he began work on them before his journey to Italy and continued on his return. It has also been pointed out that there are differences of execution between certain parts of these paintings. Thus, the faces, the horses and part of the landscapes have been said to reflect Velázquez's style, whereas the clothing, particularly that of the Queen, is said to denote a drier, more detailed manner typical of painters of the previous generation like Bartolomé González. However, these paintings are not only the result of changes made during two different periods, for further changes were made much later, when clearly visible strips of canvas were added to the sides.

The King is again "in a curvet", a symbol, as we have said, of command and majesty. Among the elements, apart from the face, that make identification possible is the large ruff, which conforms perfectly to the kind of collar in fashion during his lifetime. The river has been said to be the Tagus, in which case the city on the other side of it would be Lisbon, where Philip III made a triumphal entrance in 1619.

Both paintings adorned the Buen Retiro Palace for more than a century, after which they are mentioned in the Royal Palace inventories from 1772 on. They entered the Museo del Prado in 1819.

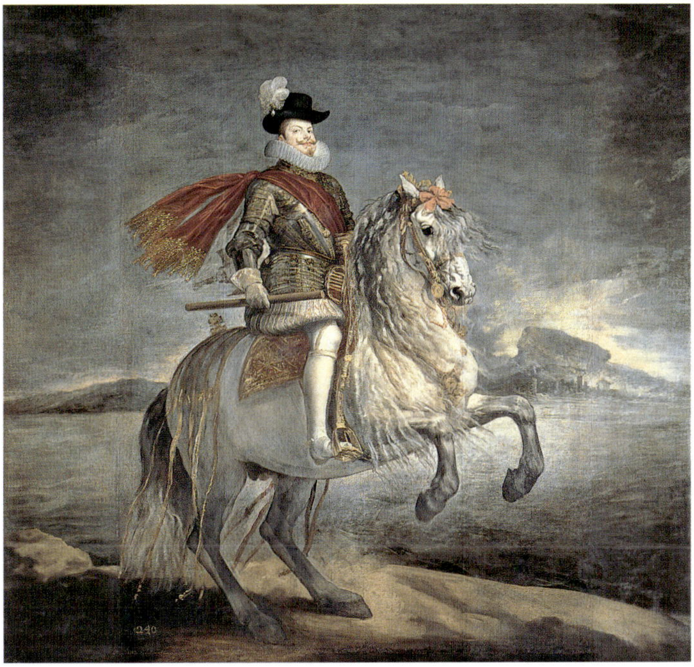
1240

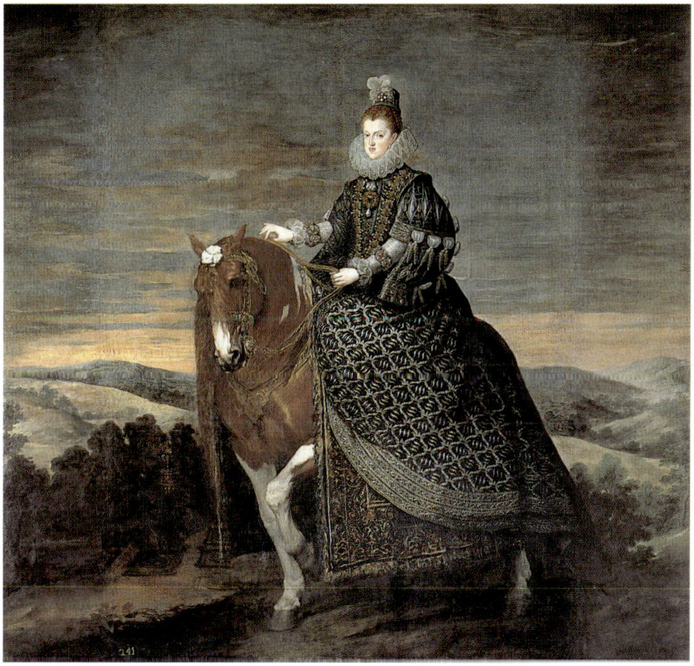
241

Philip IV on horseback

Canvas, 301 x 314 cm
Inv. 1178

Queen Isabel on horseback

Canvas, 301 x 314 cm
Inv. 1179

Opposite the two portraits discussed above and situated on either side of a door were these two paintings of the monarchs who reigned when the Buen Retiro Palace was built. As regards dates and authorship, the second, like those in the previous section, poses certain problems, and the participation of various artists in its execution is generally accepted. However, certain exceptional details of the painting – e.g. the splendid head of the horse with its beautiful cascading mane – clearly denote Velázquez's masterful touch.

Unlike the previous works, the portrait of Philip IV is considered to have been painted entirely by Velázquez and the surface displays the same level of excellence throughout. It has been suggested that it was painted over a similar picture dating from 1626. Whatever the case, the artist painted a personal reflection on a genre of great prestige in Court circles – the equestrian portrait – of which the royal collections possessed outstanding examples, including Titian's *Charles V at the Battle of Mühlberg* and a *Philip IV on Horseback* painted by Rubens during his stay in Spain in 1628 (only a copy now exists). These were doubtless in Velázquez's mind when he painted this portrait, although in a comparison between this work and those of the two masters (among the artists Velázquez most admired) the Sevillian's personality is clearly reflected. Titian painted Charles V as a victorious military hero advancing majestically with a lance – which identifies him as the embodiment of the Christian knight and the ancient hero – across the German plain. Rubens, on the other hand, painted a picture full of allegory in which the King of Spain accepts his mission as defender of the faith and is aided and encouraged by the powers of good as personified by the women in the air, who accompany his triumphant march. Velázquez, however, shunned rhetoric and without distractions concentrated on conveying the essential theme of the work: the King in general's armour who by confidently controlling his horse in a curvet shows that he is capable of holding both the reins of government and those of his own character with a firm hand. His upright posture and determined expression increase that sense of majesty devoid of rhetoric which the painter was so adept at conveying.

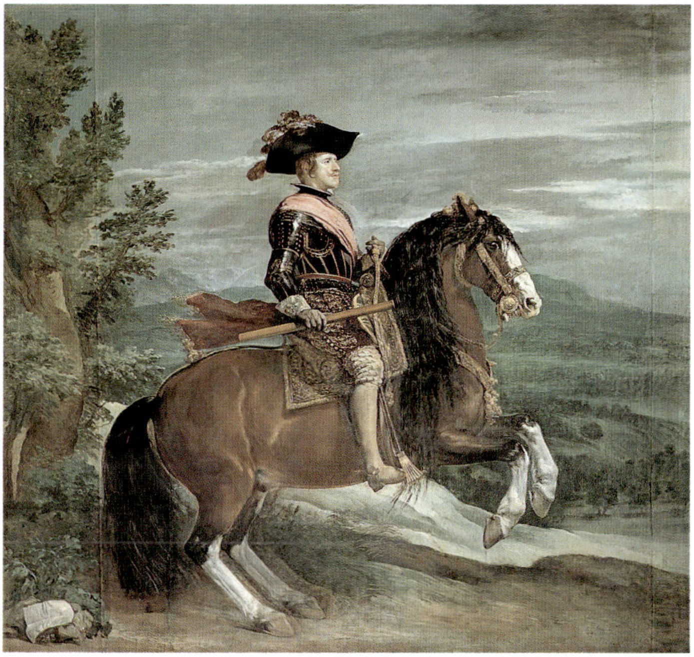

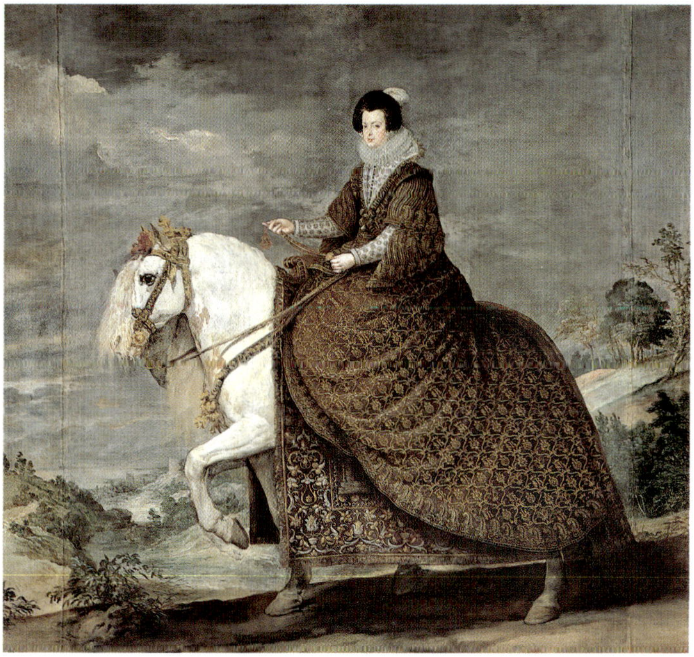

Prince baltasar carlos on horseback

Canvas, 209 x 173 cm
Inv. 1180

The idea of dynastic continuity underlying the series of paintings in the Buen Retiro Palace was continued in this portrait of Baltasar Carlos. It was originally placed between the portraits of his parents and above a door, which explains some of its formal characteristics, particularly the anatomical distortion of the horse, which was intended to be viewed from below.

Like the portrait of Philip IV, this splendid picture – which stirs memories in the contemporary spectator of childhood rides on roundabouts rather than reflections on royal majesty – has won the unanimous admiration of historians, critics, artists and visitors to the Museo del Prado. That child who seems to be playing at grown-ups is surrounded by a magnificent landscape and stands out against a background of mountains which any Madrilenian could easily identify as the La Maliciosa massif – and which María Zambrano, in a commentary on those "distances" of Velázquez's, described as "the bare mountain with the primaeval light." Such a background served Velázquez as an excuse to include elements very dear to his heart – in this case light, which floods a truly expansive painting virtually devoid of shadows. The mount, the young rider and the natural surroundings were painted with the extraordinary technical fluency typical of Velázquez's finest works.

With its great freshness, the blue enveloping both horse and rider has proved powerfully attractive to connoisseurs of painting, one being the poet Rafael Alberti, who was thinking of paintings like this one when he wrote of Velázquez:

"Y también conocía
aquel azul a quien le preguntaba:
¿Qué es ese azul que apenas
si es montaña, si es nieve, si es azul?
Y su respuesta:
-Soy, pero teniendo
por pincelada y por color el aire".

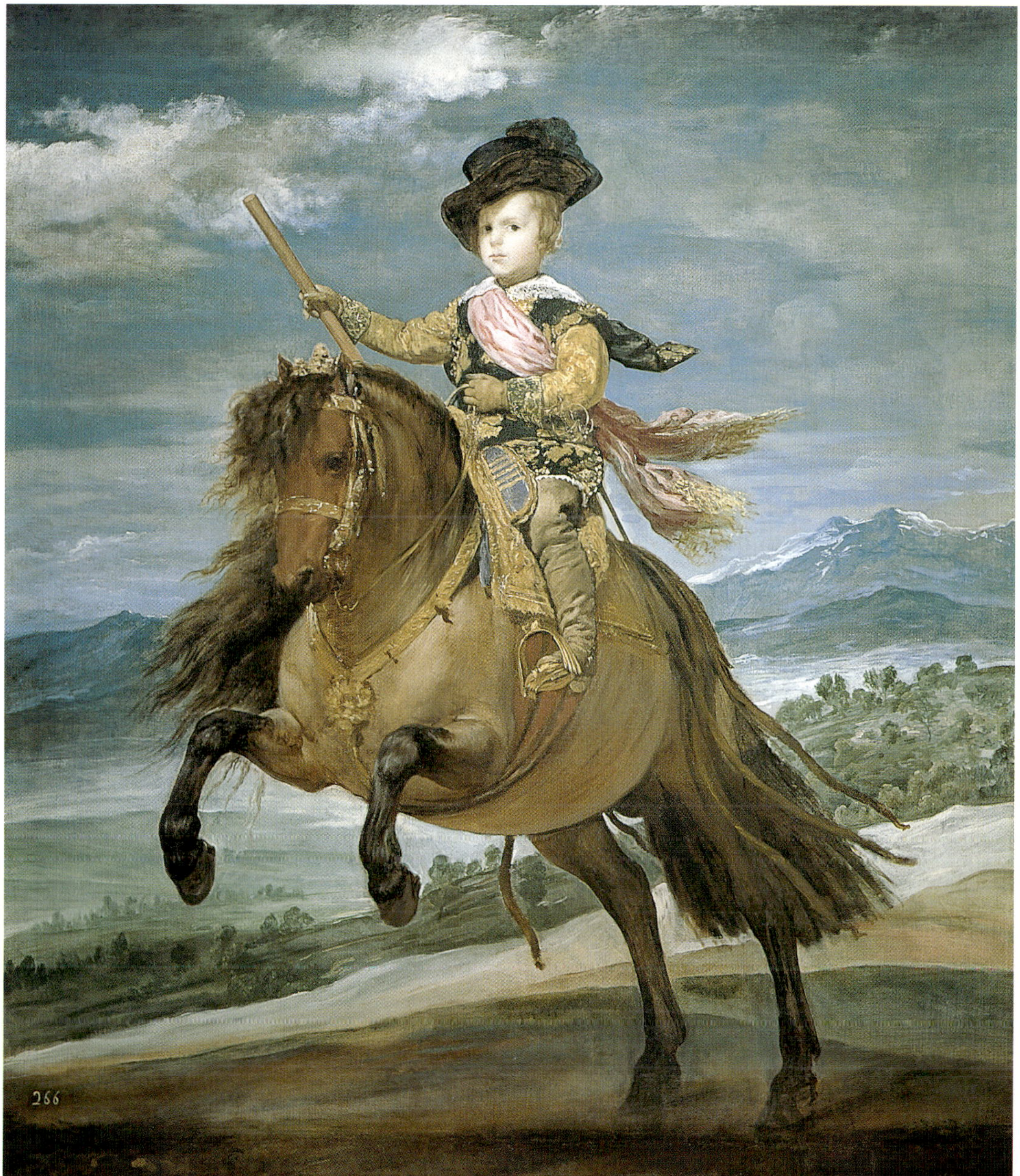
266

The Decoration of The Torre de la Parada

Philip IV as a Hunter
The Cardinal Infante Don Fernando as a Hunter
Prince Baltasar Carlos as a Hunter
Aesop
Menippus
Mars
Head of a Stag

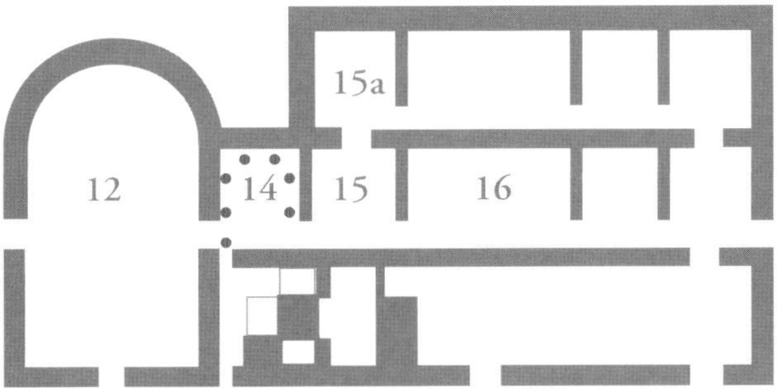

The Decoration of The Torre de la Parada

The 1630s was a very active decade for the royal collections. Spain had still not fully entered the political, economic and social crisis and the King, regarded as one of the most powerful and influential monarchs in Europe and still able to give free rein to his love of art collecting, determined to surround himself with the lavishness and splendour befitting his position. It was at this time when the Buen Retiro Palace was built, when hundreds of paintings were commissioned for it and the project of decorating certain sections of the Alcázar was implemented. The result was that a large number of paintings by the best contemporary artists in Italy and Flanders, including Lanfranco, Poussin, Claude Lorrain and Rubens, were dispatched to Madrid and Philip IV became one the greatest patrons of painting of the age. Additionally, the largest group of paintings by

Velázquez, who played an active part in most of his master's decorative projects, date from this time.

One of the buildings to benefit most from this activity was the Torre de la Parada, a hunting lodge in the El Pardo hills which was renovated between 1635 and 1638 for use by the King. Philip IV took a great interest in the progress of the work carried out there. The *Torre* served no representative function, being dedicated almost exclusively to the King's leisure during his frequent periods of hunting. For its decoration an ambitious collection of paintings was planned, to be supervised by Rubens, who was not only one of the King's favourite painters but also among the most famous artists in Europe at the time. The collection consisted of sixty-three paintings of mythological scenes and sixty of animals and hunting, the former by some of the most important painters from Antwerp working under Rubens, and the latter by Frans Snyders and Paul de Vos. Rubens himself provided all the sketches and painted more than a dozen of the canvases which were finally included. The result was one of the most important mythological cycles of the period and a veritable illustrated reflection on the history of man and the nature of his passions. At the same time, it was a display of the great Flemish artist's pictorial and narrative mastery.

Although there are no known detailed descriptions of the composition and arrangement of this collection of paintings, an inventory taken in the years immediately after the alterations (1700) is of help in this respect. It mentions one room different from the others in that it was not decorated with mythological scenes but with portraits of the royal family and scenes of Court hunts. Between Snayers's paintings of royal hunts there were as many as four pictures by Velázquez: a hunting scene, now in London (National Gallery), depicting one of the Court's customary periods of leisure in the country, and the famous portraits of Philip IV, his brother Ferdinand and his son Baltasar Carlos as hunters, all of which made this the room with the greatest political significance. As some writers have said, it was like a more relaxed and intimate equivalent of the *Salón de Reinos* in the Buen Retiro, with a "family" air about it, although this does not mean that the works exhibited were not exemplary. Indeed, that "tower" almost devoid of representative value but adorned with a complete iconographic programme through which the King and his companions could learn lessons in mythology and history was proof that painting was not regarded as frivolous or trivial during that period.

But the "exemplary" aspect of the Torre de la Parada's adornment did not only take the form of mythological paintings and royal portraits, for various other works by Rubens and

Velázquez on very different subjects were also exhibited there. Such was the case of the Flemish painter's *Heraclitus* and *Democritus* and the Sevillian's *Aesop* and *Menippus*, which offered models of philosophers with strong personalities.

However, the examples of Velázquez's work in the Torre did not end with the five paintings, for his *Mars* hung near *Aesop* and *Menippus*, just as it does today in the Museo del Prado.

Paintings Exhibited

Philip IV as a hunter

c. 1632
Canvas, 191 x 126 cm
Inv. 1184

The portraits in the *Salón de Reinos* were an allusion to dynastic continuity but those of the members of the Spanish monarchy in the Torre de la Parada did not illustrate the line of succession in the same way, first because only two generations were depicted and second because portraits of wives and mothers were absent. As this was a hunting lodge, the paintings were intended to be viewed mainly by men, who would be able to see the likenesses of the members of the male line and their feats of hunting.

The theme of the hunter-prince went beyond that of the mere sportsman, for hunting was regarded as highly appropriate to a young nobleman's education as it not only strengthened his body and provided him with a healthy pursuit in his leisure time but also inculcated into him virtues desirable for the proper exercising of power such as patience, shrewdness and prudence. Furthermore, all the literary sources of the period stress that hunting was a manifestation of the "image of war".

This painting, which is usually dated in the early 1630s, again reveals Velázquez's great mastery with an apparently very small range of pictorial and compositional resources. In fact, many of his works seem to reflect a predilection for almost flaunting his ability in this area and in turning apparent limitations into instruments of great efficiency. The English romantic traveller Richard Ford pointed this out when he wrote that Velázquez never touched the canvas without a specific idea in mind or added one brush-stroke too many. In this picture, far from avoiding the difficulties inherent in placing a brown-clad figure in brown surroundings together with a brown dog and a brown tree, Velázquez took up the challenge and composed a portrait of supreme elegance, using lighter tones to bring out the main points of expressiveness, such as the King's face, his gloves or the poised body of the dog.

This painting remained in the Torre de la Parada until well after the beginning of the 18th century. It is then mentioned in the Royal Palace inventories of 1772-1814. It had reached the Museo del Prado by 1828.

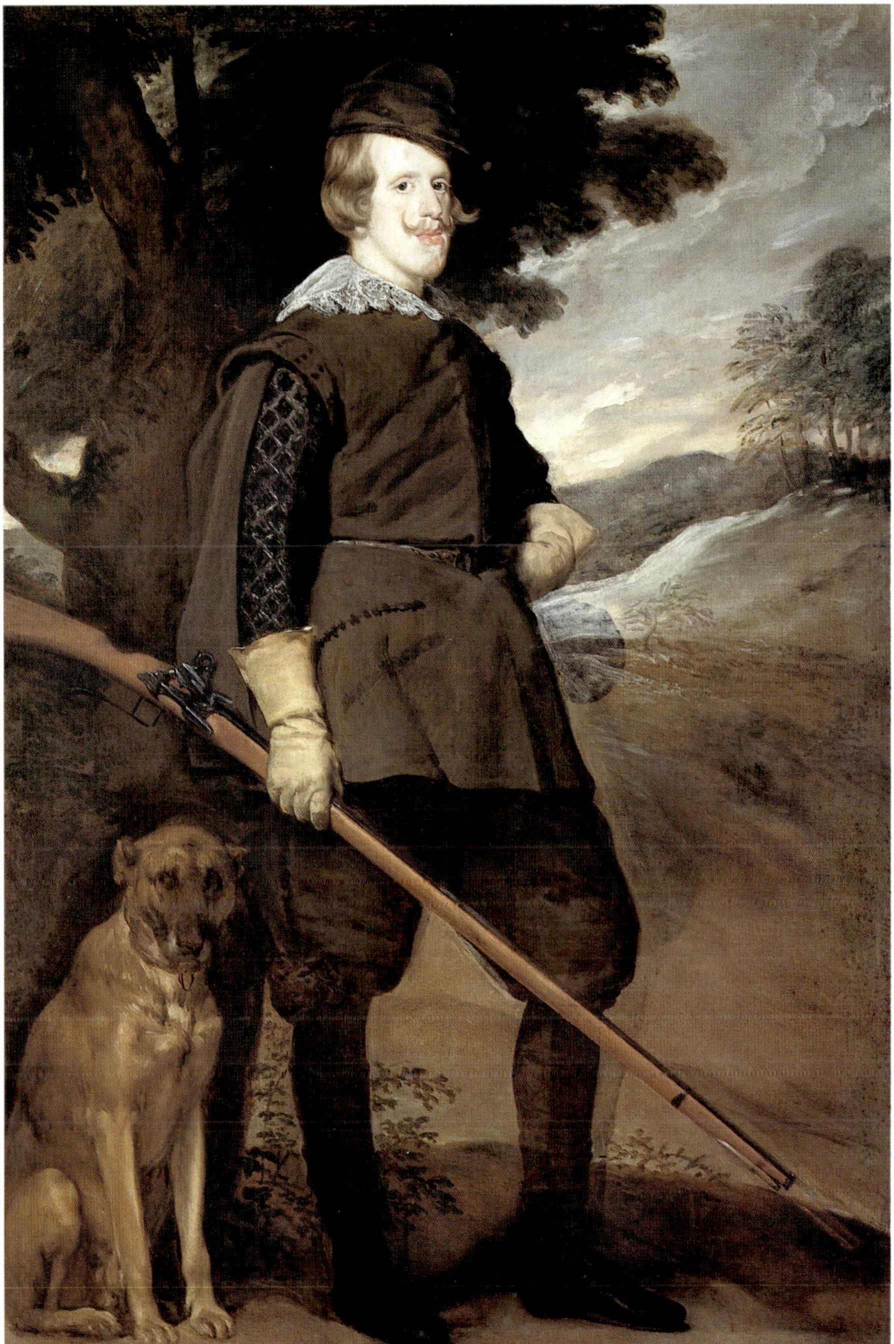

The cardinal infante don fernando as a hunter

c. 1632-1634
Canvas, 191.5 x 108 cm
Inv. 1186

The son of Philip III and Margaret of Inner Austria, the subject of this portrait was born at El Escorial in 1609. He was, therefore, Philip IV's brother and consequently held high positions: in 1619 he was invested Cardinal and in 1634 succeeded his aunt, the Archduchess Isabella Clara Eugenia, as Governor of Flanders, a position he held until his death in 1641.

The painting is usually dated 1632-1634, i.e. immediately prior to Ferdinand's departure for Flanders, although there is a great deal of discrepancy among experts. Some believe that it was painted after his departure from a drawing or a bust portrait. Whatever the case, comparison between it and the contemporary portrait of the King is very interesting. Most striking of all is the family resemblance, and for many years it was thought to be a portrait of the King himself. In this respect, we might recall that the case was similar with the portrait of Don Carlos, again due to the very distinctive features common to almost all of the members of the Austria line. Comparison also enables us to admire the painter's inventiveness: although these are portraits of two hunters in similar natural surroundings, accompanied by dogs and clad in like manner, they nevertheless convey different impressions. Velázquez placed the two subjects in different positions vis-à-vis their surroundings and depicted the King as a firm, stately figure, while that of his brother, facing more to the right, stands with a certain elegant lack of balance.

By the second half of the 18th century the painting had left the Torre de la Parada and was in the Royal Palace, Madrid. It reached the Museo del Prado in 1819.

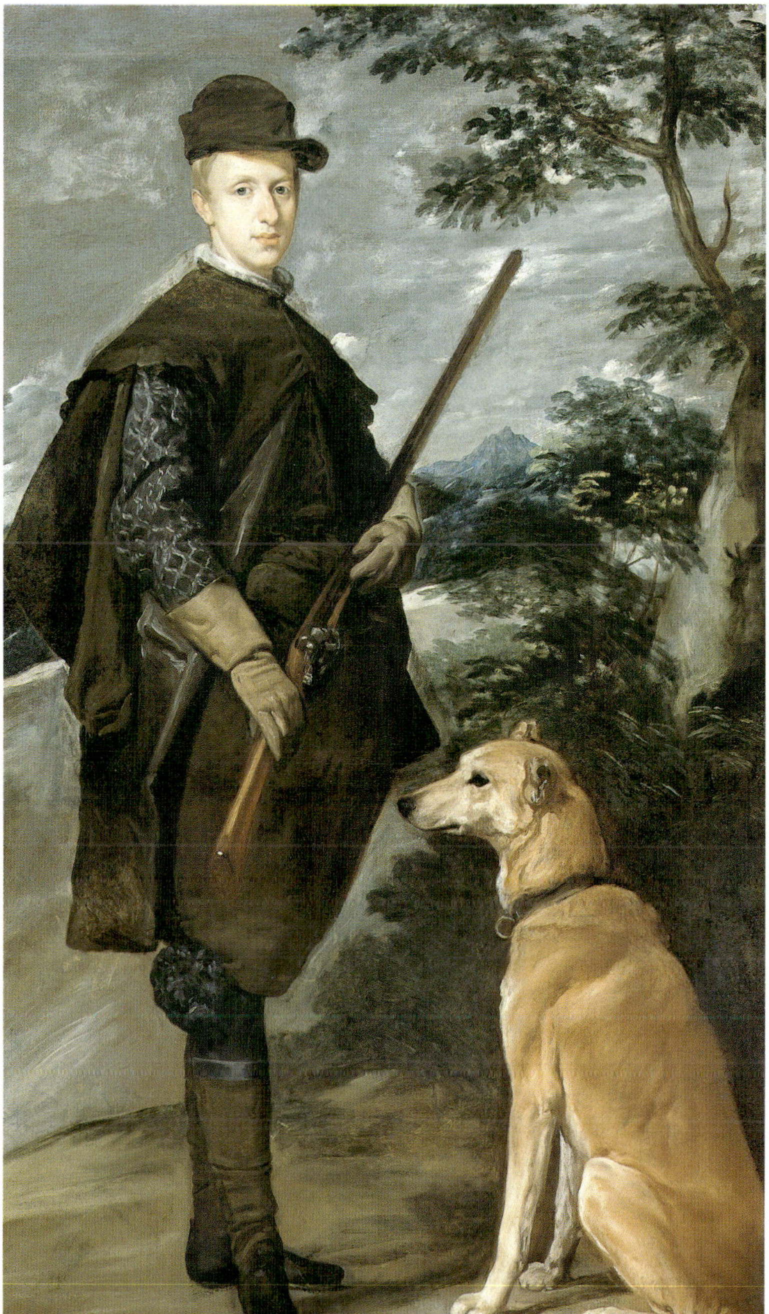

Prince baltasar carlos as a hunter

1635-1636
Canvas, 191 x 103 cm
Inscription: "Anno aetatis suae VI"
Inv. 1189

An inscription in the bottom left-hand corner of this portrait dates it between October 1635 and October 1636, by which time Velázquez, after his first visit to Italy and his long, careful study of the royal collections, had reached full artistic maturity. The subject is the young Prince Baltasar Carlos, born in October 1629 and the son of Philip IV and Elizabeth of France. All hopes of dynastic succession were placed in him. His intelligence and lively nature suggested that he would develop the qualities necessary for governing, but all such hopes were dashed with his death in October 1646. Although it may seem surprising to see such a young child dressed as a hunter, according to contemporary testimonies hunting was regarded as one of the most important aspects of a royal prince's education. Indeed, from a very early age the child had his own equipment, including the harquebus he is seen holding in his right hand, which had been a gift from the Viceroy of Navarre to Philip IV when he was a child.

In addition to being a superb testimony to Velázquez's original approach to the field of the portrait, this painting is a fine example of the interest he developed in another genre during that period – the landscape. Serving as a background to the figure, the landscape was painted with the freshness and freedom for which the painter was always so admired. In this case it was taken from life, for the tree is one of the old oaks which grow at El Pardo and any Madrilenian would recognize the mountains in the background as the blue Guadarrama. This is one of Velázquez's paintings in which an open-air sensation is at its most vivid.

Copies of this painting reveal that it was originally larger and that part of the right-hand side, which included another dog, was removed at some time. It was first hung in the Torre de la Parada but from the middle of the 18th century is referred to in the Royal Palace, Madrid. It had reached the Museo del Prado By 1819.

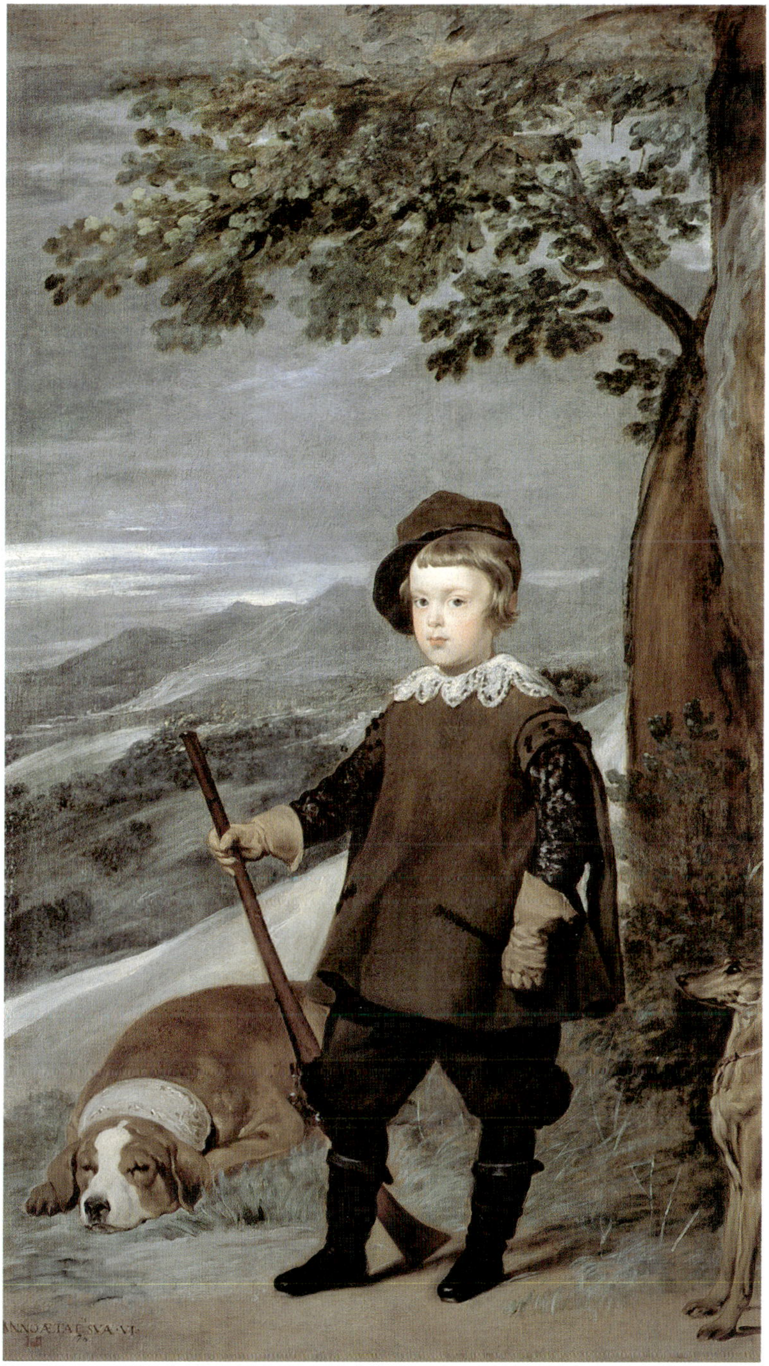
ANNO ÆTATIS SVÆ VI

Aesop

Canvas, 179 x 94 cm
Inv. 1206

One of Velázquez's most famous paintings in the 19th century was *Aesop*, and many painters, both Spanish (Goya, Fortuny, etc.) and foreign, made copies after it. It is also mentioned in almost all the books on travel written during that period, one example being that of Hans Christian Andersen, who stated that after seeing this painting it was impossible to imagine the fable writer with any other face. There were two main reasons why the painting then proved so attractive to visitors: first its very excellence, for it is one of the finest examples of Velázquez's mastery of the brush-stroke and use of a limited range of colours and his ability to paint the type of realistic picture in keeping with the tastes of 19th-century European painting with such economy. But there were also what we might call "literary" reasons, for the spectator's initial reaction of surprise at the Classical writer depicted in ragged clothing is followed by amazement on realizing just how well that tattered, tired, worn-out man staring proudly out of the painting actually embodies the philosopher.

A century later, there is not a great deal of additional information available on this work, although there has continued to be speculation, at times contradictory, about it. While many believe that underlying this painting is a similarity between the writer's wise, sceptical and ironic look and the painter's own attitude to life, a smaller group believe that the latter was mocking the former by endowing him with the features attributed in contemporary books on physiognomy to "men with the face of an ox".

Both the garments worn by Aesop in the painting and the objects around him have been interpreted as allusions to circumstances in his life. His poor clothing would therefore be a reference to his origin as a slave and his humble life and the pail to a shrewd answer to a question from his master, the philosopher Xanthus, who as a reward gave him his freedom. The baggage would be an allusion to his death: when he told the citizens of Delphi that the city's reputation was over-rated, they took revenge on him by hiding a cup in his baggage, accusing him of theft and throwing him off a cliff.

The references in this picture to Aesop's wit, independent spirit and indifference to worldly possessions as well as the serious and intelligent expression on his face and his powerful presence infuse this depiction of the philosopher with great dignity. It was probably painted to adorn one of the rooms in the Torre de la Parada together with *Menippus* and *Mars*, which are also mentioned there in 1701. It is again mentioned at various Royal Seats until 1819, by which time it had reached the Museo del Prado.

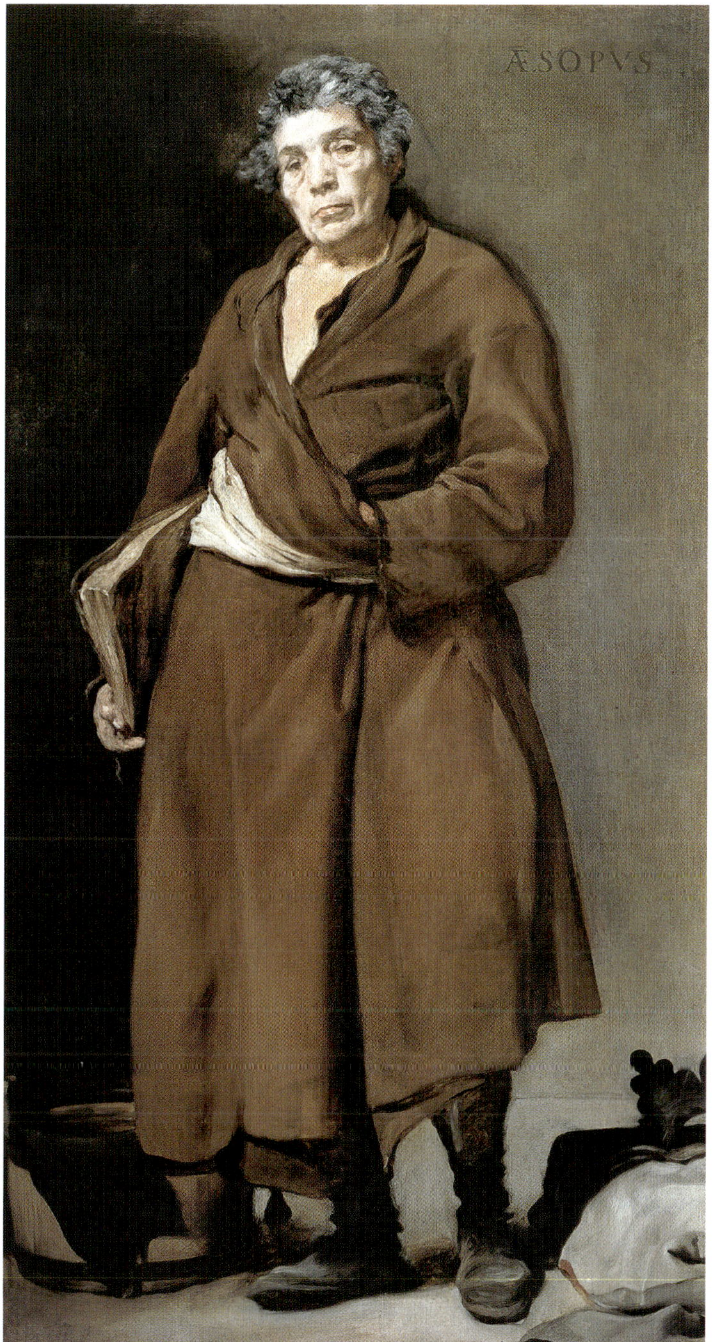
ÆSOPVS

Menippus

Canvas, 179 x 94 cm
Inv. 1207

The companion piece to the previous canvas, *Menippus* likewise depicts one of the "simple" philosophers born as slaves who wrote major works of social criticism. The two pictures are first mentioned in the Torre de la Parada together with *Mars*, which is of similar dimensions. The existence of what was probably a series has led to speculation that the three are a reflection on the vanities of the world (wealth, military might, etc.).

There is much disagreement as to the date and the circumstances surrounding the execution of *Aesop* and *Mennipus*. Although a time difference of more than ten years – 1629 to 1642 – is generally considered possible, some experts have dated *Menippus* in the last decade of Velázquez's life, citing the evident maturity of style. At the present time there is a tendency to regard the two as contemporaries painted around 1640, in view of the fact that Rubens had previously painted two other figures of philosophers – *Heraclitus* and *Democritus* – for the Torre de la Parada, where they are mentioned in 1638; the Sevillian's pictures would therefore be a kind of reply to the Flemish painter's works – and not the only one, as is evident in the case of *The Fable of Arachne*.

Like its companion, this painting has given rise to a great deal of literature attempting to decipher its meaning and using the ragged, half burlesque figure to reflect on the common people of the Spanish Golden Age – a subject on which, despite so many useful written testimonies, there is so little illustrated material.

Its history, as regards the royal collections, is similar to that of the previous painting.

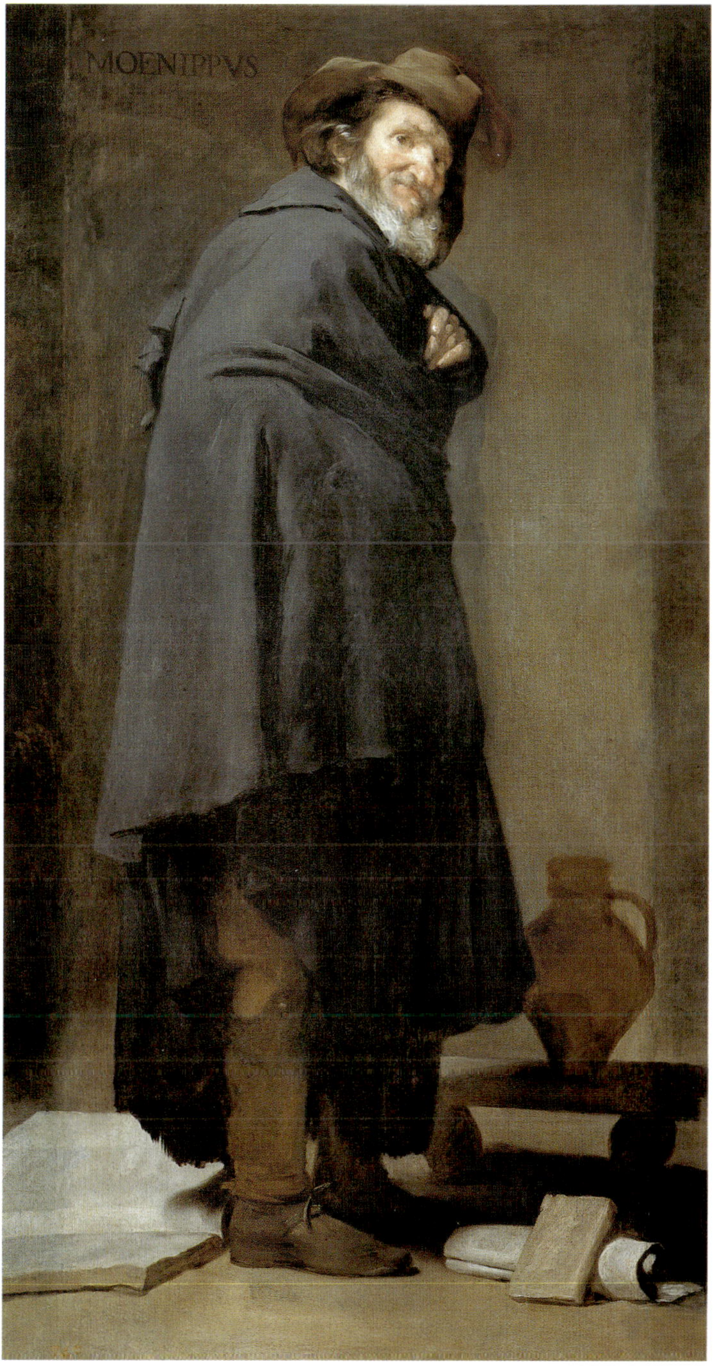
MOENIPPVS

Mars

c. 1640
Canvas, 179 x 95 cm
Inv. 1208

Mars is among Velázquez's works which best reflect his critical and highly personal approach to mythological themes. Here, instead of depicting a hardened hero, Velázquez painted a melancholic soldier with a body no longer supple and poised for battle but tired and defeated. Although out of context, three hundred and fifty years later it is very tempting to regard this painting as a symbol of a country whose armies had dominated Europe for over a century and which was now entering a long period of political and military decline. This painting has also been seen as: a continuation of the story which began with the *Forge of Vulcan* (Museo del Prado); a "mythological" portrait of the buffoon Antonio Bañules along the same lines as those of *Barbarroja* and *Don Juan de Austria*; and even a depiction of Agamemnon – although the iconographic attributes fully coincide with those of the god of war.

Any interpretation of this picture must, however, take into account that it was painted around 1640, very probably for the Torre de la Parada (where it is referred to for the first time), and in connection with *Aesop* and *Menippus*, which, as we have said, is an open invitation to place this work within a context of disillusionment or scepticism.

In *Mars* Velázquez demonstrated not only his narrative skill and capacity for painting images full of connotations but also his absolute mastery of technique – broad, free and effective strokes, colours whose freshness and boldness of combination owe a great deal to his studies of Titian, and skin tones denoting knowledge of Rubens's work. Velázquez did not lack sources for *Mars*, for the composition was inspired by previous works on the theme, and in this respect the Classical sculpture *Ares Ludovisi* (Rome, Museo Nazionale) and Michelangelo's *Il Pensieroso* on the Medici tomb (Florence, San Lorenzo) are usually cited.

The painting is referred to in the Torre de la Parada between 1701 and 1747, from where it was sent to the Royal Palace. At the end of the Peninsular War it was among the items dispatched to France with the so-called "baggage of King Joseph", but was finally returned to Spain and deposited in the Academy of San Fernando. It reached the Museo del Prado in 1827.

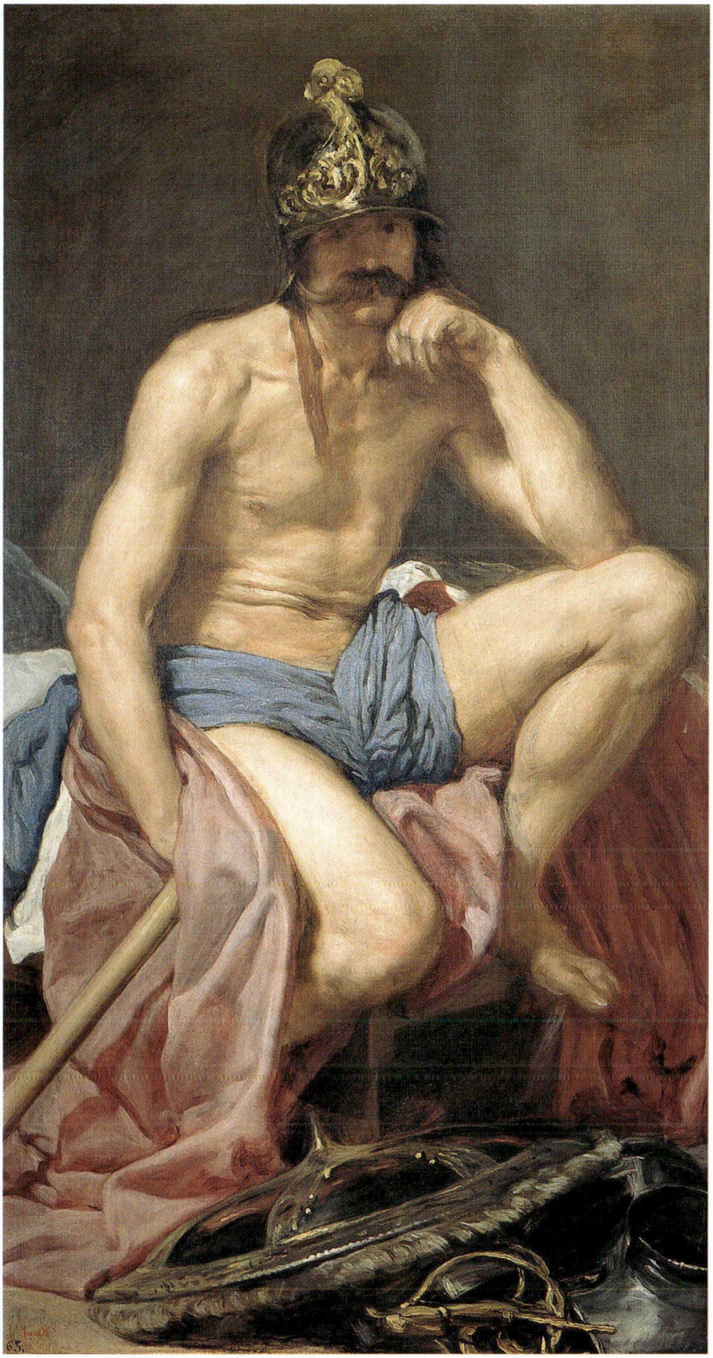

Head of a stag

1626-1636
Canvas, 58 x 44.5 cm
Inv. 3253

Although no records confirming that this picture was painted for the Torre de la Parada actually exist, the subject is an open invitation to place it among the works intended for that hunting lodge. Velázquez's style, unlike the styles of other painters, cannot be described in terms of linear progression, as many of its distinguishing features were present throughout the greater part of his career. Because of this, works which are not even minimally documented pose serious dating problems for historians. One such example is this head of a stag, which has been dated between 1626 and 1636. It is known to have been purchased in 1920 by the Marquis of Casa Torres, who donated it to the Museo del Prado in 1975, reserving it for his usufruct until his death, which took place in 1984.

The high quality of this painting and its subject and authorship all suggest that it was intended for one of the Royal Seats and some experts have pointed out that it may be the same one as that included in the Alcázar inventory of 1637 which mentions a label with the inscription: "Killed by our lord, King Philip the Fourth in the year 1626". It was included in subsequent inventories until 1747, although it is believed to have finally been released from the royal collections due to the damage it sustained in the fire in the Alcázar in 1734. The reference to 1626 has served those experts who identify it with the painting mentioned in the inventory to date the work, although others believe that the year on the label is a misprint and that it should read 1636. Yet others claim that the work mentioned in that year was *Deer's Antlers*, which now belongs to the *Patrimonio Nacional.*

Whatever its provenance, this is a painting of very high quality whose freshness, immediacy and naturalism have led to it being described as a "portrait" of an animal. The subject was a common one at the Spanish Court, as almost all the kings of Spain were passionate hunters. In this respect, we might mention the large number of hunting themes related to Court art and even poetry, examples being the paintings, mentioned above, which adorned the Torre de la Parada, and entire books like *Anfiteatro de Felipe el Grande* dedicated by its author, José de Pellicer, to the praise of a king capable of killing a bull in the Plaza Mayor in Madrid with one shot of a harquebus.

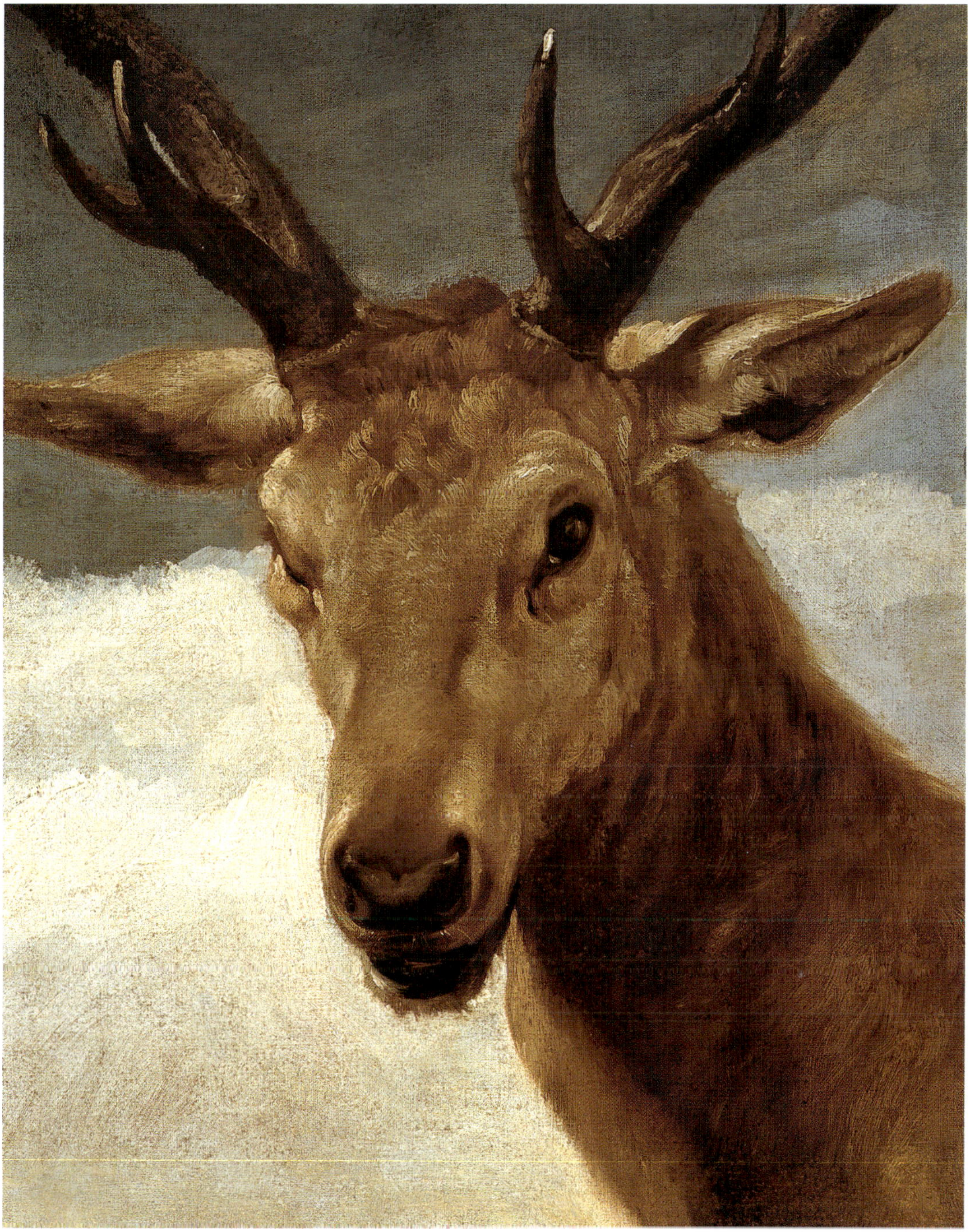

Dwarves, Buffoons and Entertainers

The Buffoon Pablo de Valladolid
The Buffoon Don Cristóbal de Castañeda y Pernia (Barbarroja)
The Buffoon Don Juan de Austria
Don Diego de Acedo, El Primo
Don Sebastián de Morra
The Dwarf Francisco Lezcano (El Niño de Vallecas)
The Buffoon Calabazas (Calabacillas)

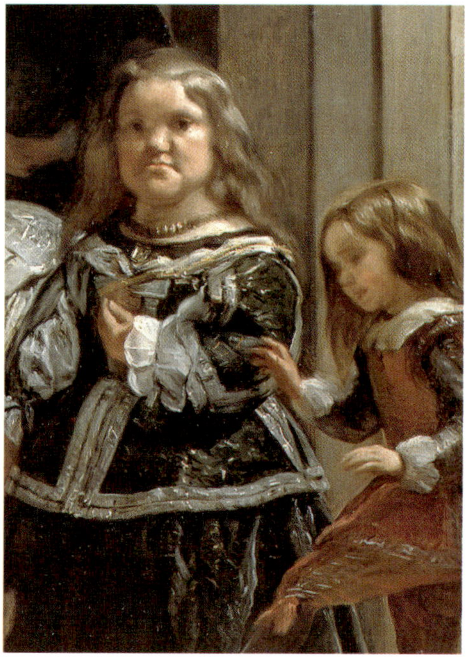

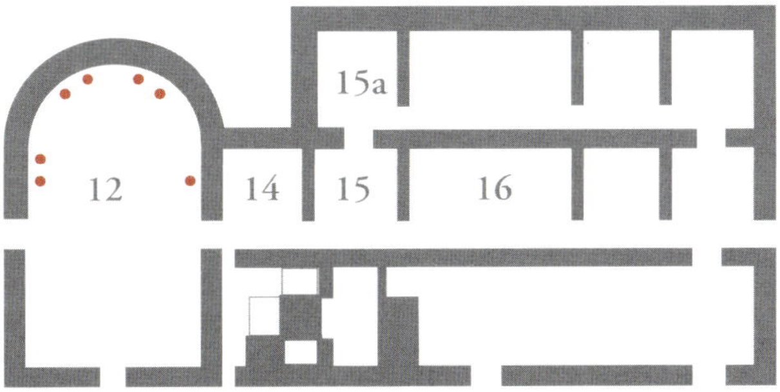

Dwarves, Buffoons and Entertainers

One of the many aspects of Velázquez which made him unique among his contemporaries was his own, very personal treatment of the various genres. He approached even those genres with centuries of tradition behind them in a new, original way. And such was the case of the portrait, a genre he devoted himself to throughout his career, using not only methods based to a certain extent on the solidly established tradition governing it but also his own, very personal approach. This is particularly evident in the portraits whose models came from the large group of "monsters, dwarfish buffoons, and entertainers" commonly found at the Spanish Court from the 16th century on who, with their physical and mental deformities, wit and personal tragedies filled the leisure time of a sector of society convinced that each man had his own specific part to play in the world. There is a relatively large amount of information on these figures who were essential members of society at any royal or aristocratic palace. The numerous portraits Velázquez painted of them pose a great many problems of interpretation and have prompted very different reactions, often in accordance with the interests of each age. Thus, in the 19th century many expressed displeasure with some of these paintings while others accused Velázquez of callously taking pleasure in portraying these creatures. Throughout the 20th century, however, many have read a more "humanistic" meaning into the paintings and, prompted by ideas of what we see today as dignity and defencelessness, stress the painter's sensitivity to human suffering. Although it is true that the dignified stare, the absence of rhetorical and anecdotal elements and the amorphous space which leads to a direct confrontation between Velázquez's buffoons and the spectator endorse this kind of interpretation, it must also be borne in mind that these pictures were painted to adorn the royal palaces and that any interpretation of them should not differ greatly from the attitude of a 17th-century courtier. In any event, these works have for many years forced the spectator to examine his or her own concept of human dignity, which makes them milestones in the history of painting and the art of painting itself a vehicle for conveying and prompting reflection on the nature of man.

Velázquez was not, by any means, the first to portray these creatures, for the Museo del Prado possesses other examples of pictures of this kind painted at the Spanish court by Sir Anthony More, Alonso Sánchez Coello and Juan Van der Hamen. Furthermore, this was not a phenomenon strictly limited to the Court, as curiosity about "freaks" of nature (the category in which many of the buffoons were included) was to be found at all levels of society, as the success of the stories and prints dedicated to them prove. While it is perhaps not surprising that they posed for portraits, it is unusual that they did so on so many occasions. Without counting the two in *Las Meninas*, the Museo del Prado possesses seven portraits of this kind, while those of Juan Calabazas (Cleveland) and Baltasar Carlos with a dwarf (Boston) belong to foreign museums. All of which makes them one of the main themes in Velázquez's production. The provenance and purpose of these portraits, however, are still not clear. The fact that the subjects served at Court and that the paintings are known to have belonged to the royal collections suggests that they were painted above all for the King, but it is not known whether they were painted on his orders or simply because Velázquez liked painting this kind of picture. Of those who believe that the latter case is true, some argue that they allowed him to adopt and diffuse a compassionate view of these creatures, while others affirm that he regarded them merely as "pictorial" motifs and, feeling no kind of responsibility towards them, used them to test his ability to capture a visual experience – just as had taken delight in accurately reproducing the volume and substance of a pitcher in his Seville period, or had set out to capture on canvas the experience of a moment in a garden in Rome. However, on evaluating such opinions it must be remembered that on no account are these pictures solely portraits, for almost all the subjects are surrounded by attributes or performing some action which adds a deeper meaning to their simple bodily traits. One is acting, another holding cards, two are disguised as warrior heroes, another has a couple of gourds by him, one is turning the pages of a large book and has writing materials at hand, another, who is standing, shows us a portrait of a woman and holds a pinwheel in his hand. Furthermore, in Velázquez's age the concept of "objective" or aseptic realism as we know it today did not exist, for the real world was full of religious and moral associations.

& Paintings Exhibited &

The buffoon Pablo de Valladolid

c. 1632-1635
Canvas, 213.5 x 125 cm
Inv. 1198

In the world of palace buffoons a distinction was made between those who were physically or mentally handicapped and those who were not and whose task was to entertain the Court with their wit. Among this second group was Pablo de Valladolid, who was born in Vallecas in 1587 and died in December 1648, having served at Court since 1632. As this painting depicts him apparently declaiming, for many years it was known as "The Comedian". In all likelihood his pose is due to the fact that one way in which he and others like him entertained the royal family (and consequently earned their living at Court) was through recitation or interpreting passages from plays.

This portrait is among those which best reflect Velázquez's mastery of painting with limited resources: although very small, the range of colours is rich in tones, the figure stands out against an indefinite space that is scarcely suggested by the faint shadow cast by the body. Far from subtracting content or lessening expressiveness, so much sobriety heightens the effect and compels the spectator, free of distractions, to face the subject before him. But the achievement of such an effect not does not depend on the painter's will alone, for he must also possess the technical skill enabling him to take the fullest advantage of such sparse resources and blend the personage into the area in which he stands.

This rhetoric of the essential was highly appreciated by late 19th-century painters, one being Edouard Manet, who said of this work that it was possibly the most astonishing piece of painting ever done and used it as the basis for his famous *Fifer*. After seeing this painting, his Dutch colleague Josef Israels wrote that Velázquez was the artist who came closest to the model of the painter one imagines when young.

The picture has been dated as *c.* 1635 but once again there is disagreement and some experts believe that it formed part of a series of pictures for the Buen Retiro Palace for which Velázquez received a fee in 1634. What is certain, however, is that in 1701 and 1716 it was in that palace, in 1772 and 1794 in the Royal Palace, in 1816 in the Academy of San Fernando and that it entered the Museo del Prado in 1827.

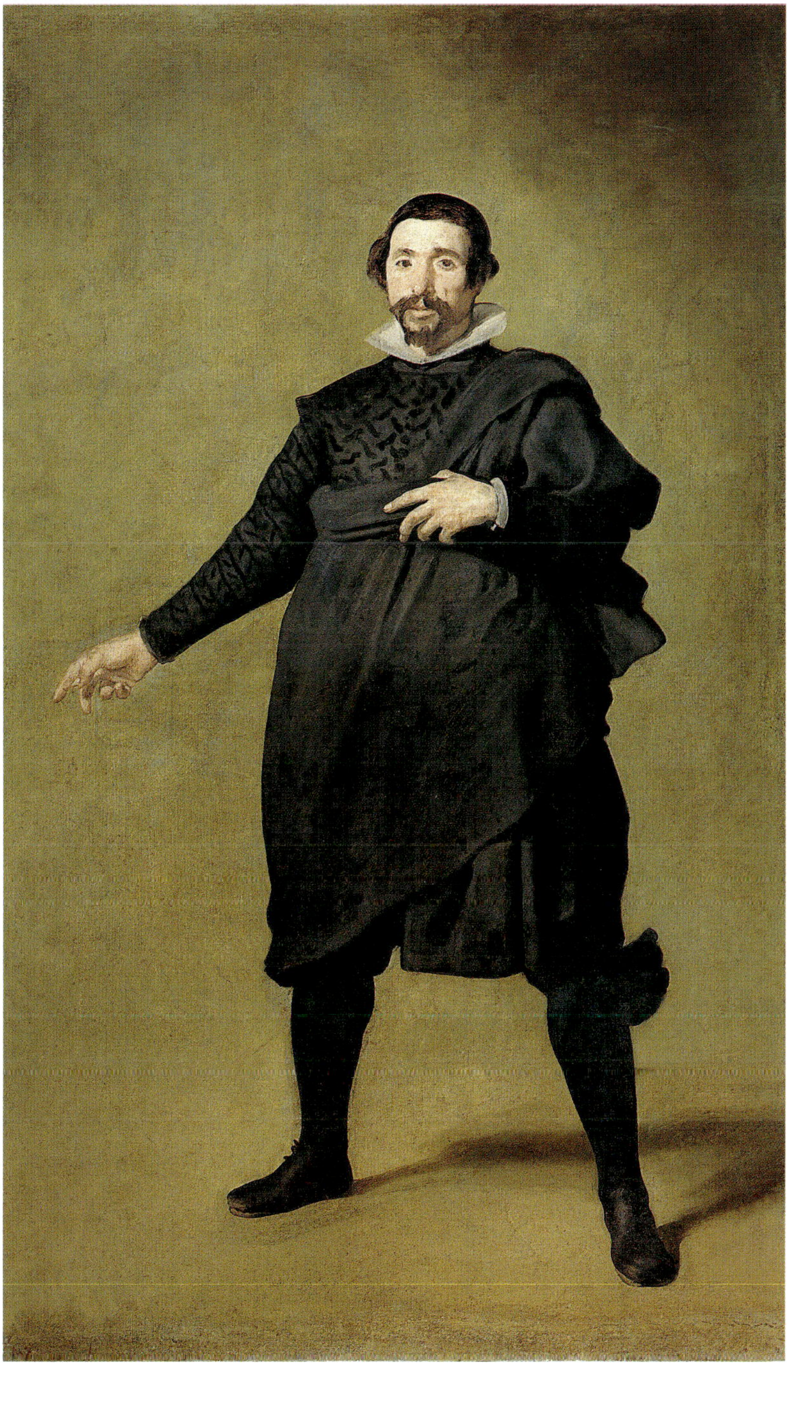

The buffoon don Cristóbal de Castañeda y Pernia (Barbarroja)

Canvas, 200 x 121.5 cm
Inv. 1199

This painting shows a man in Turkish garb firmly holding a sword and glaring out at some unknown point. The Buen Retiro Palace inventory of 1701 describes him as the buffoon "Pernia" and states that the work is unfinished.

Don Cristóbal de Castañeda y Pernia was an entertainer whose presence at the Spanish Court is recorded from 1633 to 1649. It is known that one of his various positions was emissary of the Cardinal Infante Ferdinand of Austria. What is known of his character coincides well with the impression of him conveyed in this painting, for he was famous for his quick temper and boastfulness, taking no pains to conceal them even in the presence of the King and Queen. Indeed, one impertinent response to Philip IV in 1634 cost him a period of exile in Seville. Velázquez was probably familiar with Don Cristóbal's character and reputation, and for his portrait chose the costume of Barbarossa, the famous Turkish pirate who attacked Mediterranean coastal towns during the second half of the 16th century and was defeated at Lepanto by Don Juan de Austria (impersonated by a buffoon in another of Velázquez's paintings).

This work is a prodigy of expressiveness in which the strong colour of the robe, the composition of the body and a swift and energetic brush-stroke were all used to highlight the subject's irascible nature. The fact that there is a great deal of difference between the painting of the cloak draped over the left shoulder and the rest of the work has led some experts to claim it was added at a much later time.

The same dating problems exist as with *Pablo de Valladolid.* After the first reference in the royal collections in 1701 the histories of the two are similar.

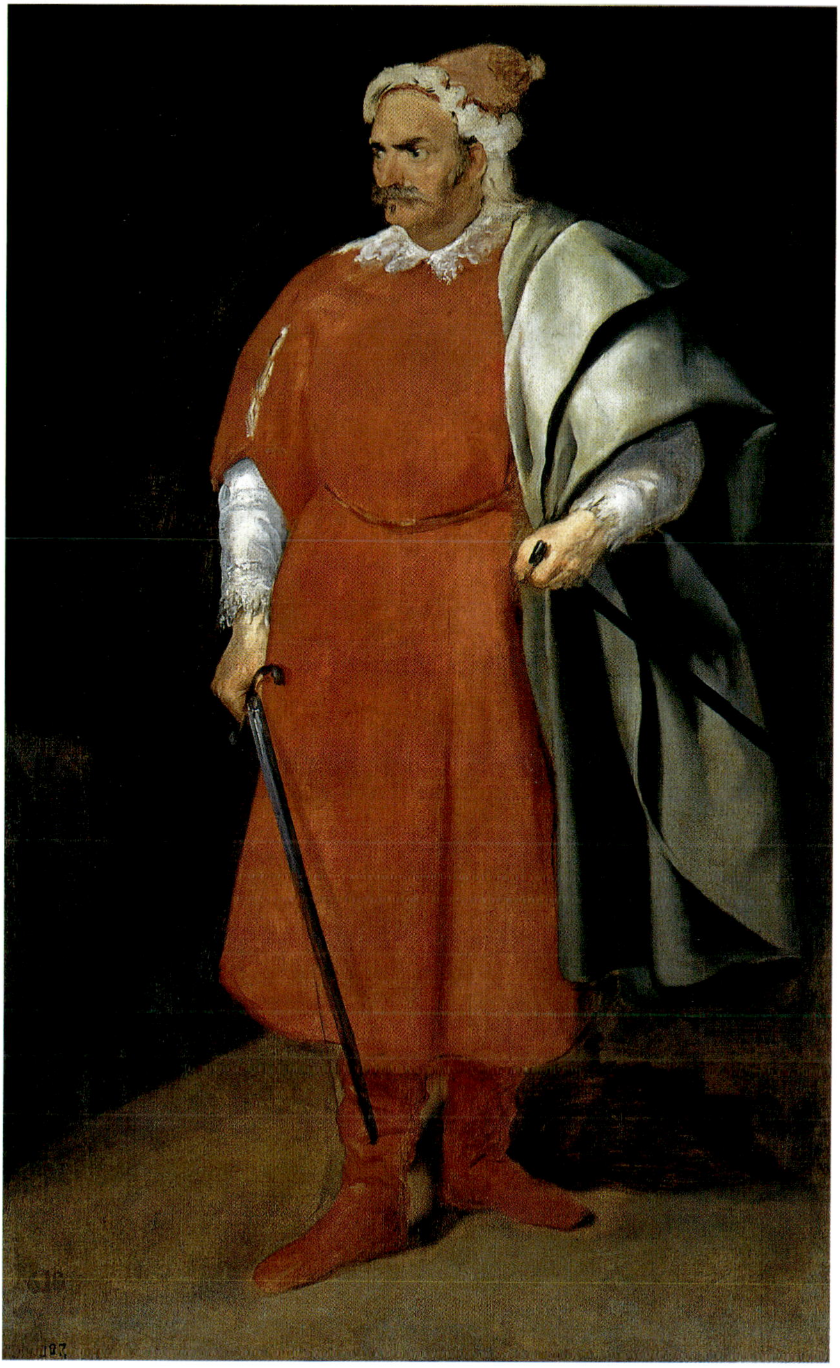

The buffoon Don Juan de Austria

Canvas, 210 x 124.5 cm
Inv. 1200

This painting was probably the companion piece to *The Buffoon Don Cristóbal de Castañeda y Pernia (Barbarroja)*, with which it can be compared in content – the soldier's costume, the connection of the personages they impersonate with the Battle of Lepanto – and yet contrasted as examples of two different aspects of human nature, the first angry and sanguineous, the second shy and passive. Here the inclusion of the costume was not due to any desire by the painter to suit the character of a buffoon to the memory of a historical hero but to something much simpler: the name by which the buffoon was known in the palace was the same as that of Charles V's son, and Velázquez took advantage of this coincidence to depict his subject as a general surrounded by objects associated with war and standing in front of a scene of a naval battle. Although this depiction is seen today as an obvious caricature, as rather unwarlike and even somewhat pathetic, this has not always been the case for in various 18th- and 19th-century inventories the painting was described as a "portrait of a general" and was even said to be of the Marquis of Pescara.

Like *Mars*, this work has been used as a reference to Spain's military decline, although such an interpretation almost certainly dates from long after the picture was painted and was not in Velázquez's mind at that time. The discovery of a delivery note dated 1632 for clothes similar to those in the picture has led some experts to claim that the painting must date from around that year; other historians, however, believe that it was painted considerably later.

Due to its technical excellence this work reveals how comfortable Velázquez felt painting portraits of buffoons, for they gave him a type of freedom not always found in his portraits of Court figures and members of the royal family. On few occasions were his strokes more fluent than in the reds of the garments in this painting and never did he achieve a greater degree of expressive freedom than in the remarkable battle taking place in the background.

The presence of Juan de Austria is recorded at Court in Madrid between 1624 and 1654. The portrait is referred to in the Buen Retiro Palace in 1701 and 1716, the Royal Palace in 1772 and 1794, and the Academy of San Fernando in 1816. It reached the Museo del Prado from the Academy in 1827.

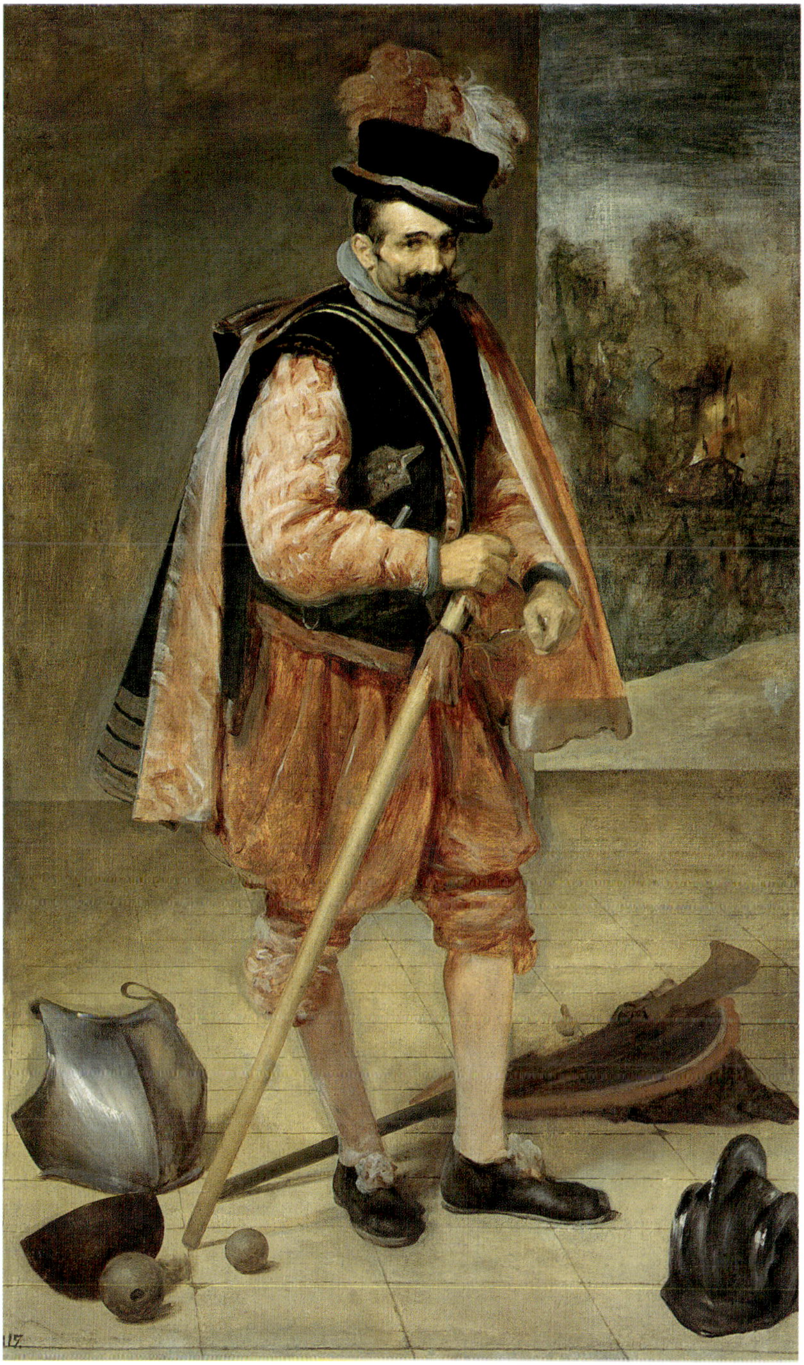

Don diego de acedo, el primo

Canvas, 107 x 82 cm
Inv. 1201

Don Diego de Acedo was a servant at the palace from 1635. In addition to his Court position as a buffoon, he was a royal courier and Keeper of the Royal Seal. Holding two such different posts was not especially unusual; for example the entertainer Agustín Profit had been Governor of the Casa de Campo in the reign of Philip II. Don Diego's duties as Keeper of the Royal Seal would explain the huge tome on his lap and the writing materials on the floor. One of Velázquez's buffoons with the greatest self-assurance, Don Diego prompted the novelist Múgica Laínez to describe him as "restless, imaginative and prying" and to write a story about him in which he practically falls in love with Titian's Danae.

There are various theories regarding the nickname "El Primo" (lit. "The Cousin"): some experts have recalled that it was the name of a rather pedantic character in *Don Quixote*, while others believe that Don Diego was a distant relation of the painter's. However, it has recently been pointed out that "Primo" was the name by which the King addressed the Grandees, who, furthermore, enjoyed the privilege – just like the buffoon in the painting – of keeping their heads covered in his presence. Bearing this in mind, the nickname could be a satire on Don Diego's airs of greatness. A few facts are known about his life, e.g. that he had a servant, that he was involved in a crime of passion in 1643, and that he died in poverty in October 1660, two months after Velázquez.

As Don Diego accompanied Philip IV on the Aragón campaign in 1644 and records prove that Velázquez painted his portrait in Fraga, some experts date the picture in that year. Others, however, believe that it was painted for the Torre de la Parada during the previous decade, basing their theory on the landscape in the background – like the portrait of Baltasar Carlos hunting, it depicts the La Maliciosa as seen from El Pardo – and on the fact that, despite other references to a now lost portrait of "El Primo" in the Alcázar inventories of 1666, 1686 and 1700, the first definite reference to it was made in the Torre inventory of 1701.

The background to the portrait is unfinished. Furthermore, it is evident that a number of vertical lines on it were made by the brush being cleaned on the canvas.

The painting is referred to at the Palace of El Pardo between 1714 and 1772 and subsequently at the Royal Palace. It reached the Museo del Prado in 1819.

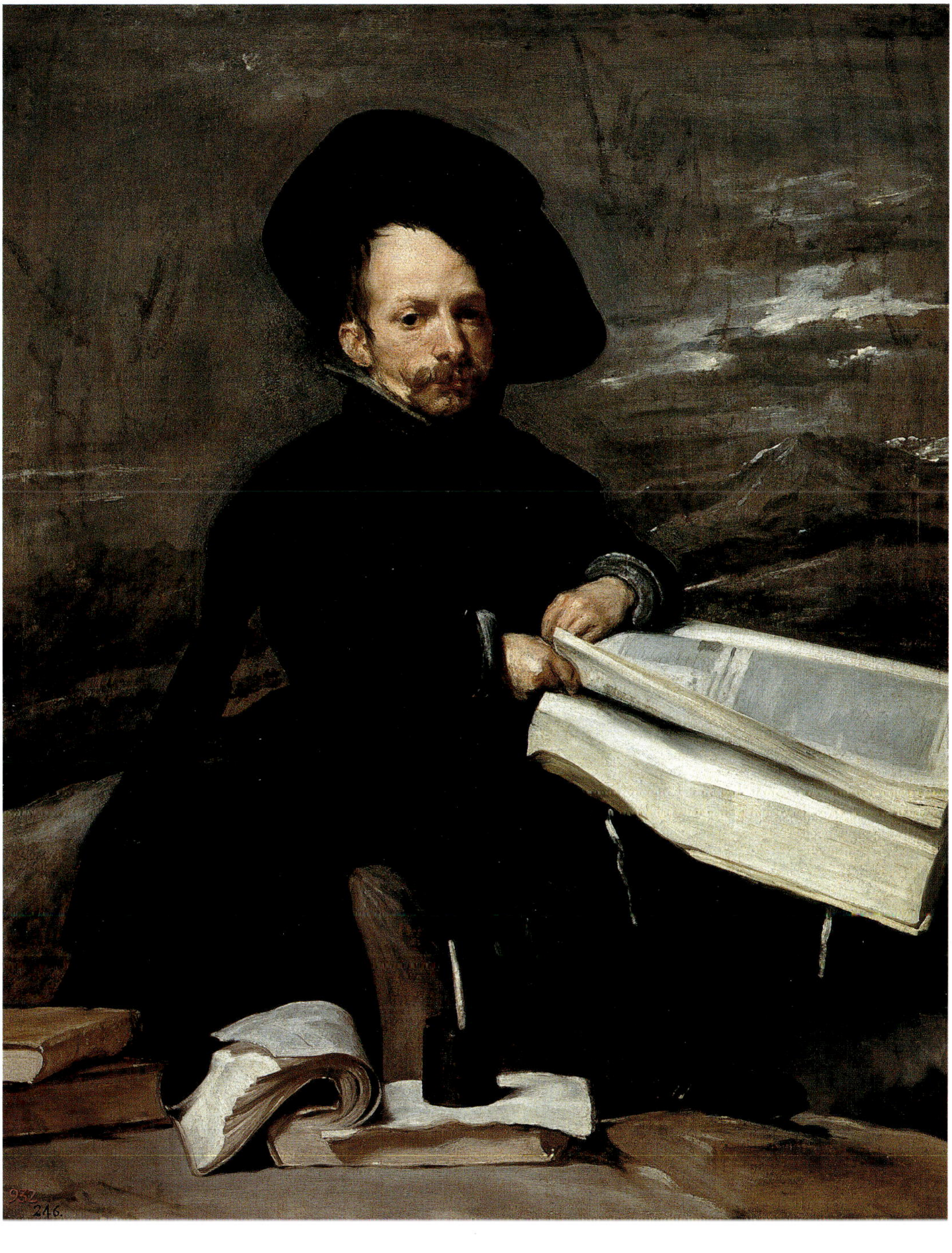
952
246.

Don sebastián de morra

c. 1643-1649
Canvas, 106 x 81 cm
Inv. 1202

Of all Velázquez's buffoons this is one of the most outstanding and striking – a fact greatly contributed to by its austere arrangement, for the very absence of space prompts the spectator to reflection and concentration. The colour is splendid, above all where Velázquez solved the problem of the contrast of the green of the suit and the ochre of the background with the red and gold of the short jacket and the silver of the sleeves and Vandyke. The subject is known to have served the Cardinal Infante in Flanders and after Ferdinand's death to have returned to Spain, where he was placed in the service of Prince Baltasar Carlos in 1643. It has been said that Don Sebastián is the dwarf pictured with the prince in the painting of the riding lesson. As the prince's will proves, Baltasar Carlos held Don Sebastián in high esteem for he left him a number of weapons and two scallops. It has been suggested that the rich garments were also a gift from his master. There is a good deal of disagreement over the date of this painting; it is mainly thought to date from around 1645, but in any event it must have been painted between 1643 and Don Sebastián's death in 1649.

In this painting Velázquez contrasted the dwarf's serious, reflexive and melancholic expression with the deformity of his almost child-like body. By so doing he has for several centuries prompted reflection extending beyond the model's personal circumstances to a definition of the human condition.

According to records, this portrait was in the Alcázar between 1666 and 1734. After the fire of 1734 it is referred to in the Buen Retiro Palace and after 1772 in the Royal Palace. It became part of the Museo del Prado collection in 1819.

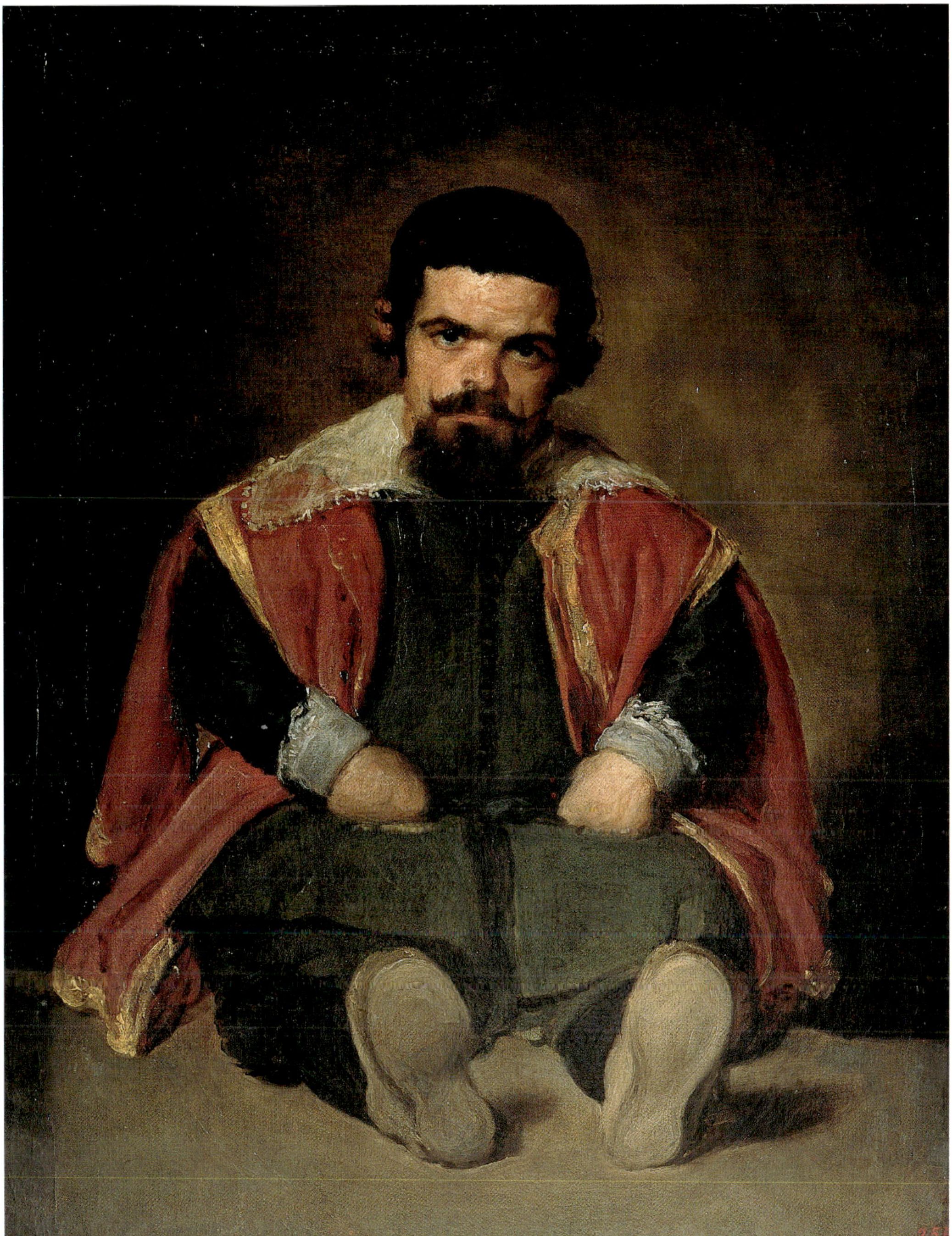

The dwarf Francisco Lezcano (El Niño de Vallecas)

Canvas, 107.5 x 83.5 cm
Inv. 1204

The subject of this portrait came from Vizcaya and is known to have been at Court from 1634, where he worked in the service of Prince Baltasar Carlos. He left Court circles between 1645 and 1648, coinciding with the Prince's death, and died in 1649. Everything suggests that he was not actually known by the nickname "El Niño de Vallecas" (lit. "the Child of Vallecas") during his lifetime as the first reference to it appears in 1794.

The buffoons painted by Velázquez were selected for employment at Court for a large number of reasons: in some cases their appearance was enough, in others their wit, and in yet others some kind of mental deficiency. In addition to his dwarfishness, Lezcano was held in esteem for his mental illness, which has been diagnosed as "cretinism with oligophrenia".

In this painting Velázquez confronts us directly with the physical and mental reality of this creature by depicting him in close-up and making the dwarf's two most expressive facets the main focuses of attention both in the picture and in the light: his face, with its ambiguous expression, and his hands, which appear to be holding a pack of cards. As regards dates, there is the usual discrepancy among historians; some believe that the portrait was painted in the mid-1640s and others ten years earlier.

Of all the portraits of buffoons, this is possibly the most frequently mentioned painting in literature, possibly due to the great potential inherent in Lezcano's defenceless figure. León Felipe made him the main character of his famous poem "Pie para el niño de Vallecas", which includes the well-known lines:

> "de aquí no se va nadie.
> Mientras esta cabeza rota
> del niño de Vallecas exista"

Another poet, Vicente Aleixandre, reflected on the old belief attributing the origin of such paintings to Velázquez's sympathy for these creatures: "This was the revelation which in Spanish life, so harsh and painful in many ways, Velázquez made with his painting and has proclaimed throughout the centuries".

The painting is first referred to in the Torre de la Parada in 1701. In 1714 it was transferred to the Palace of El Pardo and is referred to in the Royal Palace of Madrid between 1772 and 1819, when it reached the Museo del Prado.

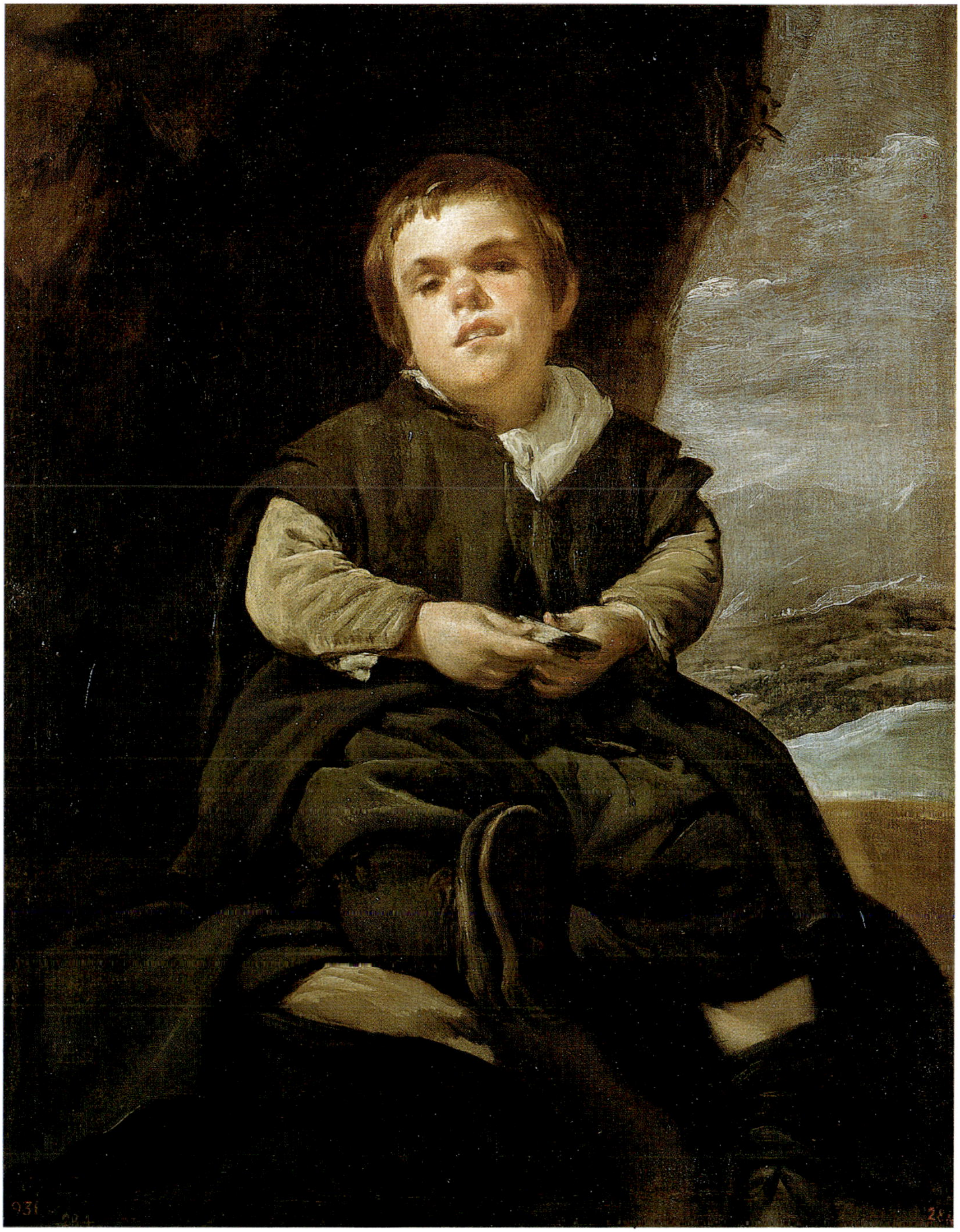

The buffoon Calabazas (Calabacillas)

Canvas, 106.5 x 82.5 cm
Inv. 1205

Although described for many years as the "Bobo de Coria", the personage almost cast aside like a rag doll on the indefinite floor in this painting is Juan Calabazas. First serving the Cardinal Infante Ferdinand as a buffoon, he transferred to the King's service in 1632 and died seven years later.

That smile halfway between stupidity and beatification and the gourds on the floor are clear indications that this buffoon was mentally retarded. Another indication is the name – one of those posthumous nicknames that are due to some physical or mental trait or some event in the person's life. According to records, from the mid-16th century the surname "Calabazas" was given to a number of buffoons in reference to some mental defect, as the word had long denoted lack of judgement. It has been very shrewdly pointed out that the association of this vegetable with stupidity may come partly from the fact that gourd shells were once commonly used in the treatment of head injuries.

This is one of the several portraits of buffoons by Velázquez whose communicative efficiency is based on the imposing presence of the personage through close-up, his position against an indefinite background, his strange and almost dislocated posture (unsuitable for any other kind of portrait) and the contrast between his physical deformity and his strange expression. Particularly striking in this picture, moreover, is the technical treatment, above all with respect to the head, which is painted diffusely and evokes two lines from Rafael Alberti's poem to the painter: "Nunca la línea se sintió más ágil / y menos responsable del contorno".

This work probably dates from before 1639 and is first referred to in the Torre de la Parada inventory of 1701; in 1772 and 1794 it was in the Royal Palace, from where it reached the Museo del Prado in 1819.

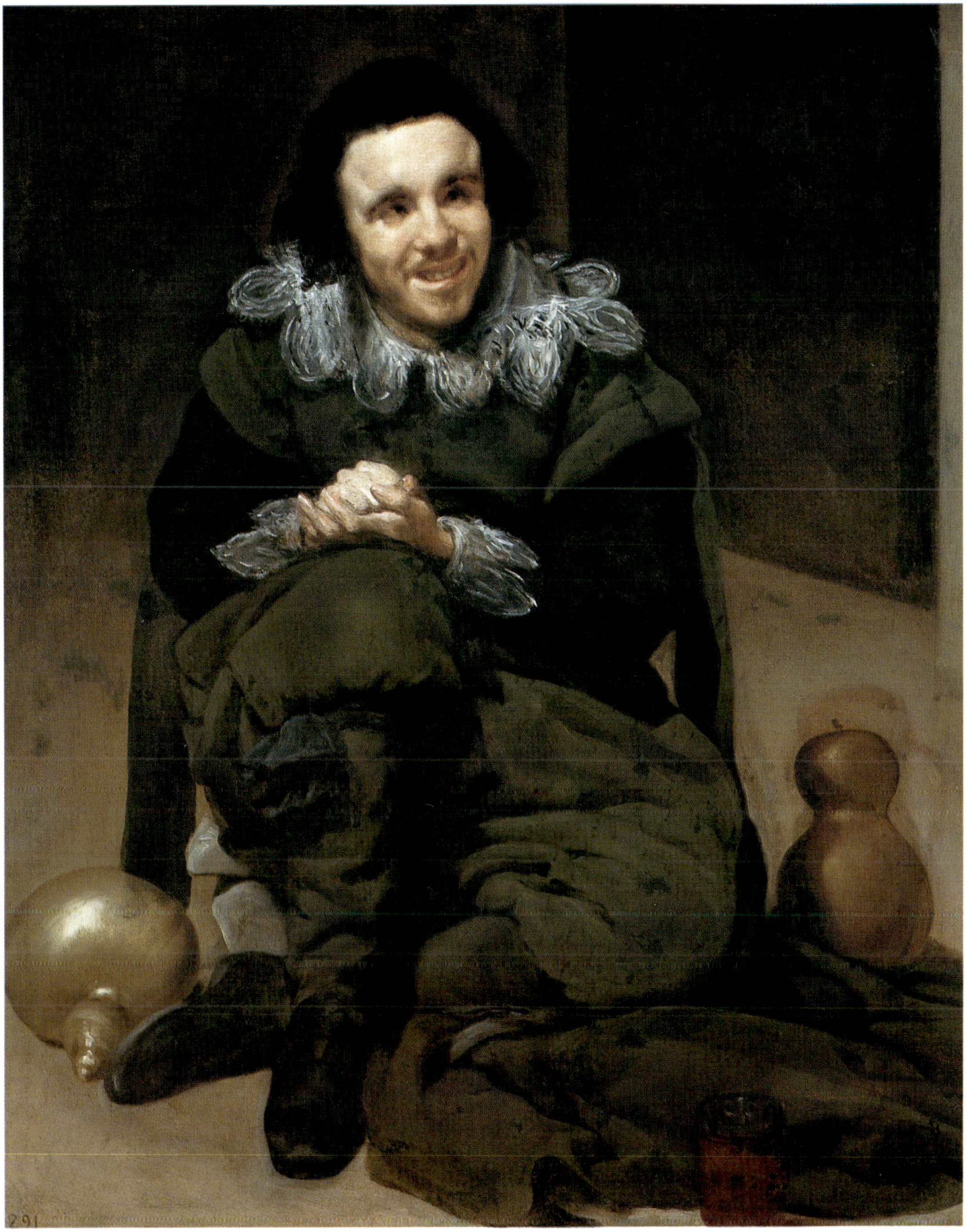
291

The Royal Family

Philip IV
Queen Mariana
Velázquez's Workshop: Philip IV in Armour
Juan Bautista Martínez del Mazo: Infanta Margarita

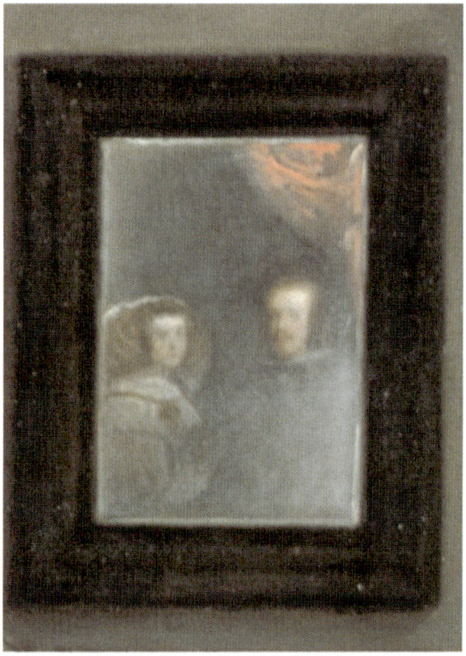

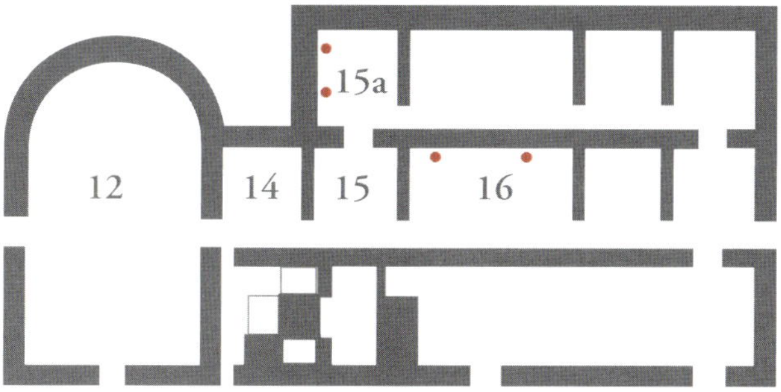

THE ROYAL FAMILY

During the Modern Age the political regime in Spain was based on the hereditary monarchy, which made the concept of the "family" the keystone of the system and its members pieces on the chessboard of European diplomacy. Thus the deaths of Queen Elizabeth of France in 1644 and of the only hope of male succession to Philip IV, their son Prince Baltasar Carlos, in 1646, came as major setbacks which made the replanning of the Spanish Austrias' matrimonial policy necessary.

In order to provide replacements for Elizabeth and Baltasar Carlos, in 1649 the King married his niece Maria Anna, who had been betrothed to Baltasar Carlos. She was expected to produce offspring promptly, if possible in the form of male heirs to the throne, but these were long in coming and when they did arrive, lived only for a short time. Consequently, for several years the

Court was busily engaged in seeking the best way of capitalizing on the few matrimonial resources it had – no more than a couple of Infantas. As the King's painter, Diego Velázquez was deeply involved in this, which explains why most of the production of his last years consists of portraits of members of the royal family. Thus even a work like *Las Meninas* cannot be fully understood if the political background to it is not taken into account.

The various functions performed by these portraits led to their final destinations being Madrid or Vienna. As is logical, the more or less official portraits of the kings plus the "home-market" paintings remained in Spain, while two types of painting were sent to Austria: those whose function was to depict the subject as marriageable and thus to help further the continuity of family links between the two courts; and those which served as testimony to the physical development of the children of Maria Anna, who, it should not be forgotten, had been raised at the Imperial Court.

Paintings Exhibited

Philip IV

Canvas, 69 x 56 cm
Inv. 1185

Despite its extreme economy, this painting of Philip IV, which is one of Velázquez's best-known portraits, reached the greatest heights in conveying the psychological profile of the subject. Indeed, through it a famous axiom of contemporary architecture – "less is more" – comes true. Such supreme competence allows us to reflect on the nature of this work and to make an observation or two on a pictorial typology with which we might venture to compare it. Here Velázquez demonstrated that the essential elements of the portrait are the features of the sitter's face. Although this may seem obvious today, it was not so in the 17th century, when the purpose of the portrait was to provide a social and professional description of the subject rather than a psychological or personal one. Thus often included in the painting were rhetorical elements relating to clothing, architecture, etc., and considered of great importance to the subject's profile.

Velázquez found a precedent to this singular definition of the portrait as a reflection of the individual in the so-called "vera effigies" – portraits, often painted in death, of personages with a reputation for holiness – whose main aim was to record the subject's facial features for posterity. Formally many were similar to this one of Philip IV, with the bust against a dark background and an almost sketchy rendering of the garments. Given the high quality of the portrait and the personality of the artist who painted it, this piece is vital to the direction the European portrait was to take in attempting to convey the model as a person with his or her own psychological profile.

Although there is doubt as to the exact date of this work, there is general agreement in placing it between 1653 – when the King wrote to Sister Luisa Magdalena de Jesús: "It is nine years since any [portrait] has been painted and I do not feel inclined to submit to Velázquez's phlegm and see myself become older" – and 1657, when the engraver Pedro de Villafranca used it as his model for the title page of a book. These were very difficult times for Philip IV, who was beginning to see his hopes of a male heir fade and Spain gradually losing political influence abroad. Significantly, it was also a time when the King immersed himself in his collection of paintings, as if turning to it for consolation. The portrait reflects this sad, rather defeated image of the King, an image also conveyed by contemporary writers such as Jerónimo de Barrionuevo, who in a letter of November 1656 wrote: "His Majesty has returned very melancholic and grave

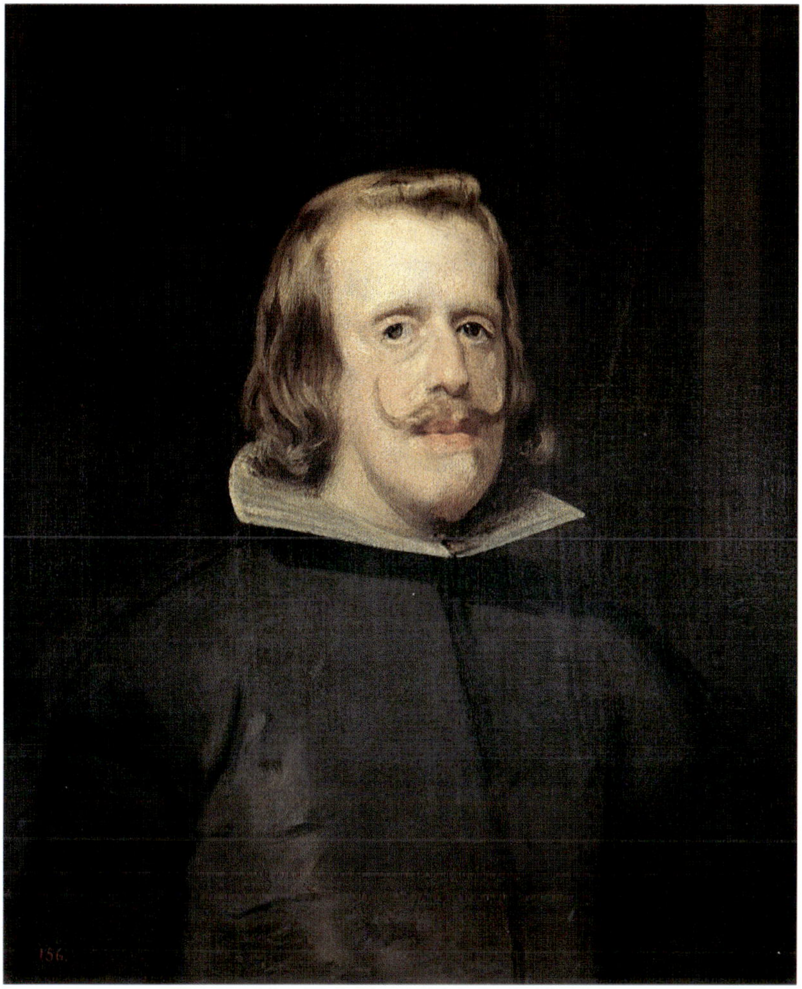

from El Escorial (...) The King was in the pantheon, behind closed doors, on his knees for two hours, not wanting a cushion, close to the niche where he is to be buried at El Escorial, and came out with his eyes red from weeping, each as large as a fist".

This painting was first hung in the Alcázar and subsequently in the Royal Palace in Madrid. It was transferred to the Royal Academy of San Fernando in 1816 and reached the Museo del Prado in 1827.

Queen mariana

c. 1652-1653
Canvas, 231 x 131 cm
Inv. 1191

As the daughter of the Emperor Ferdinand III and the Infanta Maria Anna, Queen Mariana (Maria Anna) was Philip IV's niece and she married the King in 1649 when she was scarcely fifteen years of age. She had originally been betrothed to Baltasar Carlos, but due to the prince's untimely death it was decided, for the sake of the male succession to the House of Austria in Spain, that she should marry her uncle.

As Velázquez was in Italy when the Queen arrived in Madrid for the marriage, this portrait must have been painted after his return in 1651. It is normally dated as 1652-1653, due to Mariana's age in the picture and the fact that it would have been necessary to ensure that the new queen's portrait was painted as soon as possible. Furthermore, it is highly unlikely that it was painted in 1651 as not only had Velázquez just returned from Italy but Mariana was then in a delicate state of health after recently giving birth.

This work is first referred to in 1700 at El Escorial as the companion piece to *Philip IV in Armour*, a painting believed to be from Velázquez's workshop. In all likelihood it was adapted to its new location with the addition of an extra strip of canvas to the upper part. It remained in the monastery until 1845, when it was transferred with its companion to the Museo del Prado.

This portrait is unanimously acclaimed by critics, who have stressed Velázquez's adroit combination of the symbolic elements of royal majesty with an extraordinarily skilful and detailed pictorial technique. Among the "allusive" elements are the Queen's dress, the full curtains behind her, the chair on which her right hand rests (a symbol of her status) and the clock on the table in the background (almost certainly an allusion to the prudence that must characterize a queen). Regarding the materials Velázquez used, the veritable symphony of colour is astonishing: greys, reds, blacks, silvers and ivories, applied with strokes whose extraordinary fluency and originality were to prove irresistible to the late 19th-century painters, who were astounded by Velázquez's capacity to reproduce a visual experience through a few simple brush-strokes.

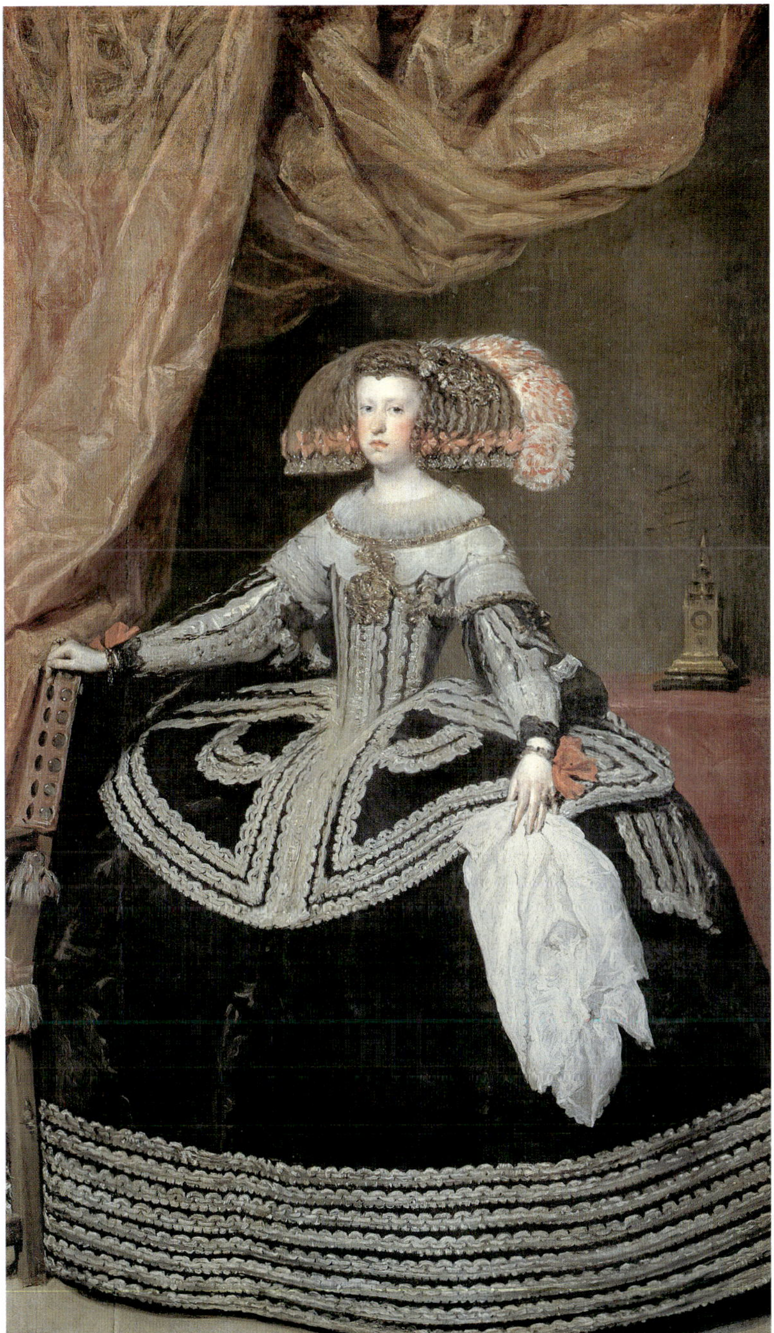

Although of doubtful authorship, two other royal portraits whose composition and style denote the work of the Sevillian painter's circle belong to the Museo del Prado collection:

VELÁZQUEZ'S WORKSHOP

Philip IV in armour

Canvas, 234 x 131 cm
Inv. 1219

According to recent laboratory tests, this portrait was painted over a previous rendering of Philip IV standing before a much more elaborate background and its dimensions and compositional characteristics were adapted in the early 1650s to match those of the portrait of Queen Mariana (1191). The two portraits were referred to as companion pieces at El Escorial in the 18th century. In accordance with its representative purpose, the painting stressed the attributes which reflected the sitter's high social rank: the King stands, he is dressed in armour and wears a general's sash, the pommel of his sword is in his left hand and the staff of command in his right... At his feet, in a clear allusion to Philip's kingly virtues, lies a lion. Few of the subjects in the royal portraits associated with Velázquez and his workshop are surrounded by greater symbolism. Another significant fact is that at the time when the portrait is believed to have been painted, Spain was deep in political and military crisis and Velázquez painted a number of direct, stark portraits of the King totally devoid of rhetoric.

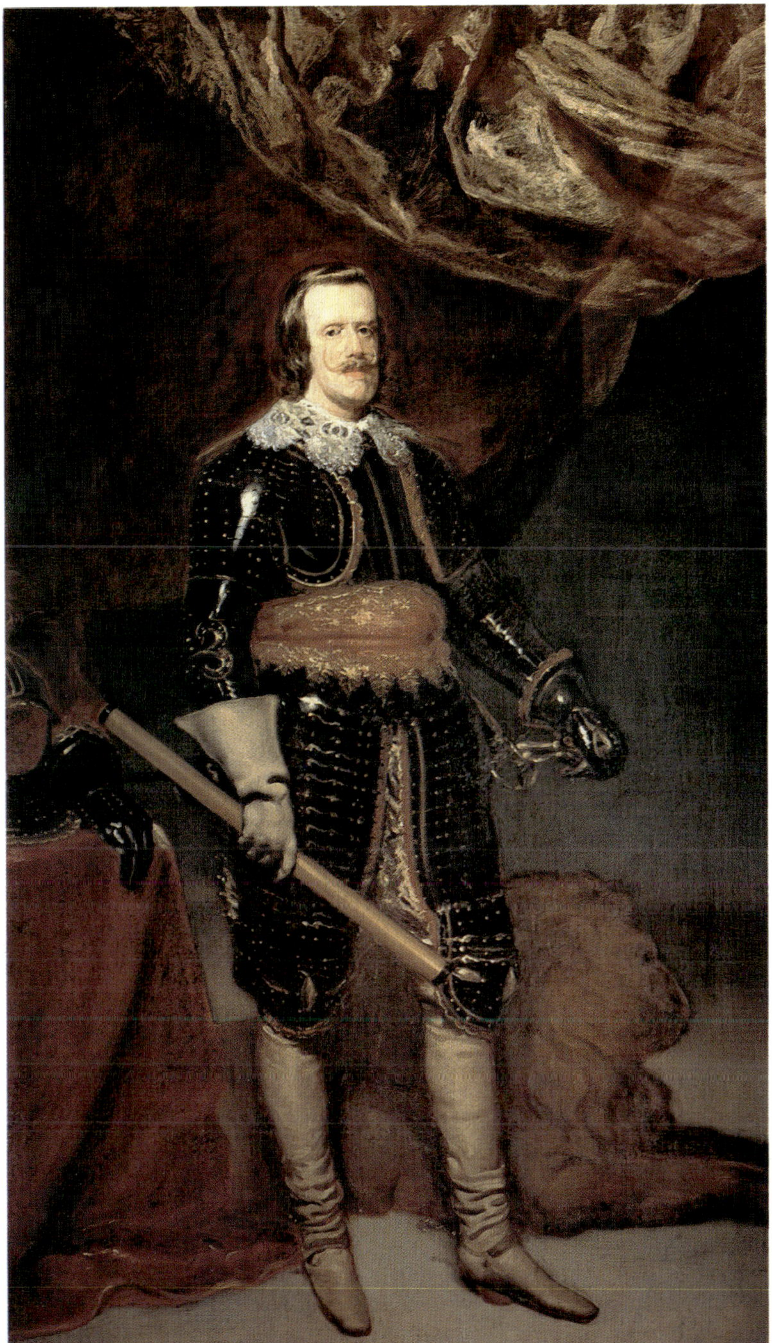

JUAN BAUTISTA MARTÍNEZ DEL MAZO

INFANTA MARGARITA
Canvas, 212 x 147 cm
Inv. 1192

Born in 1651, the subject of this portrait was the daughter of Philip IV and Maria Anna of Austria. She is also one of the main personages in *Las Meninas.* In 1666 she married the Emperor Leopold I of Austria. Many portraits were painted of her when she was young – most of them by Velázquez and his workshop – with a view to her marriage in the future.

This is among the works that have given rise to the deepest division over authorship, due not only to the interest inherent in any issue involving Velázquez but also to the extraordinarily high quality of the painting, which, furthermore, displays details of great beauty and skill. However, critics now tend to reject the idea that it was painted by Velázquez and are inclined to believe that it was actually painted entirely by Juan Bautista Martínez del Mazo, who through it proved not only his great technical skill but also how well he had assimilated his father-in-law's teachings. This view is based on a study of the composition, the appearance of the canvas itself and the subject's age in the portrait. Traditionally, however, it has been regarded as Velázquez's last painting, unfinished due to his death but completed by his son-in-law. Despite the fact that this hypothesis is supported by many magnificent details – the transparency of the handkerchief, the flowers in the Infanta's left hand, and her dress in general – the existence of other, less skilful features – such as the face or the heaviness of the curtains – have caused it to be currently regarded as extremely unlikely.

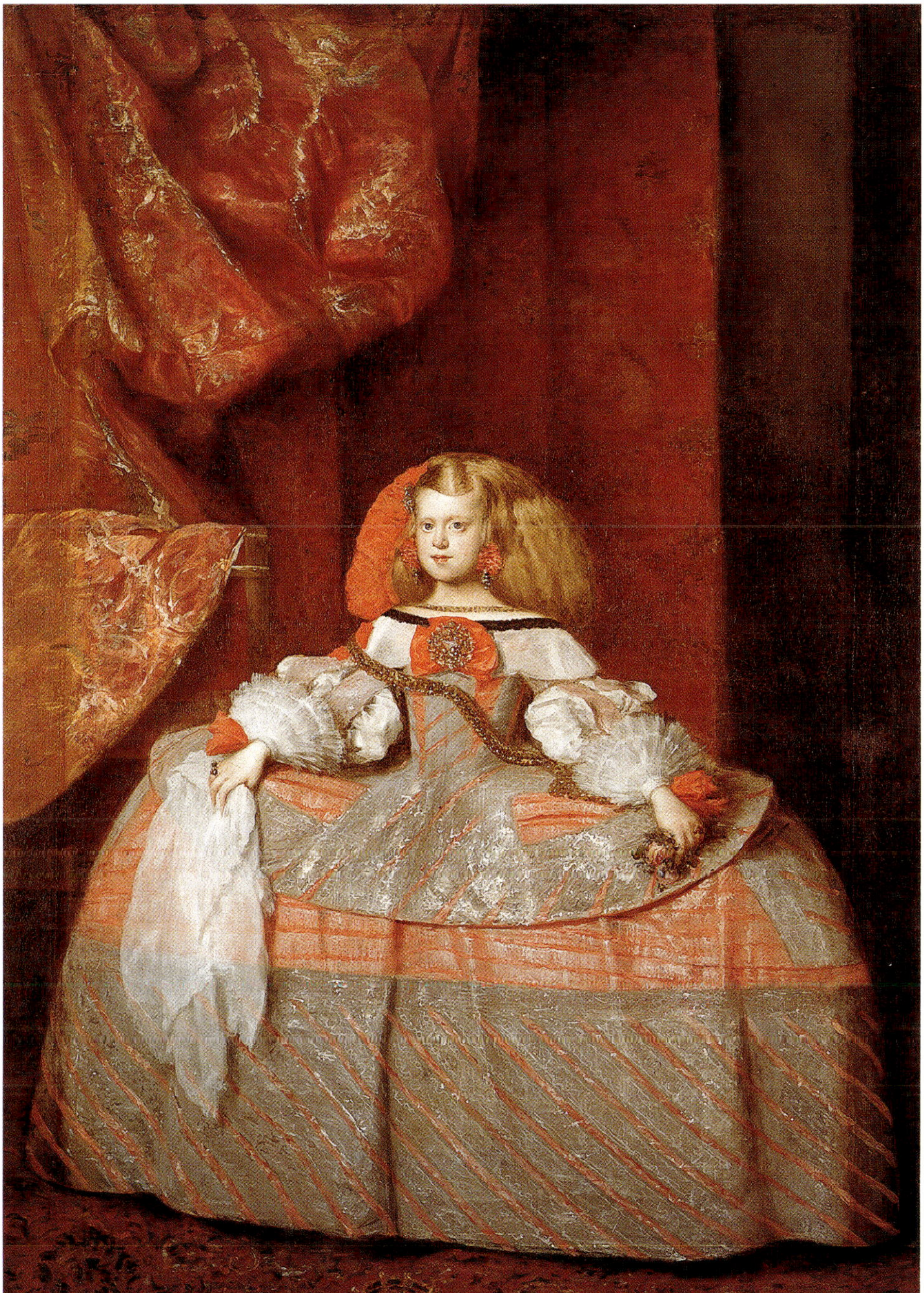

The Great Final Compositions

The Fable of Arachne
Las Meninas or The Family of Philip IV
Mercury and Argus

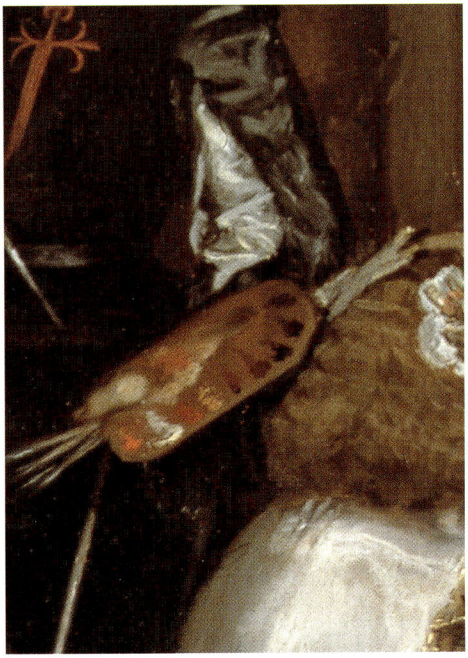

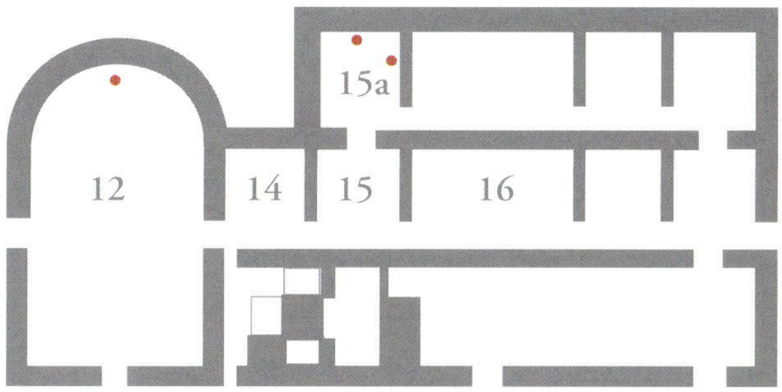

ℰ The Great Final Compositions ℰ

Although Velázquez devoted himself mainly to portraiture after he entered Court circles, his whole career is nevertheless marked by a number of great historical pictures proving his masterful approach to all genres in painting. These date from the mid-1620s to the end of his life, but the number rose significantly in his last fifteen years and include *The Fable of Arachne, Venus at Her Mirror, Las Meninas* and the paintings – of which only *Mercury and Argus* has survived – which adorned the Hall of Mirrors in the Alcázar.

This period in his career was to prove essential to his image for it saw not only some of the paintings which most increased his fame but also some of the most important events in his life. It was during this time that he made his second journey to Italy, not to study as in 1629, but to buy works of art on behalf of the King and also to prove his worth in what was still the artistic heart of

Europe. During his stay in Italy he painted some of his masterpieces of portraiture – one being the famous *Innocent X* – and demonstrated to the community of painters who lived in the city his exceptional qualities as an artist. On a personal level, his stay in Rome led to a love affair and the birth of a son.

All his known work after his return to Spain in 1651 was related exclusively to the royal family and residences. In 1652 he was appointed Chamberlain of the Palace, a post which fulfilled his ambitions to rise within the Court's administrative structure but unfortunately required his full dedication and so left him little time for painting. That is why the number of pictures of those years is so small, although all are of the highest standard and some, for example *Las Meninas*, are of great compositional complexity. Furthermore, at that time Philip IV suffered a deep personal crisis as a result of the appalling events of the previous decade, when, in addition to the serious social and political turmoil affecting the country, he was faced with the loss of his first wife and their son Baltasar Carlos, in whom he had placed all hopes of succession. Dejected and defeated, in the early 1650s Philip sought consolation in religion and that passion for collecting works of art which had filled him for so long. In those years Velázquez not only acted as the King's representative at some of the great European auctions, one example being that of the possessions of Charles I of England, but also took a special interest in the decorative remodelling of a number of the Royal Seats, especially the Alcázar in Madrid and the Monastery at El Escorial. At the Alcázar he concentrated on the most important rooms in the south wing, especially the Hall of Mirrors and the so-called "Vaults of Titian", where he brought together the breathtaking collection of nudes which, of all the paintings, was dearest to the King's heart. At El Escorial, all the rooms were rearranged and the collections were notably enriched with new acquisitions and with paintings transferred from the Alcázar. Velázquez was almost certainly involved in all of this work, for Philip IV had for a long time entrusted all matters regarding art and decoration to him.

The relationship between King and painter must have become closer in these years when both, with much experience of life now behind them, were in their prime. Furthermore, they had known each other for over twenty years and shared similar interests in painting and although we shall never know whether it is possible to use the word "friendship" in reference to their relationship, there must have been some degree of "complicity" between them, above all with respect to certain common interests. Proof of the fact that the King was familiar with some of Velázquez's most personal preoccupations and ambitions was the key part he played in procuring the habit of St James for the painter in 1658, despite the fact that circumstances were not completely in Velázquez's favour.

By attaining the habit, Velázquez saw all his aspirations of social ascent fulfilled in the culmination to a long career in the administration whose ultimate aim had been to become a member of the nobility. And these aspirations were also accompanied by a desire to prove his nobility as an artist. The part played by the Cross of St James in terms of his career at Court was the same as that played two years previously by *Las Meninas* in terms of his recognition as an artist. In this painting he had not only included himself in the same sphere as that of the royal family, to the extent that without him the composition would make no sense, but had also demonstrated his skills in two ways: on the one hand, with respect to his capacity for creating an illusion and faithfully reproducing a visual experience; on the other, regarding painting as an art of the intellect, the result of a subtle intellectual exercise, the key to which is only properly understood by those few who are capable of "judging". The great effort necessary for the fulfilment of his aspirations to the nobleman's habit is only comparable to his endeavour in painting that picture: both are the result of a lifetime of struggle with social reality on the one hand, and with visual and intellectual experience on the other. But while there have been hundreds of Knights of St James, there has only ever been one *Meninas.*

& Paintings Exhibited &

The fable of Arachne (Las Hilanderas)

Canvas, 220 x 289 cm
Inv. 1173

For generations those who have seen this work have acclaimed Velázquez's capacity to reproduce life and movement while recreating an everyday scene in a tapestry factory. Mengs said of this painting that it was painted with willpower alone. But curiously this scene that has done so much to win Velázquez recognition as the king of the realists is full of symbolic elements and has several underlying narrative levels. The discovery of the 1664 inventory of the possessions of its first owner (the King's Master of the Hounds, Pedro de Arce) confirmed the suspicions of one group of researchers: that behind that commonplace appearance lies a mythological story – the fable of Arachne.

Arachne was a mere mortal but she had an extraordinary gift for weaving tapestries which drew the curiosity and finally the jealousy of Minerva, goddess of the arts, who believed that none could match her own skill. Overwhelmed by a desire to prove her superiority, Minerva challenged Arachne to a weaving competition which ended in a draw. But the goddess gave rein to her frustration by turning Arachne into a spider, her excuse being that Arachne had dared to choose the loves of Jupiter, her father, as the theme for her tapestry.

Four different yet at the same time interrelated scenes appear in this work. The foreground contains an apparently typical scene at the Santa Isabel tapestry factory in Madrid, with five women spinning and winding the wool and a cat dozing among the balls. This area displays a large number of items – the distaff, the winding frame and the ladder leaning against the wall – believed to be of symbolic content. There are also historical and artistic references, for example the two women in the foreground, taken from nude ephebes by Michelangelo in the Sistine Chapel. In the background, a second narrative group of three ladies observes a tapestry depicting two scenes: Minerva and Arachne vying for primacy in the art of weaving and Arachne's depiction of the rape of Europa.

The scene as a whole has been interpreted as an allegory of the nobility of painting. For some, Minerva and Arachne not only appear in the tapestry in the background but are also the old woman and the young girl in the foreground performing the manual tasks involved in their trade. In this case the painting can be interpreted as a description of the creative process, which includes not only a manual phase but an intellectual one of an almost divine nature requiring illumination by the light of the idea and needing to be "judged".

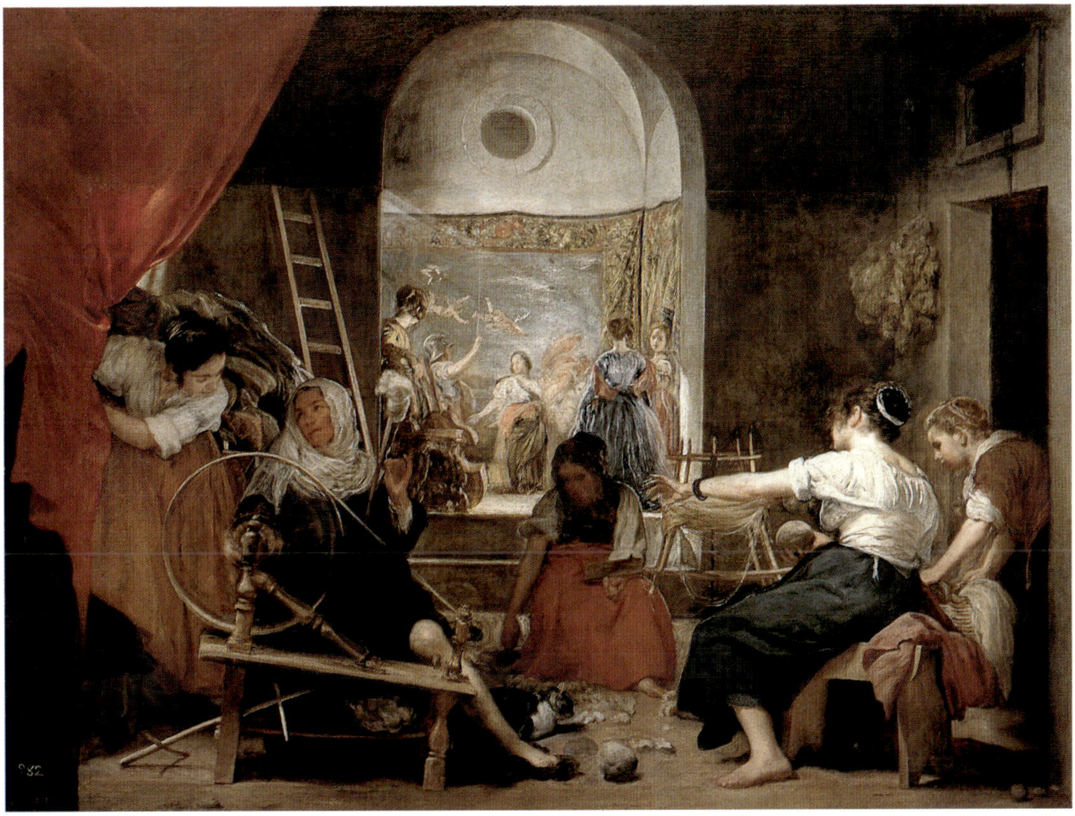

One of the keys to interpreting this work and situating it within the context of Velázquez's production lies in the scene supposedly depicted in the tapestry in the background. This is the rape of Europa, a copy of Titian's version of the scene which at that time was in the Alcázar in Madrid (today in the Isabella Stewart Gardner Museum, Boston). In this respect it has been said that Velázquez was subtly describing the Venetian's painting as "divine" as it was also on a par with Minerva's. It has also been suggested that in this way Velázquez was defending the noble and liberal nature of all painting.

But one other aspect must be taken into account vis-à-vis the rape of Europa in the scene. It had indeed been painted by Titian and belonged to the royal collections but it was not the only version Velázquez would have seen, for one of Rubens's tasks during his stay in Madrid between 1627 and 1628 was to copy works by the

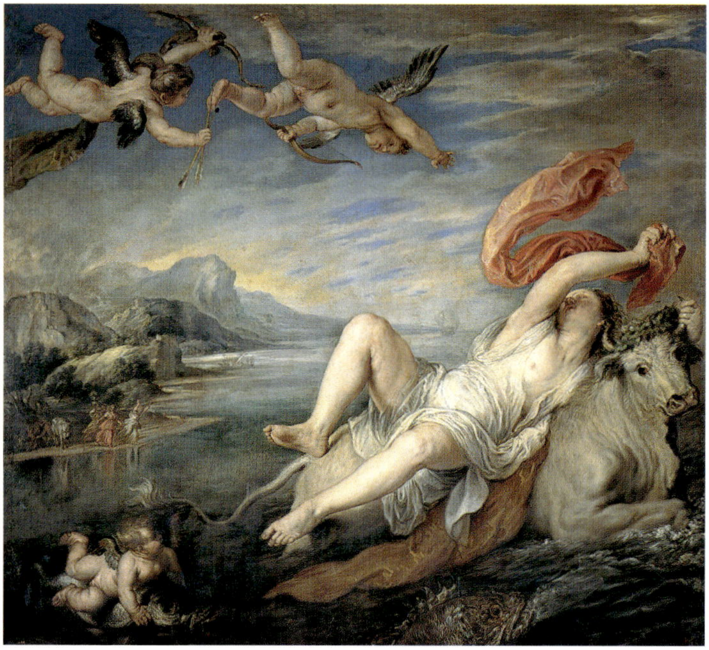

Peter Paul Rubens
The Rape of Europa,
Museo del Prado.

Venetian, including this one. Since he shared a workshop with Velázquez, it is certain that the Sevillian saw Rubens's copies. As the Flemish painter's work was purchased by Philip IV at an auction, by the time Velázquez painted *The Fable of Arachne* it had almost certainly become part of the royal collections. None of this would be of particular importance if it were no more than a simple copy, but rather than dutifully copying Titian's original, Rubens translated it into his own pictorial language in terms of emulation and competitiveness and in the conviction that his own work was one more step in the pictorial tradition to which the Venetian's also belonged.

Velázquez doubtless knew that Rubens had copied the *Rape of Europa* and that he had done so through a desire not only to learn but to compete. And perhaps he himself, in this mythological scene whose themes include the rivalry between a goddess and a mortal, also wished to emulate and compete with the two great masters. But rather than just reproduce the painting in his own style, he enveloped it in a subtle narrative plot, so proving to what extent he was an artist who took an intelligent look at the themes he painted and how fond he was of playing with

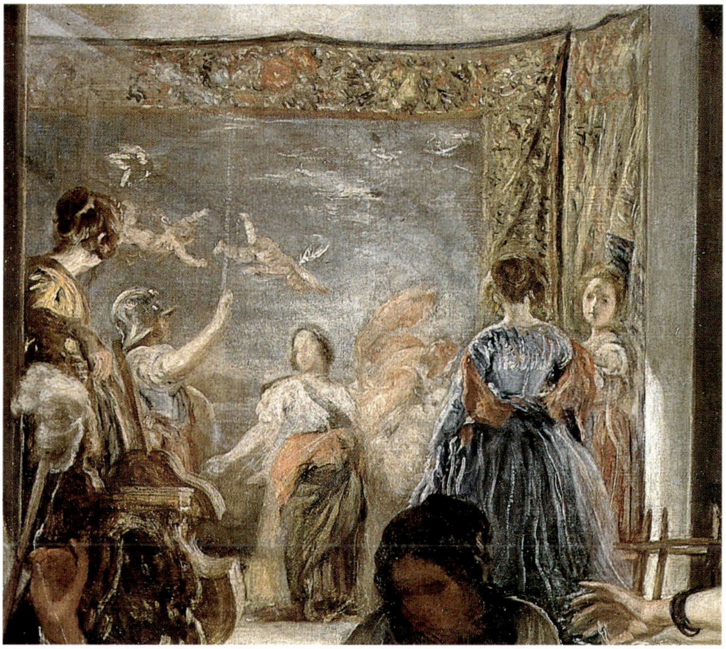

different levels of reality. "I compete too, but in my own way", he seems to be saying.

The original painting was considerably smaller, as more than fifty centimetres were later added to the top and thirty-seven to the sides. This greatly affects the composition and to a certain extent causes the focus of attention to move away from the illuminated area in the background – an area essential to an understanding of the painting's artistic and narrative aspects.

There is a great deal of discrepancy as to the date of its execution. Given its highly developed style, some experts have situated it in the last five years of Velázquez's life and subsequent to *Las Meninas*, while others, pointing out the similarities between it and *Venus at Her Mirror*, regard it as previous to the second journey to Italy.

In 1711 it was transferred from the Duke of Medinaceli collection to the Alcázar in Madrid, where it suffered considerable damage in the fire of 1734. From the Alcázar it was transferred to the Buen Retiro Palace and in 1772 is referred to at the Royal Palace, from where it reached the Museo del Prado in 1819.

Las meninas or the family of Philip IV

1656
Canvas, 318 x 276 cm
Inv. 1174

This is not only Velázquez's most famous painting but also the one which best sums up his art and is the most useful in demonstrating just how much his painting is capable of fascinating successive generations and fulfilling the expectations of each. And this is because it has been – and continues to be – constantly reinterpreted without its capacity for suggesting new visual and intellectual stimuli ever being exhausted.

For many years it was said to demonstrate a fixation on Velázquez's part with realism and that the theme he chose for his masterpiece was a single moment captured in his workshop. However, it is now regarded as the greatest example of his use of apparently realistic themes to cover an extremely complex world of meanings and relationships. Whatever the case, the fact is that in the present as in the past this painting continues to astonish us through its prodigious spatial construction – modelled through perspective and light – its magnificent composition, in which the balance of masses is not incompatible with the variety of the figures and their actions, its exquisite beauty where each and every one of the personages within it is concerned, and, in short, Velázquez's capacity to capture an instant from life and a fragment of thought on a piece of canvas.

The scene is a room in the Alcázar in Madrid and the figures in it a cross section of Court society, from the highest to those regarded as the lowest. The first figure on the left is Velázquez himself, standing back from the canvas to look and reflect, making this an allusion to the intellectual aspect of painting. Attached to his belt and clearly visible is the key testifying to his position as Chamberlain, while on his chest he displays the noble Cross of St James. Next to him kneels the *menina* or maid of honour María Agustina Sarmiento, offering a small jug on a tray to the Infanta Margarita. The Infanta was five years old at the time, as she was born in 1651, and the painting – an essential piece in the game of politics played by the House of Austria – dates from 1656. Next to her and curtsying is Isabel de Velasco, another of the Infanta's *meninas.* Finally, on the right-hand side is a trio formed by the buffoons María Bárbola and Nicolasito Pertusato and a mastiff lying quietly on the floor. Behind these an anonymous male escort stands with Marcela de Ulloa, who is dressed in "duenna's" clothing. In the background, behind the door is the Chamberlain José Nieto. But the list of figures in the painting does not end there, for the King and Queen themselves – Philip IV and Maria Anna – also appear,

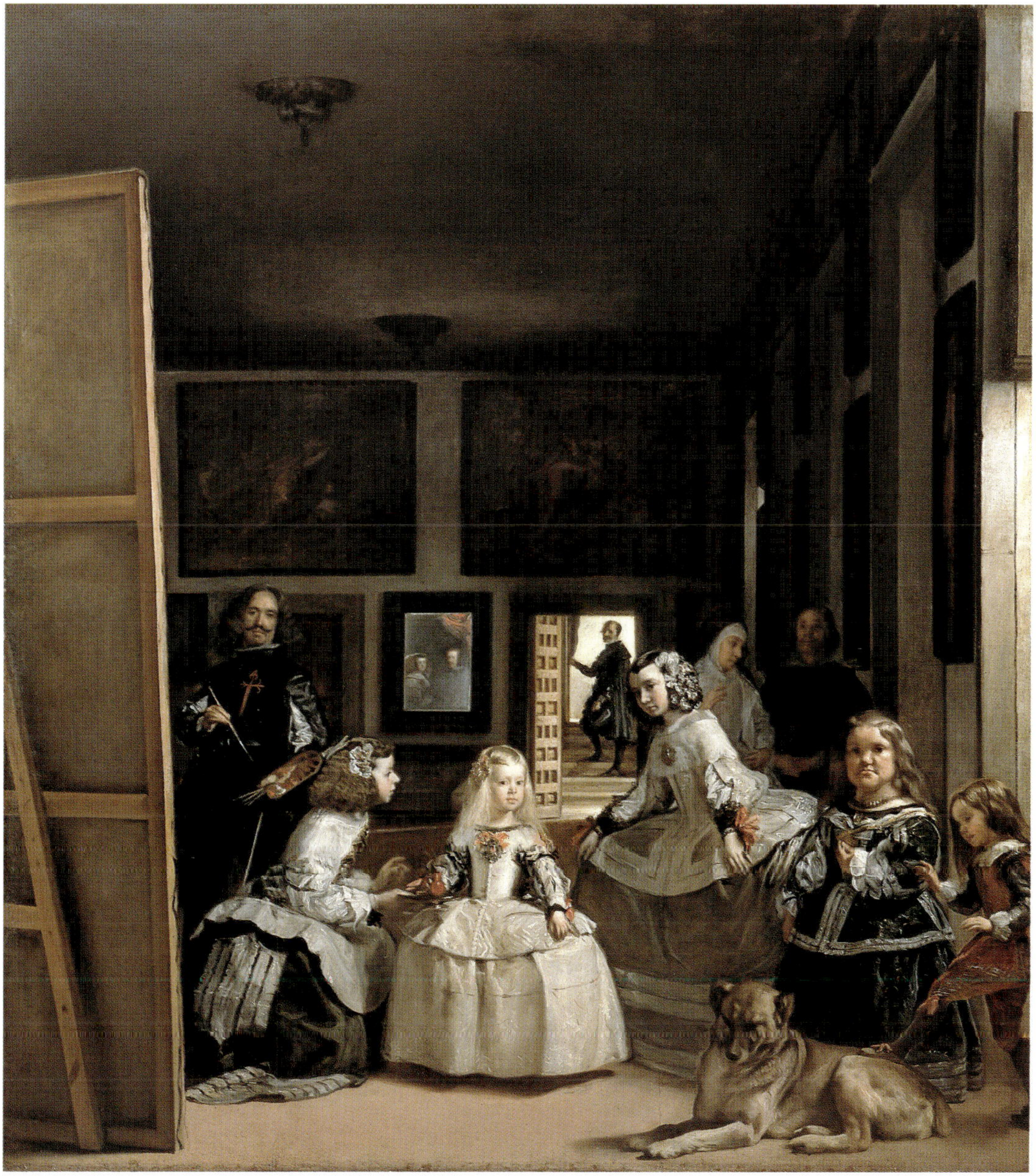

their faces in the background seen in what has been generally regarded as a mirror interpreted as a "painting within a painting".

This general description, on which there is more or less unanimous agreement, leads to multiple interpretations; interestingly these are often complementary rather than mutually exclusive and thus the painting has become enriched with new meanings. Almost all attempts to interpret it have focused on two particular aspects: the part played by Velázquez in the painting, and the inclusion of the King, the Queen and the Infanta. The presence of an artist with the attributes of his social position (the Cross of St James, the keys, etc.) who is "thinking" with the King and Queen themselves as witnesses is considered a definite avowal of the nobility of the art of painting. This idea is confirmed by the pictures in the background – copies by Martínez del Mazo of Rubens's *Minerva and Arachne* and Jordaens's *Apollo and Marsyas*, i.e. two mythological scenes also stressing the divine origin of artistic activity.

Velázquez at fifty-seven appears to be saying through this painting: "I am noble as is my art, for it is an intellectual activity worthy of the gods and placed at the service of kings, who honour it with their interest". But there is more. There is, for example, an extremely complex mathematical construction of perspective deriving from a very subtle reflection on the laws governing sight and the relationship between painted surface, suggested space and the psychological space of the observer. It is also possible to give a political reading to the painting by regarding the Infanta Margaret as the King's hope of succession. Furthermore, it has also quite rightly been said that this is a "conversation" between Velázquez and Philip IV at a time when, with over thirty years of contact, each reveals his innermost thoughts while using the observer as a witness to their dialogue.

The painting is first referred to in 1666 in the King's Summer Office in the Alcázar, Madrid, and subsequently in the royal collections. It reached the Museo del Prado in 1819.

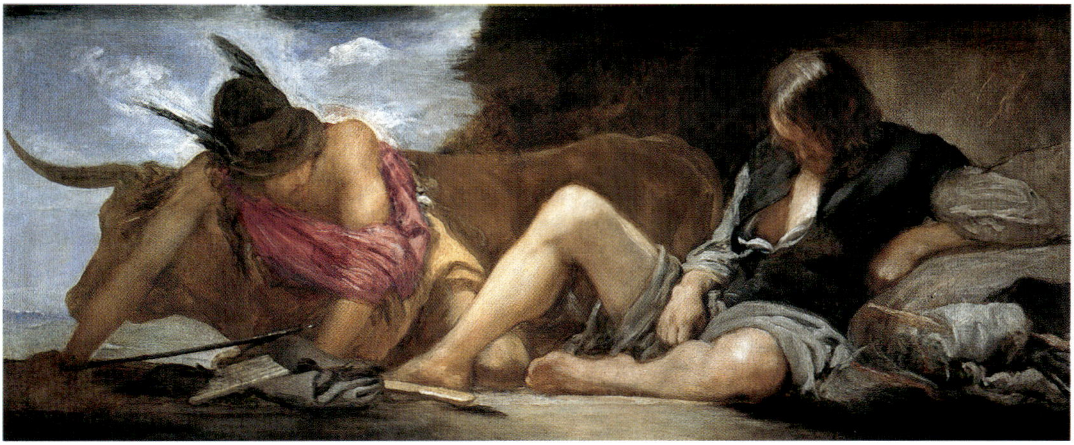

Mercury and argus
1659
Canvas, 128 x 250 cm
Inv. 1175

One of the rooms redecorated in the Alcázar in the 1650s was the Hall of Mirrors, among the areas in the old palace most frequently used for ceremonial and official occasions. In 1659 it served as the setting to the reception of a French delegation whose mission was none other than to negotiate the marriage of the Spanish Infanta María Teresa (Marie Thérèse) to Louis XIV of France. The room was specially decorated for the occasion, Velázquez painting two pairs of mythological scenes to be placed above the windows in the room. One pair was *Venus and Adonis* and *Cupid and Psyche*, and the other *Apollo and Marsyas* and *Mercury and Argus*. As the first three were destroyed in the fire of 1734, we have unfortunately been deprived of three works in a genre – that of the female nude – of which only one magnificent example by Velázquez has survived.

The date of execution and its destination explain some of this painting's characteristics: the composition is slightly forced, due to the need to adapt the scene to an oblong format, while through the technique, which is of extraordinary boldness and fluency, Velázquez inserted the figures in the painting, breaking down all limits and outlines and filling it with life. Velázquez's last known compositional work, it summarizes a lifetime of dedication to painting, masterfully combining the different ingredients which make it an art whose narrative and purely pictorial values complement each other. Furthermore, Velázquez's mastery of pictorial narrative enabled him to infuse the scene with a very subtle, highly attractive poetic air.

As always when dealing with mythological scenes, Velázquez took a very personal approach setting him apart from iconographic traditions. Were it not for Mercury's winged hat, it would be extremely difficult to describe the scene in terms other than those directly attributable to everyday experience: a cowherd appears to doze near his cattle, while another figure steals up to him. The first is Argus, designated by Juno to guard Io, who had been seduced by Jupiter and turned into a cow. For his task he had a hundred eyes, fifty of which were always watchful, but this did little to aid him against the soporific music played by the god Mercury, who approaches Argus to cut off his head and kidnap Io. Various explanations for the presence of a picture with this theme in the Hall of Mirrors have been suggested, one being that it is an allusion to the vigilance which princes must constantly exercise.

This painting was rescued from the fire in the Alcázar. It is later referred to in the Buen Retiro Palace and subsequently in the Royal Palace. It reached the Museo del Prado at some point after 1819.

Chronology, Bibliography and Index of Colour Plates

Chronology

1599, 6th June – Velázquez baptized in the Parish Church of San Pedro, Seville.

1602, 1st June – Juana Pacheco, the painter Francisco Pacheco's daughter and Diego Velázquez's future wife, born in Seville.

1609 – Velázquez enters Francisco Herrera the Elder's workshop in Seville.

1610, 1st December – Transfers to Francisco Pacheco's workshop.

1611, 27th September – Contract signed between Velázquez's father and Pacheco in which the latter undertakes to accept Diego for six years.

1617, 14th March – Velázquez becomes professionally independent and is admitted into the Seville painters' guild.

1618, 23rd April – Marries Francisco Pacheco's daughter Juana.

1619, 18th May – Baptism of Francisca, the couple's first daughter.

1620, 1st February – Admits Diego de Melgar into his workshop as a student for a period of six years.

1621, 29th January – Baptism of Ignacia, the couple's second daughter.

1622 – In the spring he travels to Madrid in the hope of entering Court circles. While there he paints the portrait of the poet Luis de Góngora and visits El Escorial.

1623 – In the summer he makes his second and final journey to Court. After painting the portrait of Juan de Fonseca, he is commissioned to paint the King.

1623, 6th October – Philip IV appoints him Court painter.

1625, 26th August – The King orders that Velázquez be entitled to the so-called "right of chamber".

1626, 19th October – Ana de Brizuela places her son Andrés as an apprentice in his workshop.

1627 – Philip IV calls his painters (Vincenzo Carducci, Eugenio Caxés, Angelo Nardi and Diego Velázquez) to a competition with the theme "The Expulsion of the Moriscos". Velázquez is declared the winner.

1627, 7th March – Appointed Usher of the Chamber.

1627 – Authorizes Pacheco to sell his house in Seville.

1628 – Rubens's second visit to Spain, during which he meets Velázquez.

1629, 28th June – The King gives Velázquez permission to travel to Italy.

1629, 10th August – Velázquez sets sail from Barcelona.

1629, 19th September – Arrives in Genoa, subsequently visiting Milan, Venice, Ferrara, Cento, Bologna and Loreto.

1629, October – Arrives in Rome, staying there for a year.

1630 – At the end of the year he arrives in Naples, where he meets Ribera. From Naples he returns to Madrid.

1631, January – Returns to Madrid.

1631, 14th May – Rents a house in the parish of Santiago.

1633, 21st August – His daughter Francisca marries his pupil Juan Bautista Martínez del Mazo.

1633 – Appointed House and Court Bailiff.

1634 – Appointed Gentleman of the Wardrobe.

1635 – Finishes *The Surrender of Breda* for the *Salón de Reinos* in the Buen Retiro Palace.

1643 – Is appointed Superintendent of Royal Works and also Gentleman of the Chamber without Duties. Death of his father-in-law and Queen Elizabeth. In June he accompanies the King to Fraga, where he paints his portrait.

1646 – Appointed Gentleman of the Chamber with Duties.

1647 – Appointed Supervisor and Accountant for the Construction of the Octagonal Room in the Alcázar.

1648, 1st November – Arrives in Malaga.

1649, 21st January – Sets sail from Malaga.

1649, 11th February – Arrives in Genoa.

1649, 10th July – Again in Rome.

1650, 17th February – Philip IV writes to his ambassador to arrange Velázquez's return in May or June.

1650, 19th March – Exhibition of the portrait of Juan de Pareja in the Pantheon.

1650, 21st June – Urgently called to Madrid.

1650, 3rd October – Called again to Madrid.

1651, 23rd June – The King informs the Duke of El Infantado that Velázquez is back in Madrid.

1652, 16th February – Appointed Chamberlain of the Royal Palace.

1656 – Paints *Las Meninas.*

1658, 12th June – Invested Knight of the Order of St James.

1660, 7th June – Attends marriage of Marie Thérèse and Louis XIV of France on Isla de los Faisanes.

1660, 6th August – Dies in Madrid.

Bibliography

Angulo, D., Velázquez. *Cómo compuso sus principales cuadros y otros escritos sobre el pintor*, Madrid, Istmo, 1999.

Beruete, A., *Velázquez* (1898), Madrid, 1987.

Bouza, F., *Locos, enanos y hombres de placer en la España de los Austrias*, Madrid, Temas de hoy, 1991.

Brown, J., *Velázquez. Pintor y cortesano*, Madrid, Alianza, 1986.

Brown, J., Elliott, J.H., *Un palacio para el rey. El Buen Retiro y la corte de Felipe IV*, Madrid, Alianza, 1981.

Calvo Serraller, F., *Las Meninas de Velázquez*, Madrid TF, 1997.

Camón Aznar, J., *Velázquez*, Madrid, Espasa-Calpe, 2 vols., 1964.

Catalogue for the *Velázquez* exhibition, Madrid, Museo del Prado, 1990.

Catalogue for the *Velázquez in Seville* exhibition, Edinburgh, National Galleries of Scotland, 1996.

Delenda, O., *Velázquez, peintre religieux*, Geneva, Editions du Cerf, 1993

Díez del Corral, L., *Velázquez, la monarquía e Italia*, Madrid, Espasa Calpe, 1979.

Gállego, J., *Visión y símbolos en la pintura española del siglo XVII*, Madrid, 1972.

Gállego, J., *Velázquez en Sevilla*, Seville, 1974.

Gállego, J., *Diego Velázquez*, Barcelona, Anthropos, 1983.

Garrido, C., *Velázquez. Técnica y evolución*, Madrid, Museo del Prado, 1992.

Gaya Nuño, J.A., *Bibliografía crítica y antológica de Velázquez*, Madrid, Fundación Lázaro Galdiano, 1963.

Gerstenberg, K., *Diego Velázquez*, Munich, Deutscher Kunstverlag, 1957.

Gudiol, J., *Velázquez, 1599-1660*, Barcelona, Polígrafa, 1973.

Harris, E., *Velázquez*, Vitoria, Ephialte, 1991.

Justi, Karl, *Velázquez y su siglo* (1888), Madrid, Istmo, 1999.

López-Rey, J., *Velázquez*, Cologne, Taschen, 2 vols., 1996.

Maravall, J.A., *Velázquez y el espíritu de la modernidad*, Madrid, Guadarrama, 1960.

Marías, F., *Diego Velázquez*, Madrid, Historia 16, (1996).

Marías, F. (ed.), *Otras Meninas*, Madrid, Siruela, 1995.

McKim-Smith, G., Newman, R., *Ciencia e historia del arte. Velázquez en el Prado*, Madrid, Museo del Prado, 1993.

Moffitt, J.F., *Velázquez, práctica e idea*, Malaga, Universidad de Málaga, 1991.

Orso, S., *Velázquez, Los Borrachos and Painting at the Court of Philip IV*, Cambridge University Press.

Ortega y Gasset, J., *Velázquez*, Madrid, Espasa-Calpe, 1963.

Stevenson, R., *The Art of Velázquez* (1895), London, 1963.

Varia Velazqueña. Homenaje a Velázquez en el III centenario de su muerte, Madrid, Dirección General de Bellas Artes, 2 vols., 1960.

Various Authors, *Obras maestras de Velázquez*, Madrid, Fundación amigos del Prado, 1999 (at press).

Index of Colour Plates

COORDINATION AND PRODUCTION
Aldeasa

COVER ILLUSTRATION
Velázquez *Prince Baltasar Carlos as a Hunter* (detail)

DESIGN
Talía Hormigo

LAYOUT
Myriam López Consalvi

PHOTOGRAPHS
Museo del Prado archives

PHOTOMECHANICAL PRODUCTION
Lucam

PRINTED BY
tf

TRANSLATION
Nigel Williams

First published June 1999

NIPO: 183-99-006-3

ISBN: 84-87317-78-2 (Museo del Prado)
ISBN: 84-8003-167-0 (Aldeasa)

LEGAL DEPOSIT: M-33105-1999

This book was printed by tf Artes Gráficas in Madrid on 6th June 1999,
feast of St Norbert and the day of the four hundredth anniversary
of the baptism of Diego Velázquez.